Teach Yourself VISUAL

Dreamweaver® CS6

D0903904

Visual

by Janine Warner

DISCARD

CARLSBAD
CITY LIBRARY
Carlsbad, CA
92011

WILEY

John Wiley & Sons, Inc.

Teach Yourself VISUALLY™ Dreamweaver® CS6

Published by
John Wiley & Sons, Inc.
10475 Crosspoint Boulevard
Indianapolis, IN 46256

CO.78
006.78
WAR

www.wiley.com

Published simultaneously in Canada

Copyright © 2012 by John Wiley & Sons, Inc., Indianapolis, Indiana

No part of this publication may be reproduced, stored in a retrieval system or transmitted in any form or by any means, electronic, mechanical, photocopying, recording, scanning or otherwise, except as permitted under Sections 107 or 108 of the 1976 United States Copyright Act, without either the prior written permission of the Publisher, or authorization through payment of the appropriate per-copy fee to the Copyright Clearance Center, 222 Rosewood Drive, Danvers, MA 01923, (978)750-8400, fax (978)646-8600. Requests to the Publisher for permission should be addressed to the Permissions Department, John Wiley & Sons, Inc., 111 River Street, Hoboken, NJ 07030, (201)748-6011, fax (201)748-6008, or online at www.wiley.com/go/permissions.

Wiley publishes in a variety of print and electronic formats and by print-on-demand. Some material included with standard print versions of this book may not be included in e-books or in print-on-demand. If this book refers to media such as a CD or DVD that is not included in the version you purchased, you may download this material at http://booksupport.wiley.com. For more information about Wiley products, visit www.wiley.com.

Library of Congress Control Number: 2012940038

ISBN: 978-1-118-25471-4 (paperback); 978-1-118-33331-0 (epdf); 978-1-118-33454-6 (emobi); 978-1-118-33049-4 (epub)

Manufactured in the United States of America

10 9 8 7 6 5 4 3 2 1

Trademark Acknowledgments

Wiley, the John Wiley & Sons, Inc. logo, Visual, the Visual logo, Teach Yourself VISUALLY, Read Less - Learn More and related trade dress are trademarks or registered trademarks of John Wiley & Sons, Inc. and/or its affiliates. Adobe and Dreamweaver are registered trademarks of Adobe Systems Incorporated in the United States and/or other countries. All other trademarks are the property of their respective owners. John Wiley & Sons, Inc. is not associated with any product or vendor mentioned in this book.

LIMIT OF LIABILITY/DISCLAIMER OF WARRANTY: THE PUBLISHER AND THE AUTHOR MAKE NO REPRESENTATIONS OR WARRANTIES WITH RESPECT TO THE ACCURACY OR COMPLETENESS OF THE CONTENTS OF THIS WORK AND SPECIFICALLY DISCLAIM ALL WARRANTIES, INCLUDING WITHOUT LIMITATION WARRANTIES OF FITNESS FOR A PARTICULAR PURPOSE. NO WARRANTY MAY BE CREATED OR EXTENDED BY SALES OR PROMOTIONAL MATERIALS. THE ADVICE AND STRATEGIES CONTAINED HEREIN MAY NOT BE SUITABLE FOR EVERY SITUATION. THIS WORK IS SOLD WITH THE UNDERSTANDING THAT THE PUBLISHER IS NOT ENGAGED IN RENDERING LEGAL, ACCOUNTING, OR OTHER PROFESSIONAL SERVICES. IF PROFESSIONAL ASSISTANCE IS REQUIRED, THE SERVICES OF A COMPETENT PROFESSIONAL PERSON SHOULD BE SOUGHT. NEITHER THE PUBLISHER NOR THE AUTHOR SHALL BE LIABLE FOR DAMAGES ARISING HEREFROM. THE FACT THAT AN ORGANIZATION OR WEBSITE IS REFERRED TO IN THIS WORK AS A CITATION AND/OR A POTENTIAL SOURCE OF FURTHER INFORMATION DOES NOT MEAN THAT THE AUTHOR OR THE PUBLISHER ENDORSES THE INFORMATION THE ORGANIZATION OR WEBSITE MAY PROVIDE OR RECOMMENDATIONS IT MAY MAKE. FURTHER, READERS SHOULD BE AWARE THAT INTERNET WEBSITES LISTED IN THIS WORK MAY HAVE CHANGED OR DISAPPEARED BETWEEN WHEN THIS WORK WAS WRITTEN AND WHEN IT IS READ.

FOR PURPOSES OF ILLUSTRATING THE CONCEPTS AND TECHNIQUES DESCRIBED IN THIS BOOK, THE AUTHOR HAS CREATED VARIOUS NAMES, COMPANY NAMES, MAILING, E-MAIL AND INTERNET ADDRESSES, PHONE AND FAX NUMBERS AND SIMILAR INFORMATION, ALL OF WHICH ARE FICTITIOUS. ANY RESEMBLANCE OF THESE FICTITIOUS NAMES, ADDRESSES, PHONE AND FAX NUMBERS AND SIMILAR INFORMATION TO ANY ACTUAL PERSON, COMPANY AND/OR ORGANIZATION IS UNINTENTIONAL AND PURELY COINCIDENTAL.

Contact Us

For general information on our other products and services, please contact our Customer Care Department within the U.S. at (877)762-2974, outside the U.S. at (317)572-3993 or fax (317)572-4002.

For technical support, please visit www.wiley.com/techsupport.

WILEY   Sales | Contact Wiley at (877) 762-2974 or fax (317) 572-4002.

NOVEMBER 2012

Credits

Senior Acquisitions Editor
Stephanie McComb

Executive Editor
Jody Lefevere

Project Editor
Dana Rhodes Lesh

Technical Editor
David LaFontaine

Copy Editor
Dana Rhodes Lesh

Editorial Director
Robyn Siesky

Business Manager
Amy Knies

Senior Marketing Manager
Sandy Smith

Vice President and Executive Group Publisher
Richard Swadley

Vice President and Executive Publisher
Barry Pruett

Project Coordinator
Sheree Montgomery

Graphics and Production Specialists
Ronda David-Burroughs
Cheryl Grubbs
Joyce Haughey
Andrea Hornberger
Jennifer Mayberry

Proofreading and Indexing
Sossity R. Smith
Potomac Indexing, LLC

About the Author

Janine Warner's best-selling books and videos about the Internet have won her an international following and earned her speaking and consulting engagements around the world.

She is the creator of DigitalFamily.com and runs a full-service interactive agency that offers web design, iPad app development, content strategy, and Internet marketing services.

Janine's skills as a "techy translator" helped her land the deal for her first book in 1996. Since then, she has written or coauthored more than 25 books about the Internet, including *Web Sites Do-It-Yourself For Dummies*, *Mobile Web Design For Dummies*, *iPhone & iPad Web Design For Dummies*, and several editions of *Dreamweaver For Dummies*. Janine has also created more than 50 hours of training videos about web design and Internet marketing.

Janine's early Internet projects included helping a creative director in Sausalito to manage a quirky team of programmers in Siberia, designing a virtual scanning system in a simulated futuristic store for Levi Strauss, and building one of the first newspaper websites in the country for the Pulitzer Prize–winning *Point Reyes Light*.

In 1998, her experience as a journalist and Internet consultant, combined with her fluency in Spanish, took her to *The Miami Herald,* first as the online managing editor and later as the director of new media. She left that position to serve as the director of Latin American operations for CNET Networks.

Janine has taught online journalism courses at the University of Miami and the University of Southern California. She has also been a guest lecturer at more than 20 other universities in the United States and Latin America, and she helped create an Internet literacy program for high school students in Central America.

She is a member of the TV Academy's Interactive Media Peer Group and has served as a judge in the Interactive Emmy Awards, the Knight News Challenge, and the Arroba de Oro Latin American Internet Awards.

Janine is a popular speaker at conferences and other events. You can learn more about her speaking topics and view a video of her in action on her website at http://JCWarner.com.

Author's Acknowledgments

Special thanks to some of the designers, artists, and photographers whose work is featured in this book, including Amy Baur of www.inplainsightart.com, David LaFontaine, and all the great photographers at http://istockphoto.com.

Thanks to all the animals who have graced me with a chance to photograph them in the wild, as well as in my living room. A special thanks to all the birds, dolphins, and deer in my California Wildlife Photography site, as well as the adorable pets featured in the photos in Chapters 11 and 12. I would send you all model releases and royalties, but my publisher does not accept paw prints. And finally, thanks to the entire team that made this book possible, most notably, my editors, Dana Lesh, David LaFontaine, and Stephanie McComb.

How to Use This Book

Whom This Book Is For

This book is for readers who have never used Dreamweaver to create websites, as well as those who have some experience and want to learn the newest features in version CS6 of this powerful program. All you need to get started is a basic understanding of how to surf the web and a desire to learn to create your own websites.

The Conventions in This Book

① Steps

This book uses a step-by-step format to guide you easily through each task. **Numbered steps** are actions you must do; **bulleted steps** clarify a point, step, or optional feature; and **indented steps** give you the result.

② Notes

Notes give additional information — special conditions that may occur during an operation, a situation that you want to avoid, or a cross-reference to a related area of the book.

③ Icons and Buttons

Icons and buttons show you exactly what you need to click to perform a step.

④ Tips

Tips offer additional information, including warnings and shortcuts.

⑤ Bold

Bold type shows command names or options that you must click or text or numbers you must type.

⑥ Italics

Italic type introduces and defines a new term.

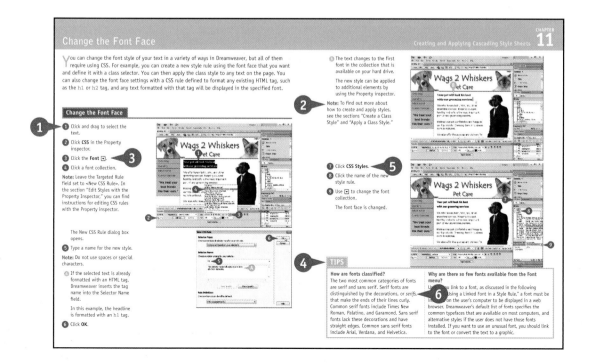

Table of Contents

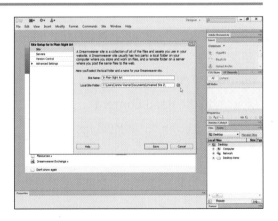

Chapter 3   Exploring the Dreamweaver Interface

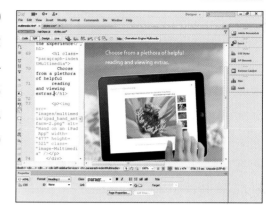

Chapter 4   Working with HTML

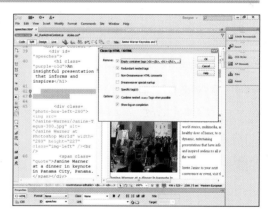

Table of Contents

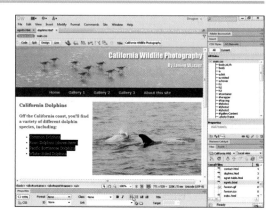

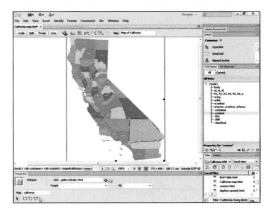

Table of Contents

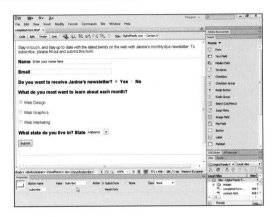

Chapter 11 | Creating and Applying Cascading Style Sheets

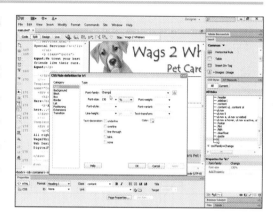

Table of Contents

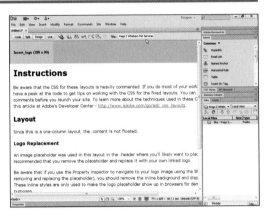
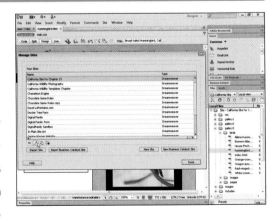

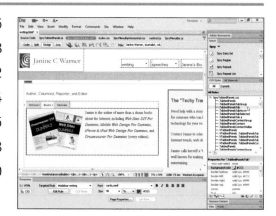

CHAPTER 1

Getting Started with Dreamweaver

This chapter describes the World Wide Web (WWW), introduces the different types of information that you can put on a website, and shows you how to get started with Dreamweaver.

Introducing the World Wide Web

You can use Dreamweaver CS6 to create, edit, and publish pages on the World Wide Web (WWW) using the Hypertext Markup Language (HTML) and Cascading Style Sheets (CSS). You can create web pages on your computer and test them in a web browser, such as Microsoft Internet Explorer, Apple Safari, Mozilla Firefox, or Google Chrome, before publishing them on the web. However, before your web pages can be viewed over the Internet, they must be transferred to a web server.

The World Wide Web

The *World Wide Web* — or simply the *web* — is a global collection of documents located on Internet-connected computers. You can access the web by using a web browser, such as Internet Explorer, Safari, Chrome, or Firefox. Web pages are connected to one another by hyperlinks that you can click.

A Website

A *website* is a collection of linked web pages stored on a web server. Most websites have a *home page* that introduces the site and provides a place where visitors can start their exploration of the site's information. A good website includes links that make it easy to find the most important pages.

Dreamweaver

Adobe Dreamweaver is a program that enables you to create and edit web pages with hyperlinks, text, images, multimedia, and more. You can design web pages on your computer and then, when you are finished, use Dreamweaver to transfer the finished files to a web server where others can view them on the web.

HTML, HTML5, and XHTML

HTML is the formatting language that is used to create web pages. The Extensible Hypertext Markup Language (XHTML) is a stricter version of HTML that meets today's web standards. HTML5 is the newest version, but it has not yet been finalized by the World Wide Web Consortium (W3C), which sets

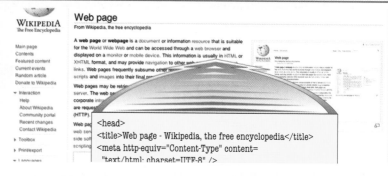

standards for the Internet, and the Web Hypertext Application Technology Working Group (WHATWG), which has been working to create HTML5 as the "living standard." You can use Dreamweaver to create web pages without knowing HTML because Dreamweaver writes the HTML code for you behind the scenes.

A Web Server

A *web server* is a computer that is connected to the Internet and has software that serves web pages to visitors. Each web page that you view in a browser on the World Wide Web resides on a web server somewhere on the Internet. You do not have to run your own web server to create a website because there are

many web hosting companies that provide web server space for a small monthly fee. When you are ready to publish your pages on the web, you can use Dreamweaver to transfer your files to such a web server.

A Web Browser

A *web browser* is a program that interprets HTML and other code and then displays the web page text and any associated images and multimedia described in that code. You can download most popular web browsers for free, including Microsoft Internet Explorer, Mozilla Firefox, Apple Safari, and Google Chrome.

Explore the Many Ways to Design a Web Page

In the early days of the Internet, web design was a lot easier, but it was also vanilla boring. You could use text and images on a web page, but the formatting options were extremely limited. Today, there are many more ways to design web pages, but first you have to decide which approach is best for your site. This section introduces you to a few of the most common options that you can choose from and provides tips for when it is best to use tables, Cascading Style Sheets (CSS), Flash, and other more advanced options.

Text and Images

Dreamweaver makes it easy to insert text and images into your web pages. You can then use Dreamweaver to change the size, color, and font of the text; to organize your text into paragraphs, headings, and lists; and to change its alignment. However, if you want to create a more complex design, you need to use one of the other options described in this section.

Multimedia

Websites can include audio, video, and animation files, collectively called *multimedia*. You can use Dreamweaver to add these files to web pages. Some of the "flashiest" sites on the web have been created using Adobe Flash, a vector-based design program. Although Flash has been popular for years, many designers no longer use it because the .flv and .swf files that it creates are not visible on the Apple iPad or iPhone. Using a video hosting service, such as YouTube or Vimeo, is a better way to add video to your web pages today.

Tables

Tables used to be a popular choice for creating page designs. By merging and splitting table cells and turning off the border setting, you could create complex page layouts. Today, designing with Cascading Style Sheets is the best option, and tables are recommended only when you are formatting tabular data, such as the kind of information you would find in a spreadsheet program or a database.

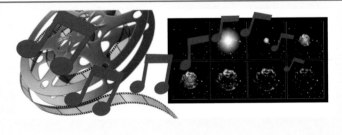

Sun Perennials	Shade Perennials
Echinacheas	Helleborus
Sedums	Hydrangeas
Daisies	Hostas
Daylilies	Ferns

AP Divs

Dreamweaver's AP Divs, called *layers* in earlier versions of Dreamweaver, use absolute positioning to create "boxes" that you can use to position images, text, and other content on a page. AP Divs are very intuitive to use: You just click and drag to create a box anywhere on a web page. However, AP Divs have many limitations, among them that you cannot center a design created with AP Divs, which is a popular trick for making your design appear to float on the page on different screen sizes. Another limitation is that, although they seem to give you precise design control, their display can vary dramatically from browser to browser.

CSS Layouts

Many professional web designers today recommend creating page layouts using CSS. Although AP Divs are technically created with CSS, they receive very special treatment in Dreamweaver and have very significant limitations. In general, when web designers refer to *CSS layouts,* they mean designs that do not use absolute positioning — or that use it very sparingly. Using CSS is one of the most challenging web design options, but it brings some powerful benefits, such as greater accessibility and flexibility, which can help your site look better to more people on a greater range of devices. When used effectively, pages designed with CSS are also faster to download and easier to update.

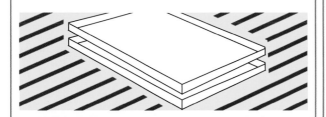

Dynamic Websites

At the highest end of the web design spectrum, you can connect a website to a database, Extensible Markup Language (XML) files, or another data source to create highly interactive sites with features such as shopping carts, discussion boards, and more. Most blogs are created using a database and a program such as WordPress, Drupal, or Joomla. Database-driven sites are especially useful when a website grows to more than 100 pages or so because they are more efficient to update.

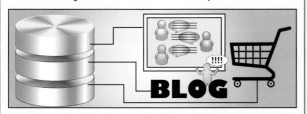

Sample Websites

To help you appreciate the many ways to create websites and to follow along with the exercises in this book, you can find a collection of sample websites that you can download and use at www. DigitalFamily.com/tyv; follow the instructions there to find these bonus materials.

Plan Your Website

Before you start building a website, taking a little time to plan what you will place on your pages and how you want your website visitors to move from one page to another can help to ensure that your finished website looks great, is well organized, and is easy to navigate. Before you create your first page, organize your ideas and gather all of the images, text, and other materials that you will need to create your site.

Organize Your Ideas

Build your website on paper before you start building it in Dreamweaver. Sketching out a website map, with rectangles representing web pages and arrows representing links, can help you to visualize the size and scope of your project. Use sticky notes if you want to move pages around as you plan your website.

Gather Your Content

Before you start building your web pages, gather all the elements that you want to use. This process may require writing text, taking photos, and designing graphics. It can also involve producing multimedia content, such as audio and video files. Gathering all your material together in the beginning makes it easier for you to organize your website when you start building it in Dreamweaver.

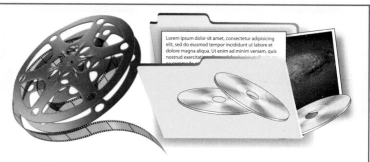

Define Your Audience

Identifying your target audience can help you to decide what kind of content to offer on your website. For example, you may create a very different design for small children than for adults. Similarly, a website for a business audience may require a more professional design, whereas a site for gamers may warrant a more playful approach.

Host Your Finished Website

To make your finished website accessible over the Internet, you need to store, or *host,* your site on a web server. However, you do not have to set up your own web server. Most people have their websites hosted on a web server at a commercial Internet service provider (ISP) or at their company or university.

Start Dreamweaver on a PC

Y ou can use Dreamweaver on a PC running the Windows operating system. Most web designers begin by creating web pages on their local computer and then publishing those pages to a web server after they are completed. If you do not already have Dreamweaver, you will need to purchase and install the program. If you want to try the program before you buy it, you can also download a fully functional, free trial version that will work for 30 days from Adobe's Dreamweaver web page, www.adobe.com/dreamweaver.

Start Dreamweaver on a PC

1 Click **Start**.

2 Click **All Programs**.

3 Click **Adobe Dreamweaver CS6**.

Note: Your path to the Dreamweaver application may be different, depending on how you installed your software and your operating system.

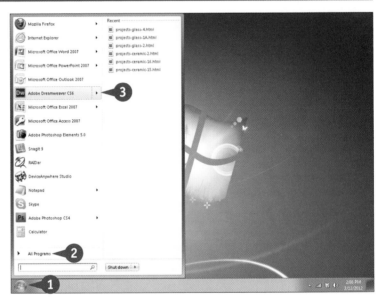

The Dreamweaver start screen appears.

Just before Dreamweaver starts, you may be prompted with a dialog box that gives you the option of making Dreamweaver the default editor for many kinds of file types, including CSS, XML, and PHP. If you want to open these kinds of files automatically in Dreamweaver, click **OK**.

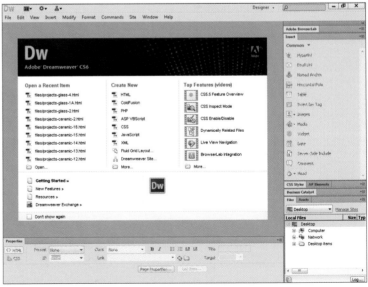

Start Dreamweaver on a Macintosh

You can use Dreamweaver on a computer running the Macintosh operating system, and you can create web pages on your Mac and test them before you publish your site on the web. If you do not already have Dreamweaver installed on your Macintosh, you will need to purchase and install the program. You can also download a fully functional, free trial version that will work for 30 days from Adobe's Dreamweaver web page, www.adobe.com/dreamweaver.

Start Dreamweaver on a Macintosh

1 Double-click your hard drive icon.

2 Click **Applications**.

3 Click **Adobe Dreamweaver CS6**.

Note: The exact location of the Dreamweaver folder depends on how you installed your software.

4 Double-click **Adobe Dreamweaver CS6**.

The Dreamweaver start screen appears.

Just before Dreamweaver starts, you may be prompted with a dialog box that gives you the option of making Dreamweaver the default editor for many kinds of file types, including CSS, XML, and PHP. If you want to open these kinds of files automatically in Dreamweaver, click **OK**.

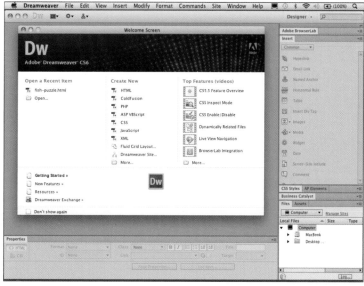

Tour the Dreamweaver Interface on a PC

When you open Dreamweaver CS6 on a PC, you will see a variety of windows, panels, and inspectors. Opening and closing panels and reading the names of the features in the various menus are great ways to get familiar with the program. You can move panels and other items around in the interface to make the features that you like best more accessible. Dreamweaver includes several workspace layouts. This book primarily shows the Designer layout option. To make your program appear the way that it does in the figures in this book, click **Window**, then **Workspace Layout**, and then **Designer**.

Ⓐ Menus

Contain the commands for using Dreamweaver. Many of these commands are duplicated within the windows, panels, and inspectors of Dreamweaver.

Ⓑ Toolbar

Contains shortcuts to preview and display features and a text field where you can specify the title of a page.

Ⓒ Insert panel

Provides easy access to common features. There are several different Insert panels that you can select, depending on the type of features that you want to insert into your page.

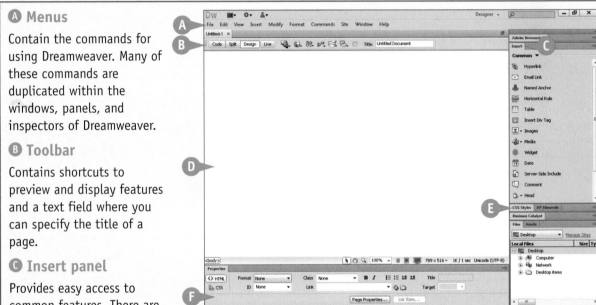

Ⓓ Document window

The main workspace where you insert and arrange the text, images, and other elements of your web page.

Ⓔ Panels

Can be docked or floated and provide access to many common tools in Dreamweaver, including the Insert, CSS Styles, AP Elements, Business Catalyst, Files, and Assets features.

Ⓕ Property inspector

Used to display and edit the attributes of any element selected in the Document window.

Tour the Dreamweaver Interface on a Macintosh

Dreamweaver CS6 on a Macintosh likewise features a variety of windows, panels, and inspectors. Opening and closing panels and reading the names of the features in the various menus are great ways to get familiar with the program. You can move panels and other items around in the interface to make the features you like best more accessible. Dreamweaver includes several workspace layouts on the Macintosh. This book primarily shows the Designer layout option. To make your program appear the way that it does in the figures in this book, click **Window**, then **Workspace Layout**, and then **Designer**.

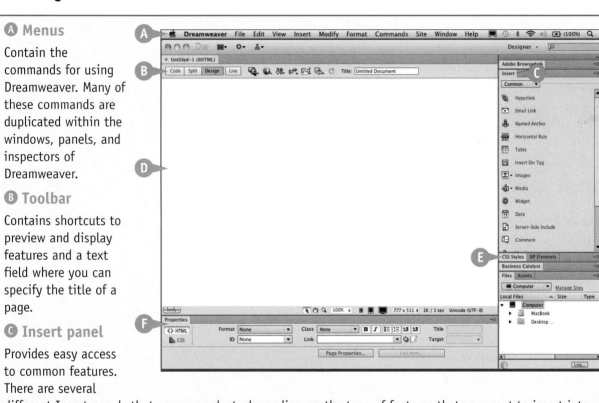

Ⓐ Menus

Contain the commands for using Dreamweaver. Many of these commands are duplicated within the windows, panels, and inspectors of Dreamweaver.

Ⓑ Toolbar

Contains shortcuts to preview and display features and a text field where you can specify the title of a page.

Ⓒ Insert panel

Provides easy access to common features. There are several different Insert panels that you can select, depending on the type of features that you want to insert into your page.

Ⓓ Document window

The main workspace where you insert and arrange the text, images, and other elements of your web page.

Ⓔ Panels

Can be docked or floated and provide access to many common tools in Dreamweaver, including the Insert, CSS Styles, AP Elements, Business Catalog, Files, and Assets features.

Ⓕ Property inspector

Used to display and edit the attributes of any element selected in the Document window.

Show or Hide Features

Y ou can show or hide features in Dreamweaver, called *windows*, *panels*, and *inspectors*, by choosing options from the Window menu. Panels and inspectors provide access to the many tools. For example, the Files panel displays all the files in a website, and the Property inspector displays the properties for any selected item on the page. For these and most other features to work in Dreamweaver, you must have a document open in the program. You can create a new document or open any existing web page.

Show or Hide Features

Show a Window

1 Click **Window**.

2 Click the name of the window, panel, or inspector that you want to open.

This example opens the Property inspector.

Ⓐ ☑ next to a name indicates that the window, panel, or inspector is open.

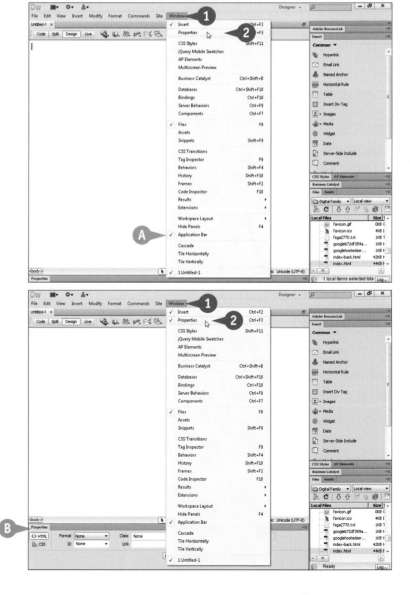

Ⓑ Dreamweaver displays the window that you chose.

Hide a Window

1 Click **Window**.

2 Click the check-marked (☑) name of the window that you want to hide.

Note: You can click **Window** and then click **Hide Panels** to hide everything except the Document window and toolbar.

Exit Dreamweaver

You can exit Dreamweaver to close the program when you are finished working on the pages in your website.

You should always exit Dreamweaver and any other programs that are open before turning off your Macintosh or Windows computer. Make sure that you close all open files before exiting the program. Turning off your computer while you still have files open in Dreamweaver can cause you to lose any work that you have not yet saved in the program. Exiting Dreamweaver is a quick and easy process.

Exit Dreamweaver

1 Click **File**.

2 Click **Exit**.

Before quitting, Dreamweaver alerts you to save any open documents that have unsaved changes.

3 Click **Yes**.

Dreamweaver exits.

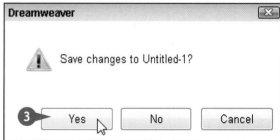

Get Help

Throughout this book, you will find instructions and tips for using the many great features in Dreamweaver, and you can find additional help on the Help menu. The Dreamweaver Help menu includes many options, including the Spry Framework Help option, shown here. All of the help options are searchable, which makes it easy to find answers to your questions or to learn new techniques. You must be connected to the Internet for most of the Help features to open.

Get Help

① Click **Help**.

② Click the Help option that you want, such as **Spry Framework Help**.

Ⓐ You can also click the Tab Group icon (▦) in the Property inspector and choose **Help**.

The selected Help page opens and displays information related to the feature that you selected.

Ⓑ You can click any topic that you want help with.

③ Type one or more keywords about the topic that you want help with.

Note: You can narrow your search by separating keywords with +.

④ Click **Search** or press Enter (Return).

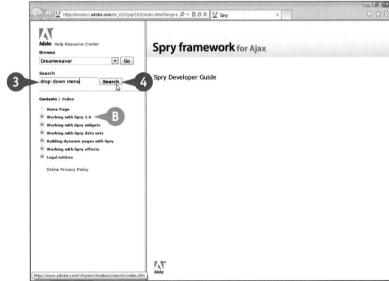

A list of topics appears.

⑤ Click a topic from the search result list.

Information appears on the topic that you selected.

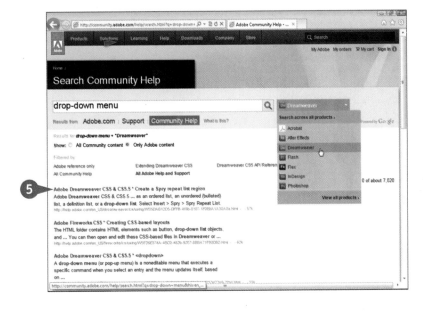

TIP

Are there different ways of opening the Help tools and other options in Dreamweaver?
Very often, yes. As with many programs, there is often more than one way to do the same task. For example, you can access many tools and commands, such as Modify Page Properties, by using either a menu or the Property inspector. You can also use the Split or Code view commands to view and edit the HTML code directly, if you know how to write HTML.

CHAPTER 2

Setting Up Your Website

You start a project in Dreamweaver by defining a local root folder where you will store all the files in your website on your computer. You can then create your first page and save it in the root folder. This chapter shows you how to set up your website.

Define a New Website

Before you create or edit web pages, you need to define your site in Dreamweaver and set up a local site folder where you can store all the files in your site. Defining a local site folder enables Dreamweaver to manage your files in the Files panel and properly set links. As you set up your site, you can create a new folder on your hard drive or select an existing folder as your local site folder. For more information on the Files panel, see Chapter 13, "Publishing a Website."

Define a New Website

1. Click **Site**.

2. Click **New Site**.

The Site Setup dialog box appears.

3. Type a name for your site.

4. Click 📁 to search for your website folder.

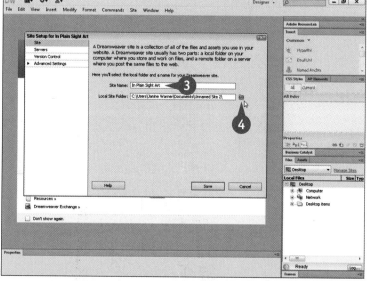

The Choose Root Folder dialog box appears.

⑤ Click here and select the folder that stores your web pages.

Ⓐ You can create a new folder for a new site by clicking 🖻, typing in a new name for the folder, and then selecting the new folder.

⑥ Click **Select**.

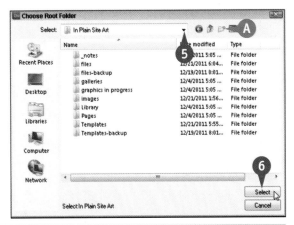

You are returned to the Site Setup dialog box.

⑦ Click **Save**.

If you are setting up an existing site, you will be prompted with a message stating, "The cache will not be re-created." Click **OK**.

Note: Creating a cache enables Dreamweaver to work more efficiently.

Ⓑ The process can take a few seconds. When complete, the files and folders of the selected site are listed in the Files panel.

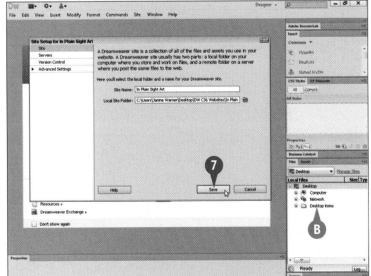

TIP

Why is it important to keep all my website files in the same root folder on my computer?
Keeping everything in the same root folder on your local computer enables you to easily transfer your website files to a web server without changing the organization of the files. If your website files are not organized on the web server in the same way that they are organized on your local computer, hyperlinks may not work, and images may not be displayed properly. For more information about working with website files and publishing your site to a server, see Chapter 13.

Create a New Web Page

There are many ways to create a new page in Dreamweaver CS6. When you launch the program, the initial start page includes useful shortcuts that you can use to create new HTML pages and other kinds of files. If you want the maximum number of options when you create a new page, use the New Document dialog box, covered in this section. In the New Document dialog box, you can choose from a long list of page types, including HTML, HTML Template, CSS, XML, and more advanced programming options, such ColdFusion and PHP.

Create a New Web Page

1 Click **File**.

2 Click **New**.

The New Document dialog box appears.

3 Click **Blank Page**.

4 Click **HTML** to specify the type of page.

5 Click **None** to create a blank page.

You can also create preformatted pages by choosing any of the other options under Layout in the New Document dialog box.

6 Click **Create**.

Dreamweaver displays a new Document window.

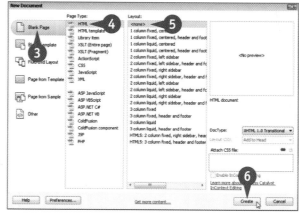

Add a Title to a Web Page

I t is easy to forget to add a page title to each of your pages, but do not skip this important step. A web page title appears in the title bar or tab when the page opens in a web browser. The title is also important to search engines, which are known to put special value on the keywords in title text. The words in your title also get saved in a user's Bookmarks or Favorites list if he or she bookmarks your web page.

Add a Title to a Web Page

When you create a new document, an untitled document appears in the main workspace.

Note: The page name and filename are "Untitled" until you save them.

① Type a name for your web page in the **Title** text box.

② Press **Enter** (**Return**).

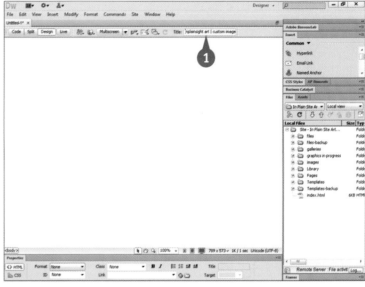

Ⓐ The web page title appears in the title bar when the page is displayed in a web browser.

Ⓑ If the browser supports tabbed browsing, the title also appears on the tab.

Save a Web Page

Save early and often. It is a good practice to save your web page as soon as you create it — and again before closing the program. It is also a good idea to save all your files any time you make a significant change to prevent work from being lost due to power outages or system failures. When you preview a page in a browser or transfer pages to a web server, Dreamweaver automatically saves your page for you. For information about transferring pages to a server, see Chapter 13.

Save a Web Page

Save Your Document

1 Click **File**.

2 Click **Save**.

Ⓐ You can click **Save As** to save an existing file with a new filename.

If you are saving a new file for the first time, the Save As dialog box appears.

3 Click here and select your local site folder.

Note: Your local site folder is where you want to save the pages and other files for your website.

4 Type a name for your web page.

5 Click **Save**.

B Dreamweaver saves the web page, and the filename and path appear in the title bar.

C You can click ⊠ to close the page.

Revert to an Earlier Version of a Page

1 Click **File**.

2 Click **Revert**.

The page reverts to the previously saved version. All the changes that you made since the last time you saved the file are lost.

Note: If you exit Dreamweaver after you save a document, Dreamweaver cannot revert to the previous version.

TIP

Why should I name the main page of my site index.html?
You should name your main website or home page index.html because that is the filename that most web servers open first when a user types a domain name into a web browser. If you name your main page index. html and it does not open as your first page when your site is on the server, then check with your system administrator or hosting service. Some servers use default.htm or index.htm instead of index.html.

Preview a Web Page in a Browser

You can see how your web page will appear to the visitors to your website by previewing it in a web browser. The Preview in Browser command works with any web browser that is installed on your computer and set up in Dreamweaver's browser list. Although Dreamweaver does not ship with web browser software, Internet Explorer is preinstalled on most Windows computers, and Safari is preinstalled on most Macintosh computers. You can download the Firefox web browser for free from www.mozilla.com/firefox, and you can download the Chrome web browser from www.google.com/chrome.

Preview a Web Page in a Browser

Launch a Web Browser

1 Click the Preview in Browser button (⚙).

2 Click a web browser from the drop-down menu that appears.

You can also preview the page in your primary web browser by pressing F12.

The web browser launches and opens the current page.

When you preview a web page in a browser, you can follow links by clicking them, just as you normally would when viewing websites.

Add a Browser

1 Click **File**.

2 Click **Preview in Browser**.

3 Click **Edit Browser List**.

The Preferences dialog box appears.

4 Click ⊞.

The Add Browser dialog box appears.

5 Type a name for your web browser.

6 Click **Browse** and select any web browser on your computer's hard drive.

7 Click **OK**.

You are returned to the Preferences dialog box.

8 Click **OK**.

The newly added web browser will appear in the browser list.

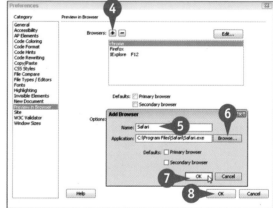

TIP

Why should I use more than one web browser for previews?

Dreamweaver makes it easy for you to add more than one web browser because not all web browsers display web pages the same way. For example, Internet Explorer and Firefox sometimes display web pages differently. As a result, it is important to test your pages in a variety of browsers to ensure that they will look like you want them to for all your visitors. By using the browser list, you can easily test your web page in a different web browser with just a few mouse clicks and adjust your designs until they look good in all the browsers that you think your visitors may use.

CHAPTER 3

Exploring the Dreamweaver Interface

In this chapter, you will take a tour of the panels and windows that make up the Dreamweaver interface. You will discover all the handy tools and features that make this an award-winning web design program.

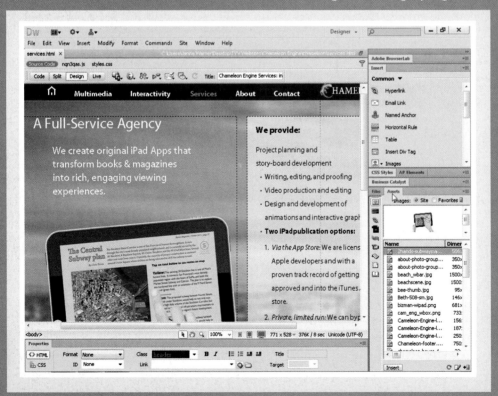

Choose a Workspace Layout

In Dreamweaver CS6, you can choose from 11 different workspace layout options. Each layout is optimized for a different task or work style. If you consider yourself a designer and have more experience working with graphics programs, you will probably prefer the Designer layouts, which focus on the design features in Dreamweaver. If you are a programmer or most of your experience has been writing code, you will probably prefer the Coder or App Developer layouts, which are optimized for those who prefer to work in Code view. Most of the figures in this book show the Designer layout.

Choose a Workspace Layout

1 Click ▼ to select a layout option.

2 Click **Designer Compact**.

The workspace changes to the Designer Compact layout with the panels diminished on the side of the workspace.

3 Click ▼ to select a different layout option.

4 Click **Coder**.

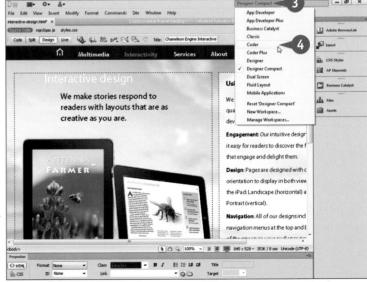

The workspace changes to the Coder layout, with the Code view open in the workspace.

⑤ Click ▼ to select a different layout option.

⑥ Click **Designer**.

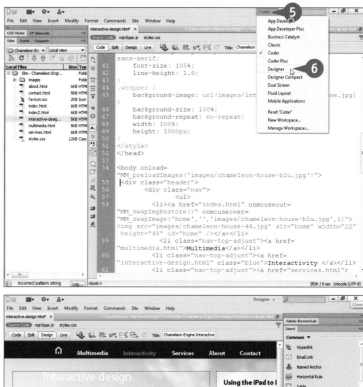

The workspace changes to the Designer layout, my personal favorite and the layout option I use throughout this book.

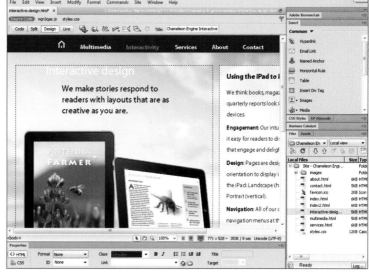

TIP

Which layout is right for me?

This depends on the way that you work. Dreamweaver CS6 includes many preset workspace layouts. Each is designed to optimize the workspace based on common ways of working in the program. Experiment with the various options, choose the one you like best, and remember that you can click and drag to rearrange the panels and inspectors to change the workspace to best accommodate your preferences.

Customize the Document Window

After you choose the layout that you want to use in Dreamweaver CS6 (see the preceding section, "Choose a Workspace Layout"), you can customize your workspace further to create an interface that makes your favorite features accessible. You can open and close dialog boxes and inspectors, rearrange and dock panels, and expand or minimize panels and windows. When you get all of these features the way that you want them, you can save one or more custom layouts for future use. See the section "Open and Customize the Insert Panel" later in this chapter for more information, and consider creating different layouts for different tasks.

Customize the Document Window

1 Click **Split**.

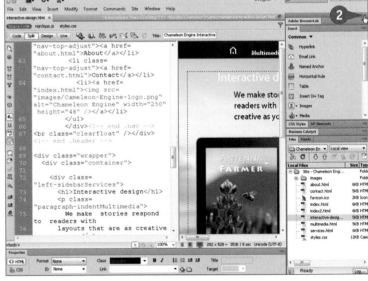

The Code view window opens in the left half of the workspace.

2 Click ▶▶ to minimize the panels.

The panels are minimized.

Ⓐ You can click ◄◄ to expand the panels.

③ Double-click anywhere in the gray bar above the Property inspector.

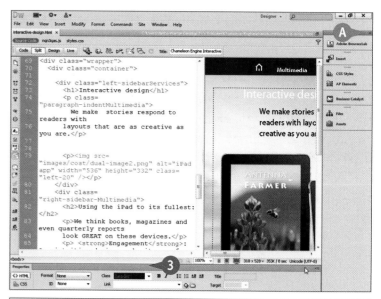

The Property inspector is minimized.

Ⓑ You can double-click anywhere in the gray bar again to expand the Property inspector.

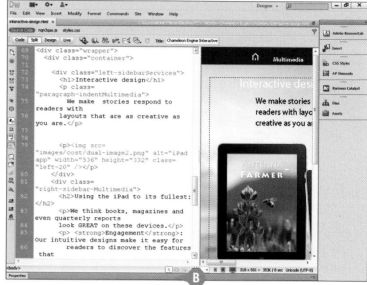

TIP

How can I keep my favorite features handy?

You can open or close any of the panels and inspectors in Dreamweaver so that your favorite features are handy when you need them and so that others are out of the way when you do not need them. Most of the panels and other options are available from the Window menu. For example, to open the CSS Styles panel, you click **Window** and then click **CSS Styles**. As you work, you may choose to have different panels opened or closed to give you more workspace or to provide easier access to the features that you are using.

Format Content with the Property Inspector

The Property inspector enables you to view the properties associated with any object or text that is currently selected in the Document window. Click to select an image, and the image properties appear in the Property inspector. Click to select text, and the text properties appear. Use the text fields, drop-down menus, buttons, and other fields in the Property inspector to modify the properties of any selected element, such as the font size or font family of text on the page.

Format Content with the Property Inspector

Format an Image

1 Click to select the image.

A The image properties appear.

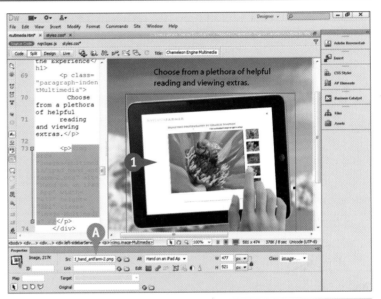

B If the code is visible, the image source code is highlighted in Code view.

You can change many image properties in the Property inspector, such as the image size and Alt text.

2 Type text in the **Alt** field.

Note: In HTML, *Alt* stands for *alternate*. This text is used as an alternative and is displayed in the browser only if the image is not visible. Alt text is recommended for accessible web design. Alt text is read aloud by screen readers, which are used by the blind or those with limited vision.

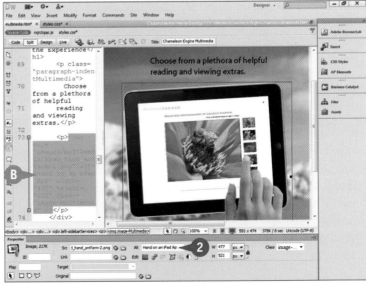

C The text is added as an attribute of the image tag in the HTML code.

Format Text

3 Click and drag to select the text.

4 Click the Format ▼.

5 Click to select a heading option, such as **Heading 1**.

Note: The heading tags are an ideal choice for formatting headlines. Heading 1 is the largest, and Heading 6 is the smallest.

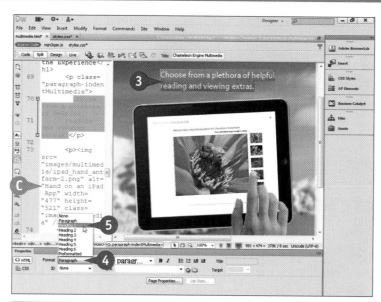

D Your text automatically changes to reflect your formatting choices in the Property inspector.

You can change many text properties in the Property inspector.

E The Property inspector includes HTML and CSS options.

Note: For many formatting choices, such as font and size, you must create styles. You can find instructions for creating styles using Cascading Style Sheets in Chapter 11, "Creating and Applying Cascading Style Sheets."

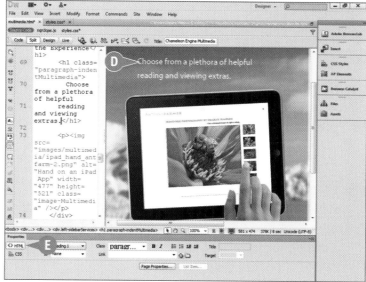

TIP

When would I use more than one font on a web page?
When you choose a font face in Dreamweaver, the program offers fonts in groups of three. For example, one option is Arial, Helvetica, and Sans-Serif, and another option is Times New Roman, Times, and Serif. Dreamweaver provides these collections because the fonts that are displayed on a web page are determined by the available fonts on the visitor's computer. Because you cannot guarantee what fonts a user will have, web browsers use the first font that matches in a list of fonts. Thus, in the first example, the font will be displayed as follows: in Arial if the Arial font is on the visitor's computer; in Helvetica if Arial is not available; and in any available sans-serif font if neither of the first two fonts is available.

Open a Panel

Dreamweaver features a highly customizable workspace. You can move panels around the screen by clicking the top bar of a panel and dragging it to a new position in the workspace. All the panels can float or lock into place at the side of the program. You can open or close and expand or collapse a panel by clicking and dragging on the bottom of the panel. To find additional panel options, click the tabs at the top of each panel.

Open a Panel

1 Click **Window**.

2 Click the name of the panel that you want to open, such as **Files**.

Ⓐ The panel appears; in the example of the Files panel, it displays all the files in the website.

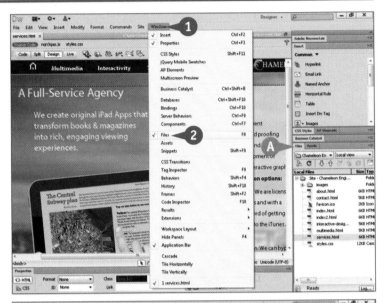

3 Click a tab to open a related panel, such as the **Assets** panel.

The panel appears.

Ⓑ In the Assets panel, you can click any of the buttons to display the assets that it represents, such as the Images button (🖼).

4 Click 🖼.

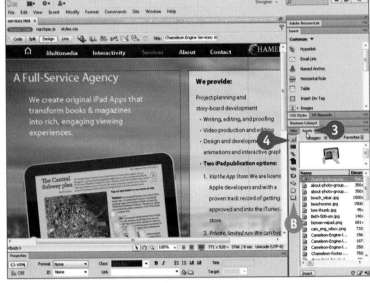

C All the available images in the site appear in the Assets panel.

5 Click any image filename to preview the image in the display area at the top of the Assets panel.

6 Double-click anywhere in the gray bar at the top of the Files panel to close the panel.

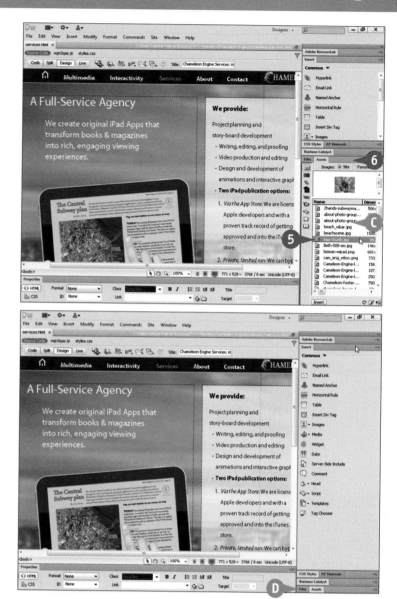

In this example, the Files and Assets panels collapse.

Note: When you collapse a panel such as the Files panel, other panels become more visible.

D You can double-click the gray bar on any panel to open it and then click any tab in an open panel to make it active.

TIP

How can I keep track of my assets?

The Assets panel provides access to many handy features, such as the Colors assets, which list all the colors that are used on a site. For example, this is useful if you are using a particular text color and you want to use the same color consistently on every page. Similarly, the Links assets make it easy to access links that are used elsewhere in your site so that you can quickly and easily set frequently used links.

Open and Customize the Insert Panel

One of the most commonly used panels in Dreamweaver is the Insert panel. When you choose the Designer layout, as shown in the first section of this chapter, "Choose a Workspace Layout," the Insert panel is located at the top right of the workspace. The Insert panel features a drop-down menu that reveals options such as Common elements, Forms, and Text. You can use the features in the Common Insert panel to insert a variety of elements in your web pages, including images, links, tables, divs, video, and audio files.

Open and Customize the Insert Panel

1 Click **Window**.

2 Click **Insert**.

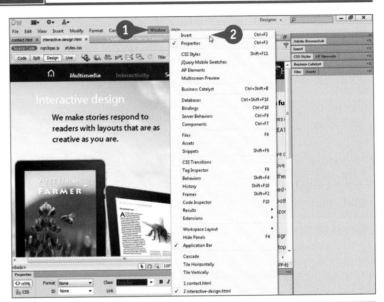

A The Insert panel appears.

3 Click here.

4 Click **Hide Labels**.

B The labels are no longer visible, and the icons are rearranged to take up less space.

5 Click the gray bar above any panel and drag it to enlarge or reduce the size.

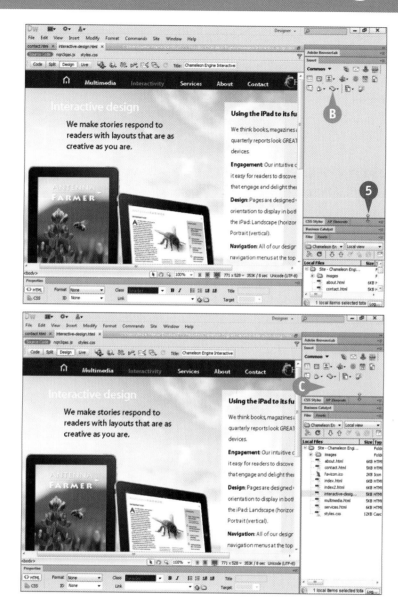

C The panel adjusts to fill the space based on where you dragged it.

Note: You can adjust the panels to be as large or small as you like.

TIP

How can I save the workspace after I get it the way I want it?

After you have all the panels and inspectors the way that you want them in Dreamweaver, you can save the entire workspace as a custom layout. Click **Window**, then **Workspace Layout**, and then **New Workspace**. In the New Workspace dialog box, give the layout a name. Then you can select the custom layout just as you would select any other workspace layout.

Set Preferences

You can easily change many options in Dreamweaver by changing the settings in the Preferences dialog box. This enables you to modify the interface and many default options to customize Dreamweaver to better suit how you like to work. For example, you can change the font family and size used to display the code to make the code more readable in Code view. You can also change the version of HTML code used in your pages, the colors used for color coding, and many other style options.

Set Preferences

① Click **Edit**.

② Click **Preferences**.

If you are using a Macintosh computer, click **Dreamweaver** from the top menu and then click **Preferences**.

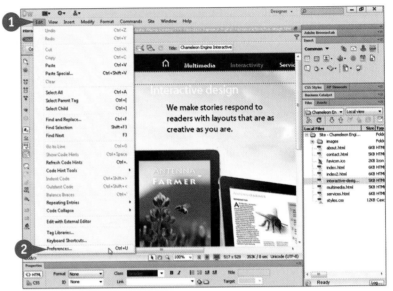

The Preferences dialog box appears.

③ Click a Preferences category, such as **Fonts**.

Ⓐ Options appear for the category that you selected.

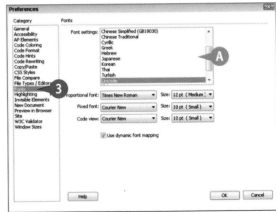

④ Change the settings for the property that you want to alter.

Ⓑ In this example, the **Code View Size** drop-down menu is used to change the font size to 14 pt.

⑤ Click **OK**.

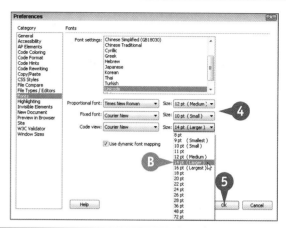

The changes take effect immediately.

Ⓒ In this example, the text in Code view is enlarged to display in a 14 pt font size.

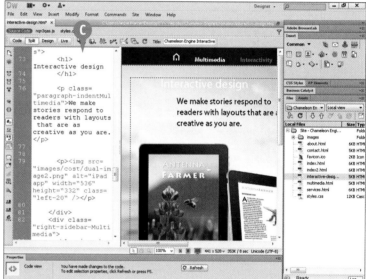

TIP

How do I ensure that Dreamweaver does not change my HTML or other code?
You can select options in the Code Rewriting category in the Preferences dialog box to ensure that Dreamweaver does not automatically correct or modify your code. For example, you can turn off the error-correcting functions, specify the files that Dreamweaver should not rewrite based on file extension, and disable the character-encoding features.

CHAPTER 4

Working with HTML

Dreamweaver helps you to build web pages by automatically writing the HTML code as you insert images, format text, and add other features to your pages in Design view. This chapter introduces you to the HTML code behind your pages, as well as some of the tools in Dreamweaver that you can use to edit, add, and remove HTML code.

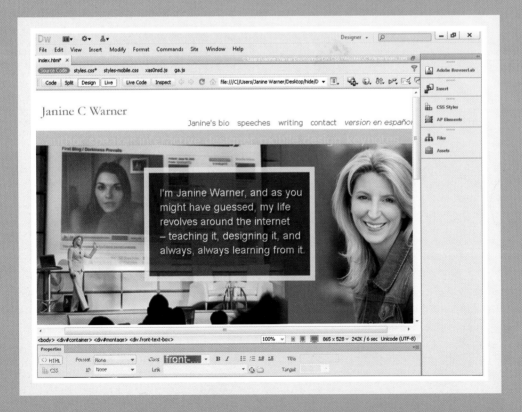

Introducing HTML

You do not have to learn HTML if you use Dreamweaver to create your web pages. Dreamweaver writes the HTML code for you, which can save you time and trouble. However, learning the basics of HTML can help you better understand how web design works and make it easier for you to troubleshoot conflicts and code errors when they occur. You can create pages in Design view, but remember that you always have the option of writing or editing HTML in Code view.

HTML and XHTML

Hypertext Markup Language (HTML) is a formatting language that you can use to create web pages. When you open a web page in a web browser, the HTML code tells the web browser how to display the text, images, and other content on the

page. By default, Dreamweaver CS6 writes code in the version of HTML known as *XHTML 1.0 Transitional* because it is a stricter version of HTML that complies with contemporary web standards.

HTML Tags

The basic unit of HTML is called a *tag*. You can recognize HTML tags by their angle brackets:

```
<h1>This is a
headline</h1>

<p>It is followed
by some plain
text in a
paragraph tag.
```

```
<b>This text will appear bold because it is surrounded by the bold tag.</b> This text will not be bold.</p>
```

You can format text and other elements on your page by placing them inside the HTML tags. When you use the formatting tools in Dreamweaver, the program automatically inserts tags in the code.

How Tags Work

Some HTML tags work in pairs. Open and close tags surround content in a document and control the formatting of the content, such as when the `<strong>` and `</strong>` tags set off bold text. Other tags can stand alone, such as the `<br />` tag, which adds a line break. HTML tags must have a closing tag, even if there is only one tag, and close tags always contain a forward slash (/). This is why the line break tag in HTML looks like this: `<br />`. HTML must be written in lowercase letters.

Create Web Pages without Knowing HTML

Dreamweaver streamlines the process of creating web pages by giving you an easy-to-use, visual interface with which you can generate HTML code. You specify formatting with menu commands and button clicks, and Dreamweaver takes care of writing the underlying HTML code. When you build a web page in the Document window, you can see your page as it will appear in a web browser instead of as HTML code.

Edit HTML Documents in a Text Editor

Because HTML documents are plain-text files, you can open and edit them with any text editor. In fact, in the early days of the web, most people created their pages with simple editors such as Notepad (in Windows) and SimpleText (for the Macintosh). If you use Dreamweaver, you have the advantage of being able to write HTML code when you want to or letting Dreamweaver write it for you.

HTML Code

```
<head>
<title>Diamond Jubilee of Elizabeth II
<p>The <b>Diamond Jubilee of Queen
Elizabeth II</b> is the international
celebration throughout 2012 marking
the 60th anniversary of the accession
```

Direct Access to the HTML Code

Dreamweaver allows you direct access to the raw HTML code. This is helpful if you want to edit the code directly. In Dreamweaver, you can work in Code view, Design view, or Split view, which enables you to see the Code and Design views simultaneously. You can also use the Quick Tag Editor to edit code without switching to Code or Design view.

Code View

```
<p>On 23 September 1896, Victoria
surpassed her grandfather <a href="/wiki/
George_III_of_the_United_Kingdom"
title="George III of the United
Kingdom">George III</a> as the longest-
reigning monarch in English, Scottish, and
British history. The Queen requested that
any special celebrations be delayed until
1897, to coincide with her <a href="/wiki/
```

Design View

Queen Victoria in her Di

Work in Design View and Code View

You can switch to Code view in the Document window to inspect and edit the HTML and other code on the web page. You can use the Split view to see both the HTML code and Design view at the same time.

You will probably do most of your work in Design view, which displays your page the way that it will appear in most web browsers, but it is a good practice to use Split view because it can help you learn HTML.

Work in Design View and Code View

1 In the Document window, click the **Split** view button.

A You can click the **Code** view button to display the source code of your page in the Document window.

B You can click the **Design** view button to hide the code and view only the page design as it would appear in a web browser.

C You can click the **Live** view button to preview the page as it will appear in the latest version of the Google Chrome or Safari web browsers. Live view enables you to test rollover images and other interactive features without leaving Dreamweaver.

Both Code view and Design view appear in the Document window when you click **Split**.

D The HTML and other code appear in the left pane.

E The Design view appears in the right pane.

2 Click and drag to select some text in the Design view pane.

F The corresponding code becomes highlighted in the Code view pane.

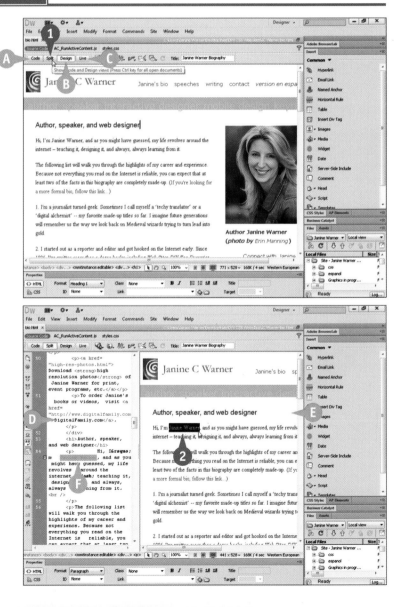

③ Type to edit the text in the Code view pane.

Ⓖ The corresponding text is automatically updated in the Design view pane.

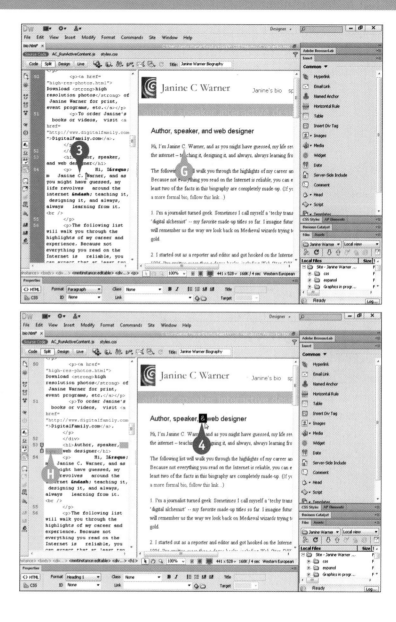

④ Click in the Design view pane and type to make changes.

Ⓗ The content in the Code view pane is updated as you make your changes.

TIP

How do I change Split view to horizontal instead of vertical?
In Dreamweaver CS6, the default Split view is split with the code on the left and the design on the right, when you choose the Split workspace layout. You can change the Code view to horizontal (as it was in versions prior to CS4) by clicking **View** and then **Split Vertically**, which deselects the vertical view and causes Dreamweaver to split the Code and Design views horizontally.

Explore Head and Body Tags

Every HTML document contains head and body tags. The head tags contain elements that do not display in the browser window, such as CSS style rules and JavaScript code. The text, images, and other elements that appear within the browser window are included between the open body tag, <body>, and the close body tag, which includes a forward slash and looks like this: </body>. To view the HTML code of a web page, you can click the **Code** view button in the Document window, or you can click **Window** and then click **Code Inspector**.

Ⓐ DOCTYPE

The DOCTYPE describes the document and identifies that it was created with XHTML 1.0 Transitional, which is currently recommended for most web pages.

Ⓑ <html> tags

Open and close <html> tags begin and end every HTML document.

Ⓒ <title> tags

Open and close <title> tags display the content that appears in the title bar of a web browser.

Ⓓ <body> tags

All the content that is displayed in the web browser window is contained within the open and close <body> tags.

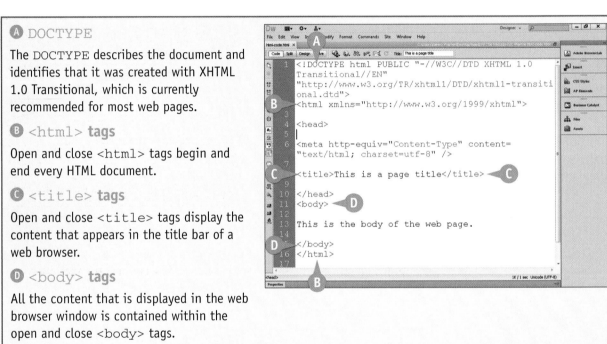

Explore Block-Formatting Tags

HTML is made up of many different types of tags, each designed to specify a particular kind of formatting. Some of the most commonly used tags are the `<div>` tag, which is used to divide sections of a page; the paragraph, `<p>`, and break, `<br>`, tags; and the headline tags: `<h1>` through `<h6>`. To help you identify these common tags, the same page is displayed in the two following figures, first in Code view and then in Design view.

Code View

This page is displayed in Code view in Dreamweaver.

Ⓐ `<div>` tag

The `<div>` tag is used to divide content and is often combined with styles that are created in CSS.

Ⓑ `<h1>` to `<h6>` tags

The heading tags are ideal for formatting headlines. The `<h1>` tag creates the largest heading style, whereas the `<h6>` tag is the smallest.

Ⓒ `<em>` tags

The `<em>` tags provide emphasis by making text appear in italics.

Ⓓ `<p>` tags

The open and close `<p>` tags separate paragraphs of content and add a space between images and other elements.

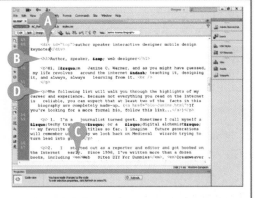

Design View

This is the same page displayed in Design view.

Ⓐ `<div>` tag

The `<div>` tag is displayed in Design view as a box. The width and centering of the container is defined with a CSS style.

Ⓑ `<h1>` to `<h6>` tags

The `<h1>` tag makes the headline text large and bold.

Ⓒ `<em>` tags

The `<em>` tags provide emphasis by making text appear in italics.

Ⓓ `<p>` tags

The `<p>` tag separates content into paragraph blocks and adds space around images and other elements.

Clean Up HTML Code

Dreamweaver can optimize the code for your web pages by deleting redundant or nonfunctional tags. This can decrease the page file size and make the source code easier to read in Code view.

It is easy to create unused tags when you do things such as copy and paste content in Design view because if you do not select the tags when you copy the text, the tags get left behind in the code. To keep formatting more consistent, it is a good idea to delete unused tags by running the Clean Up XHTML command.

Clean Up HTML Code

1 Click **Split** to display the Code view and Design view at the same time.

Ⓐ In this example, there are two empty <h1> tags.

Ⓑ The extra <h1> tags add blank space to the top of the page in Design view.

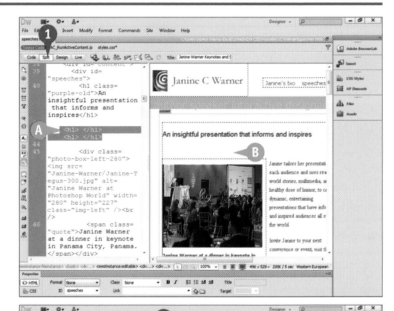

2 Click **Commands**.

3 Click **Clean Up XHTML**.

The Clean Up HTML/XHTML dialog box appears.

④ Click the options for code that you want to remove or clean up (☐ changes to ☑).

⑤ Click **OK**.

Ⓒ The cleaned-up HTML code appears in Code view. In this example, the two empty <h1> tags were removed.

Ⓓ The corresponding changes are also visible in Design view. In this example, there is no longer any extra space at the top of the page.

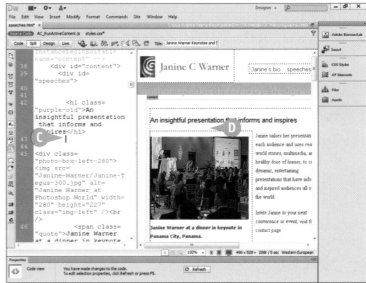

TIP

Does Dreamweaver fix invalid HTML code?

By default, Dreamweaver rewrites some instances of invalid HTML code. When you open an HTML document, Dreamweaver rewrites tags that are not nested properly, closes tags that are not allowed to remain open, and removes extra closing tags. If Dreamweaver does not recognize a tag, it highlights it in red and displays it in the Document window, but it does not remove the tag. You can change or turn off this behavior by clicking **Edit**, then clicking **Preferences**, and then selecting the category **Code Rewriting**.

View and Edit Head Content

reamweaver offers you various ways to view, add to, and edit the head content of a web page. Elements such as meta tags are not visible when the page is displayed in a web browser, but they are still very important. For example, meta tags store special descriptive information about the page that can be used by search engines. Although not all search engines use meta tag information, including this content in your pages can improve search engine results.

View and Edit Head Content

Insert Meta Keywords

1. Click **Insert**.

2. Click **HTML**.

3. Click **Head Tags**.

4. Click **Keywords**.

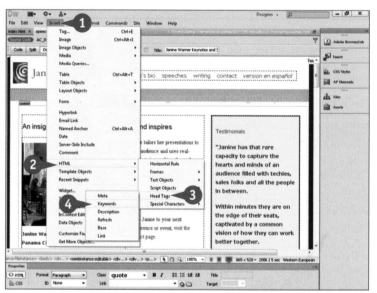

The Keywords dialog box appears.

5. Type a series of keywords, separated by commas, that describe the content of the page.

6. Click **OK**.

The keywords are added to the code.

Note: Keywords are not displayed in Design view or in a web browser.

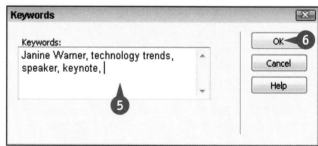

Insert a Meta Description

1 Click **Insert**.

2 Click **HTML**.

3 Click **Head Tags**.

4 Click **Description**.

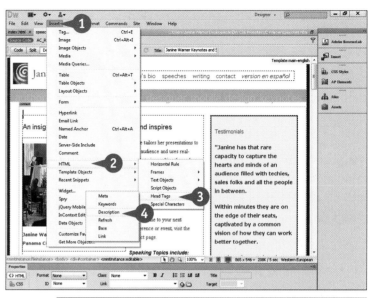

The Description dialog box appears.

5 Type a brief description of the content of the page.

6 Click **OK**.

The description is added to the code.

Note: Descriptions are not displayed in Design view or in a web browser.

TIP

How can I influence how search engines rank my pages?
Some search engines give greater importance to the description and keyword information that you add to the head content of HTML documents than others, but it is always a good practice to include it. You can also improve search engine ranking by including keywords in the title tag of the page.

Make Quick Edits to HTML Tags

The Code and Split view options are best when you want to do extensive work in the HTML code, but if you just want to get quick access to HTML and other code, you can use the Quick Tag Editor. The *Quick Tag Editor* is a handy tool for making quick changes to tags without using the Code view. The Quick Tag Editor is ideal for making minor changes, such as renaming a class or ID style or changing an <h1> tag to an <h2> tag.

Make Quick Edits to HTML Tags

Use the Quick Tag Editor

1. Click to place your cursor in an area of the page that you want to edit, or click and drag to select a section of text.

2. Right-click (Control + click) the tag that you want to edit in the Tag selector.

3. Click **Quick Tag Editor**.

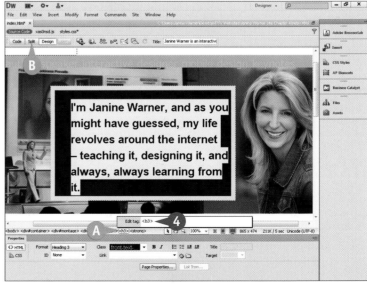

4. Click to select the tag and type to replace, delete, or add more text.

5. Press Enter (Return).

A. The tag is automatically changed in the HTML code, and the change becomes visible in the Tag selector and in the formatting in Design view.

B. You can click **Split** to view the code if you want to check your work.

Remove a Tag

1 Click to place your cursor in an area of the page that you want to edit, such as this bold text formatted with the <strong> tag.

Note: It is not necessary to select the entire text section or image to select the tag.

2 Right-click (Control + click) the tag that you want to remove in the Tag selector.

3 Click **Remove Tag**.

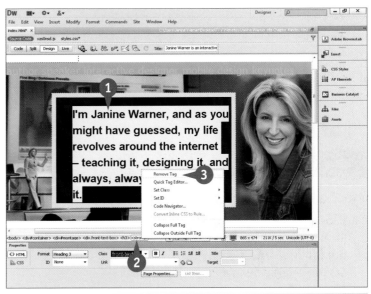

C The tag and any related formatting is removed. In this example, the text is no longer bold.

Note: When you want to change the way text or other content is formatted, removing a tag before adding more formatting is a good practice because it can prevent multiple tags from being applied to the same content.

4 Click **Live** to view the page as it will appear in the latest web browsers.

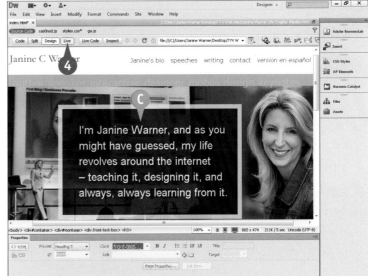

TIPS

Does Dreamweaver support all HTML tags?
Dreamweaver CS6 includes the vast majority of HTML tags in its many menus and panels. You can also write your own tags in Code view if you want to use tags that are not supported in Dreamweaver's features. When you write HTML in Code view, Dreamweaver automatically provides assistance with its code-completion features.

What does the text *Lorem ipsum dolor* mean that appears in web templates?
The text is Latin, a commonly used language for *dummy text*, which is used as a placeholder when laying out pages. Although Latin text is often used as placeholder text in designs, its meaning generally has nothing to do with its usage. The idea is that using Latin text will make it obvious that the text still needs to be replaced.

Using Code Snippets to Add Special Formatting

Y̶ou can insert short pieces of prewritten code from the Snippets panel. Like other panels, you can open the Snippets panel by selecting it from the Window menu. This is a handy feature for adding special formatting and for storing commonly used formatting options where they are easy to apply to the page. Snippets can be especially useful if you are working with a team of developers with varying skill sets. More experienced programmers can create snippets that less experienced programmers can then use when formatting pages.

Using Code Snippets to Add Special Formatting

1 Click **Window**.

2 Click **Snippets**.

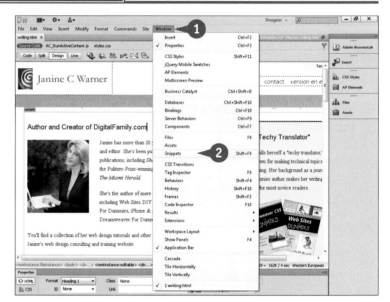

Ⓐ The Snippets panel appears.

3 Click to place your cursor where you want the snippet to appear in your page.

4 Click + to open a snippet collection.

5 Double-click a snippet to insert it.

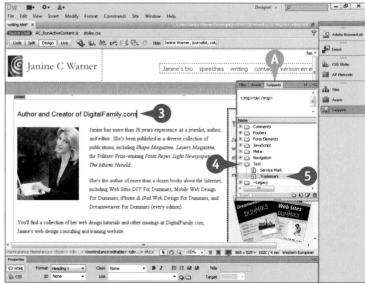

Ⓑ The snippet is inserted into the document.

6 Double-click the gray bar at the top of the panel group to close the Snippets panel.

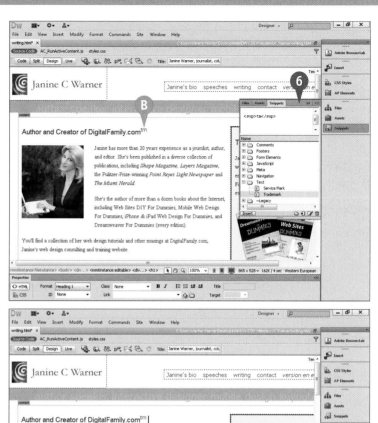

Ⓒ The panel group closes.

TIPS

How many snippets can I use?

You can create your own snippets to make it easy to add frequently used pieces of code to your pages, and you can add as many snippets as you like to Dreamweaver. You can also choose from a variety of snippets included with Dreamweaver.

What types of snippets are included in Dreamweaver?

When you open the Snippets panel in Dreamweaver, you will find eight folders of snippets. Each folder contains a collection of text and code snippets that you can use for common tasks. For example, the Footer folder contains a snippet with text that you can use for a copyright notice.

CHAPTER 5

Formatting and Styling Text

Text is the easiest type of information to add to a web page using Dreamweaver. This chapter shows you how to create and format headlines, paragraphs, bulleted lists, and stylized text.

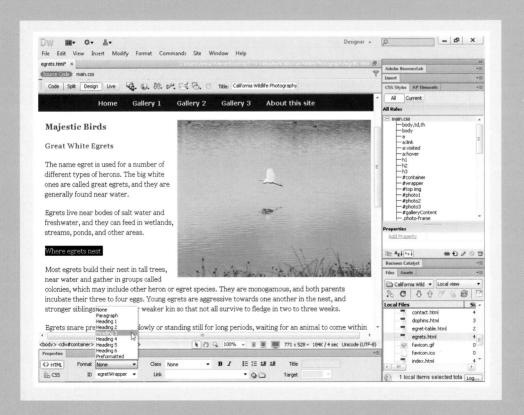

Create a Heading

The best way to format headlines is with heading tags because they can help you create a hierarchical structure for the content in your pages. There are six heading tags: Heading 1 is the largest, and Heading 6 is the smallest. By default, the Heading 1 tag makes text extra large and bold. The rest of the headings format text in progressively smaller sizes. In this section, you learn how to apply the heading tags to text. In Chapter 11, "Creating and Applying Cascading Style Sheets," you find out how to use CSS to change the formatting style of the heading tags.

Create a Heading

1. Click and drag to select the text that you want to use for a main heading.

2. Click the **Format** ☐.

3. Click **Heading 1**.

Ⓐ The font size changes to the largest heading size, and the text changes to bold. White space separates it from other text.

4. Click and drag to select text that you want to use for a second-level heading.

5. Click the **Format** ☐.

6. Click **Heading 2**.

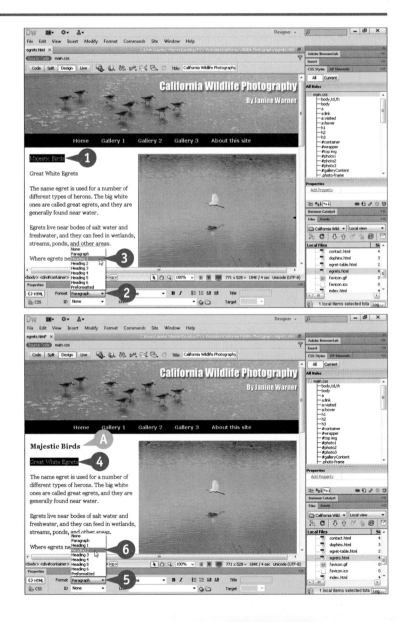

60

B The text changes to second-level headline, with a size slightly smaller than the first, and it also becomes bold.

Note: The higher the heading number, the smaller the text formatting.

7 Click and drag to select text that you want to use for a third-level heading.

8 Click the **Format** ▾.

9 Click **Heading 3**.

C The headline changes to a size smaller than the Heading 2 size but remains bold.

Note: Using CSS, which is covered in Chapter 11, you can change the size, font family, and other formatting features of text formatted with the heading tags.

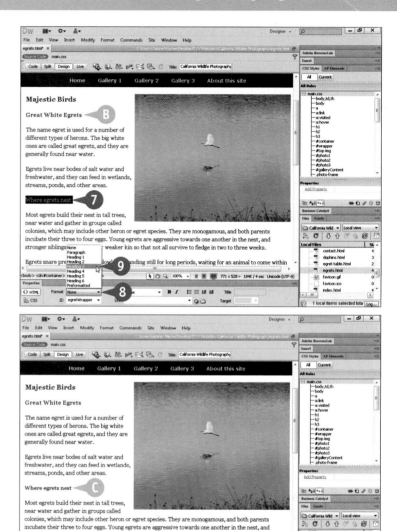

TIPS

What heading levels should I use to format my text?

Headings 1, 2, and 3 are often used for titles and subtitles. Heading 4 is similar to a bold version of default text. Headings 5 and 6 are often used for smaller text, such as copyright or disclaimer information.

Why are my headlines different sizes when I see them on another computer?

Size can vary from one computer to the next, and some users set their web browsers to display larger or smaller type on their computers. Browsers use the default text size to determine the size of the heading. By default, Heading 1 text is three times larger than the default text size, and Heading 6 text is one-third the default size.

Create Paragraphs

You can organize the text on your web page by creating and aligning paragraphs. When you press Enter (or Return for a Mac), you add a paragraph tag to the code, which creates a line break and space between paragraphs. As you discover in the next section, "Create Line Breaks," when you do not want a full paragraph break, you can hold down the Shift key and press Enter (or the Shift key and Return for a Mac) to create a single line break.

Create Paragraphs

1. Type the text for your web page in the Document window.

2. Position ▷ where you want a paragraph break.

3. Press Enter (Return).

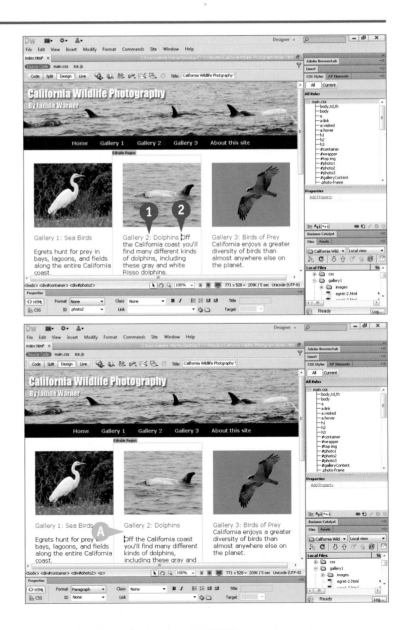

Ⓐ A blank line appears between the blocks of text, separating the text into paragraphs.

62

Note: Paragraphs align left by default.

④ Click and drag to select the paragraph that you want to align.

⑤ Click **Format**.

⑥ Click **Align**.

⑦ Choose an alignment option to align your paragraph.

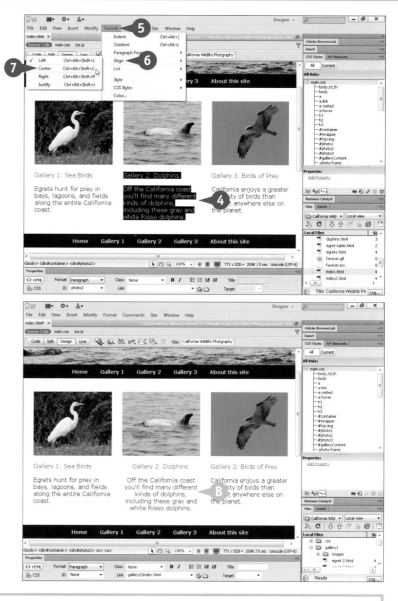

Ⓑ The paragraph aligns on the page.

Note: In this example, the text is centered. You can also control the alignment of text, images, and other content using Cascading Style Sheets, covered in Chapters 11 and 12.

TIPS

What controls the width of the paragraphs on my web page?
The width of your paragraphs depends on the width of the web browser window or the container that surrounds your text. You can use tables or `div` tags with CSS to control the width of your paragraphs. If you do not, when a user changes the size of the browser window, the widths of the paragraphs will also change. For more information on tables, see Chapter 8. For more information on CSS, see Chapters 11 and 12.

What is the HTML code for paragraphs?
In HTML, paragraphs are surrounded by opening `<p>` and closing `</p>` tags. You can click the **Code** view button to view the HTML code of the page.

Create Line Breaks

When you do not want a full paragraph break, you can use line breaks to keep lines of text adjacent. When you hold down the **Shift** key and press **Enter** (or the **Shift** key and **Return** for a Mac), you create a single line break. Single line breaks are commonly used between each line in a street address or when you want two lines of text to be grouped together — for example, when you have a list of names and titles and want to keep both lines close together.

Create Line Breaks

1 Click where you want the line of text to break.

2 Press **Shift** + **Enter** (**Return**).

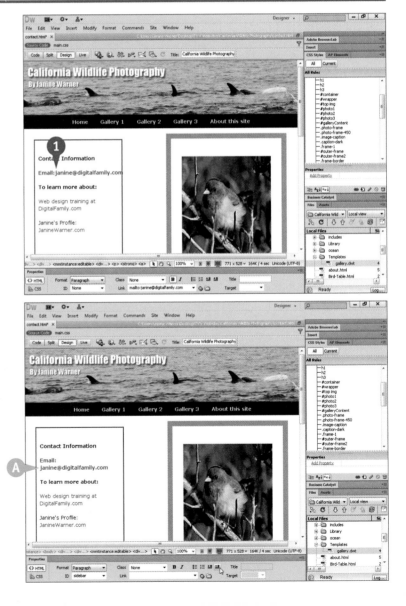

A Dreamweaver adds a line break.

Note: You can combine paragraph and line breaks to add more space between lines of text.

Indent Paragraphs

HTML includes a tag called `<blockquote>`, which can be used to indent text. Technically, this tag should be reserved only for long quotes, commonly called *block quotes*. However, many web designers use the `<blockquote>` tag as a quick-and-easy way to indent any line or paragraph of text. Indenting text is a standard way to make selected paragraphs stand out from the rest of the text on your web page in much the same way that you would use the **Tab** key, or indent feature, in a word-processing program.

Indent Paragraphs

1 Click and drag to select a paragraph or series of paragraphs.

2 Click 🔲 to indent the text.

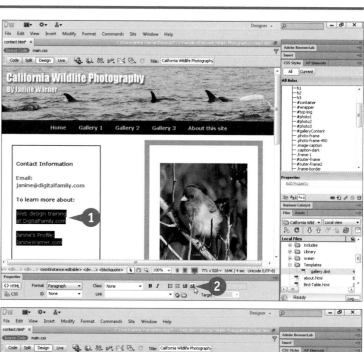

A Additional space appears in both the left and right margins of the paragraph.

You can repeat steps **1** and **2** to indent a paragraph further.

B You can outdent an indented paragraph by clicking 🔲.

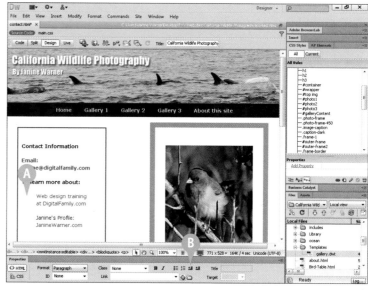

Create Lists

If you have text on the web that people commonly scan for information more than read it, a great way to organize it is to format the text items as ordered and unordered lists. *Unordered lists* have items that are indented and bulleted. This option works well when you have a list of items that do not have to be followed sequentially. *Ordered lists* have items that are indented and numbered or lettered, which is ideal for step-by-step exercises, top 10 lists, and other lists for which order and priority are important.

Create Lists

Create an Unordered List

1 Type your list items in the Document window.

2 Click between the items and press `Enter` (`Return`) to place each item in a separate paragraph.

3 Click and drag to select all the list items.

4 Click the Unordered List button (icon) in the Property inspector.

A The list items appear indented and bulleted.

B To remove the bulleted formatting, click and drag to select all the list items and then click (icon) again.

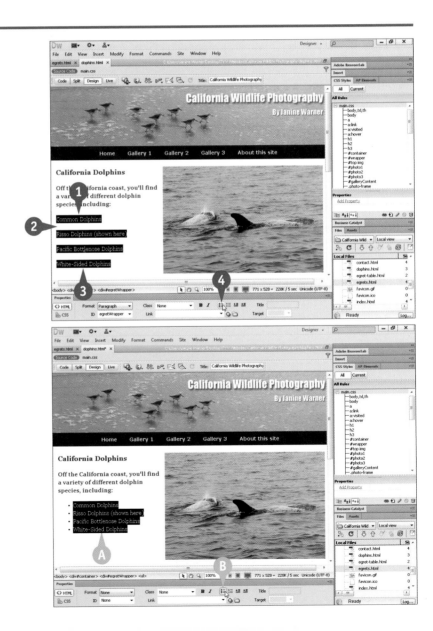

Create an Ordered List

1 Type your list items in the Document window.

2 Click between the items and press **Enter** (**Return**) to place each item in a separate paragraph.

3 Click and drag to select all the list items.

4 Click the Ordered List button (▦) in the Property inspector.

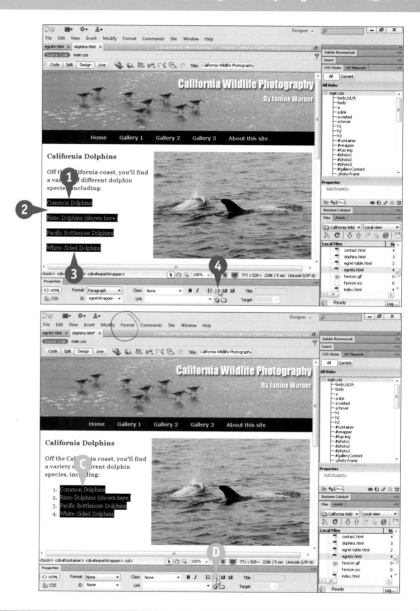

C The list items appear indented and numbered.

D To remove the numbered formatting, click and drag to select all the list items and then click ▦ again.

TIPS

Can I modify the appearance of my unordered list?

Yes. You can modify the style of an unordered list by highlighting an item in the list and clicking **Format**, then clicking **List**, and then clicking **Properties**. The dialog box that appears enables you to select different bullet styles for your unordered list.

Can I modify the appearance of my ordered list with CSS?

Yes. You can create CSS style rules for the ul, ol, and li tags and change the spacing, alignment, and other formatting elements of lists. You can find instructions for creating CSS styles in Chapters 11 and 12.

Insert Common Special Characters

You can insert special characters into your web page that do not appear on your keyboard, such as the copyright symbol, trademark symbol, and letters with accent marks. Although you can indicate a copyright or trademark using the written words, adding the symbols is more professional and accurate. When you are writing in a language other than English, accent marks and other special characters can be essential because many words, such as ano and año in Spanish, have different meanings when written without special characters.

Insert Common Special Characters

1 Click where you want to insert the special character.

2 Click **Insert**.

3 Click **HTML**.

4 Click **Special Characters**.

5 Click the special character that you want to insert.

Ⓐ The special character appears in your web page text.

The HTML code that defines that special character is inserted into the HTML code of the page.

Ⓑ You can add space, edit, and format special characters as you would any other text on your web page.

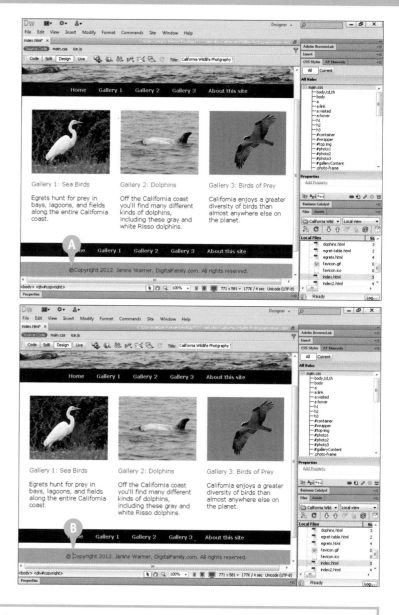

©Copyright 2012. Janine Warner, DigitalFamily.com. All rights reserved.

© Copyright 2012. Janine Warner, DigitalFamily.com. All rights reserved.

TIP

Why do special characters look strange in my web browser?

Although most web browsers display quotation marks without problems, many seemingly standard punctuation marks are considered special characters in HTML and require special code. If the browser you are using to view a page does not support the special character code or if there is an error in the code, those characters may not be displayed properly. For example, the HTML code `&copy;` creates a copyright symbol (©) in most web browsers. Similarly, the code `&#8364;` creates the symbol for the European currency, the Euro, which is this: €.

Insert Other Special Characters

You can add a long list of special characters, including the accent marks used in Spanish and French, umlauts used in German, and many other characters and symbols. As you learn in this section, you can add these special characters to your web page by choosing the **Other** option from the **Special Characters** list and then scrolling through the list of characters. When you find the one that you want to use, you click to select it, and Dreamweaver automatically inserts it into your web page.

Insert Other Special Characters

1. Click where you want to insert the special character.

2. Click **Insert**.

3. Click **HTML**.

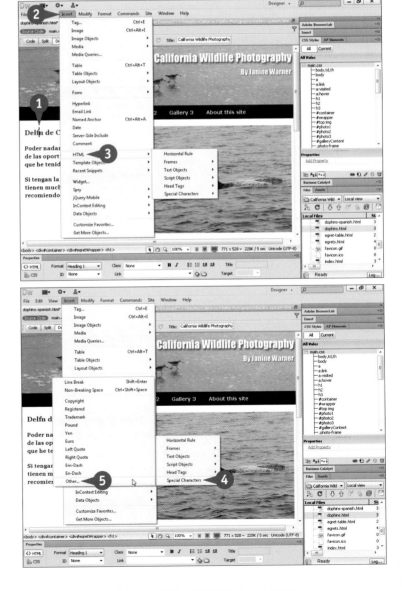

4. Click **Special Characters**.

5. Click **Other**.

The Insert Other Character dialog box appears, displaying a wide variety of special characters.

6 Click a special character.

7 Click **OK**.

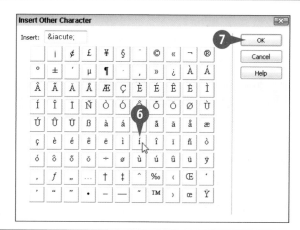

A The special character appears in your web page.

The HTML code that defines that special character is inserted into the HTML code of the page.

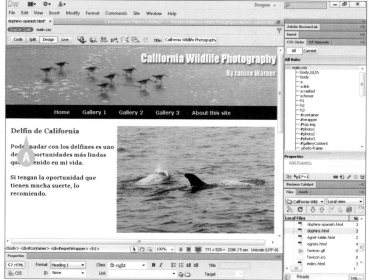

TIP

How do I include non-English-language text on my web page?
Many foreign languages feature accented characters that do not appear on standard keyboards. Dreamweaver CS6 supports spell check and all of the common characters in 37 languages, including Dutch, French, German, Polish, Russian, Spanish, Swedish, and Turkish. You can insert most of these characters using the Special Characters feature described in this section.

Copy Text from Another Document

You can save time by copying and pasting text from an existing document into Dreamweaver, instead of typing it all over again. This is particularly convenient when you have a lot of text in a word-processing program such as Microsoft Word or data in a spreadsheet program such as Excel. When you paste text in Dreamweaver, you have multiple options about how the original formatting of the text is included when it is added to your page.

Copy Text from Another Document

1 Click and drag to select text in the original file, such as this document created in Microsoft Word.

2 Click the Copy button.

Alternatively, you can press Ctrl + C (⌘ + C).

3 In Dreamweaver, click where you want to insert the text.

4 Click **Edit**.

5 Click **Paste Special**.

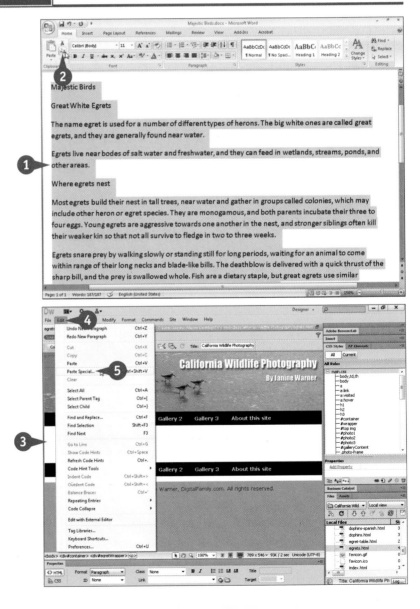

The Paste Special dialog box opens.

6 Click a Paste option.

7 Click **OK**.

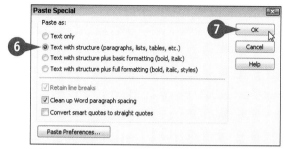

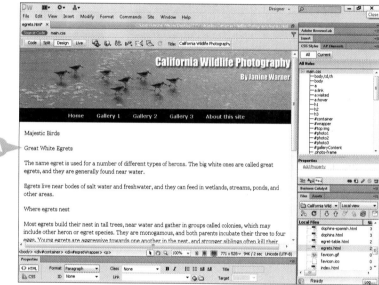

A The text is inserted into the HTML file.

Dreamweaver automatically formats the text in HTML, based on the formatting option that you selected in the Paste Special dialog box.

TIP

When is it a good idea to copy and paste text?
Even if you type at speeds of over 100 words per minute, you can save time if you do not have to retype all your documents. If your original text file was created using a word-processing program such as Microsoft Word, you can speed up the process by importing the Word document into Dreamweaver. You can also copy and paste text from Excel documents, and Dreamweaver automatically builds tables to duplicate the formatting from Excel. After you have pasted the content into Dreamweaver, you can edit and format the text or other data as you normally would.

CHAPTER 6

Working with Images and Multimedia

You can make your web page more interesting by adding multimedia elements. You can download the files featured in this chapter from www.DigitalFamily.com/tyv.

Insert an Image into a Web Page

Images are one of the most common, valuable, and eye-catching additions to any web page. You can insert many different types of images into your pages, including photos, graphics, clip art, and scanned images. Before you insert an image into a web page, you must save the image in one of three web formats: GIF, PNG, or JPEG. This section shows you how to add images in any of those formats to your web pages using Dreamweaver's Insert Image features.

Insert an Image into a Web Page

1 Click to position ⌖ where you want to insert the image.

2 Click **Insert**.

3 Click **Image**.

Ⓐ You can also click the Images button (🖼) in the Common Insert panel.

The Select Image Source dialog box appears.

4 Click ▾ and select the folder that contains the image.

5 Click the image file that you want to insert into your web page.

Ⓑ A preview of the image appears.

Ⓒ You can insert an image that exists at an external web address by typing the address in the **URL** field.

6 Click **OK**.

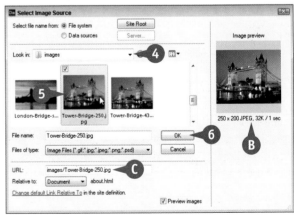

The Image Tag Accessibility Attributes dialog box appears.

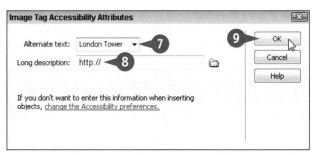

⑦ Enter a description of the image.

Note: Alternate text is displayed only if the image is not visible. It is important for visually impaired visitors who use screen readers to read web pages to them.

⑧ Enter a URL for a longer description, if available.

⑨ Click **OK**.

Ⓓ The image appears where you positioned your cursor on the web page.

Ⓔ To delete an image, click the image and press Del.

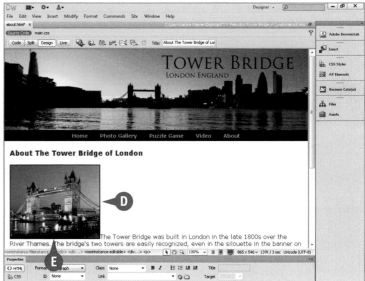

TIP

What file formats can I use for web images?

The majority of the images that you see on web pages are GIF, PNG, or JPEG files. All three of these file formats can be optimized, a process that makes them smaller than other image files and therefore download faster. The GIF and PNG formats are best for images that have a limited number of colors, such as cartoons or line art. The JPEG format is best for photographs and other images with millions of colors. You can insert GIF, PNG, and JPEG files into your web page using the steps shown in this section.

Wrap Text around an Image

You can wrap text around an image by aligning the image to one side of a web page. In previous versions of Dreamweaver, you could align images using the alignment properties, but those properties are no longer part of HTML and were removed from the Property inspector in Dreamweaver CS6. In this section, you learn how to apply a CSS rule to align an image to the left or right of a page. In Chapter 12, "Designing a Website with CSS," you learn how to create CSS rules that can be used for aligning images.

Wrap Text around an Image

With the Image on the Left

1. Click the image to select it.

2. Click the **Class** ▼.

3. Click the class style fltlft to position the image on the left side of the page.

Note: All the CSS layouts included in Dreamweaver CS6 include alignment styles named fltrt (float right) and fltlft (float left).

Ⓐ The text flows around the right of the left-aligned image.

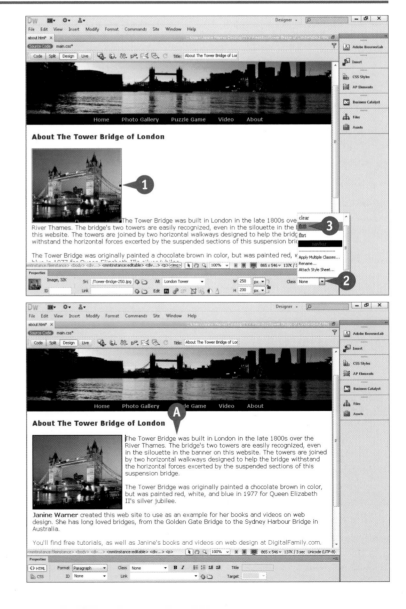

With the Image on the Right

1 Click the image to select it.

2 Click the **Class** ▾.

3 Click the class style `fltrt` to position the image on the right side of the page.

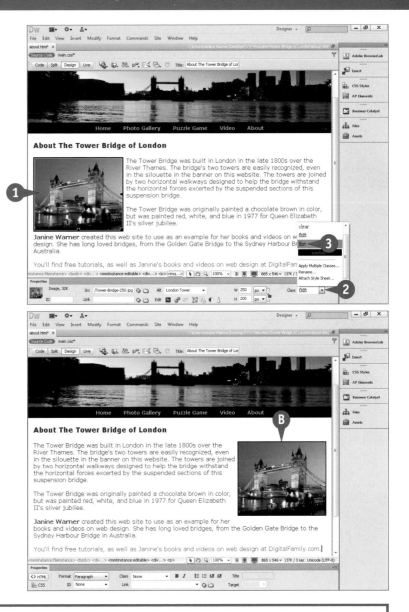

B The image is aligned to the right of the page, and the text flows around the left of the image.

Note: To learn how to create styles to align images, see the section "Using Floats to Align Elements" in Chapter 12.

TIPS

How can I determine the download time for my web page?

The total size of your web page appears in kilobytes (KB) on the status bar at the bottom of the workspace. The total size includes the size of your HTML file, the size of your images, and the size of any other elements on the web page. Next to the size is the estimated download time for the web page.

What is the ideal size of a web page?

Most web designers feel comfortable putting up a page with a total size under 200KB. However, there are exceptions. For example, you may want to break this rule for an especially important image file. The 200KB limit does not apply to multimedia files, although multimedia files should be kept as small as possible.

Add Space around an Image

You can create margins to add space around an image and separate the image from any text or other images on your web page. This creates a cleaner page layout and makes it easier to read the text that wraps around an image. Using Cascading Style Sheets, you can add as much or as little margin space as you want in your designs. In this section, you learn how to alter the amount of margin space in a CSS rule that has already been created. In Chapters 11 and 12, you find instructions for creating CSS rules.

Add Space around an Image

1 Click **Window**.

2 Click **CSS Styles**.

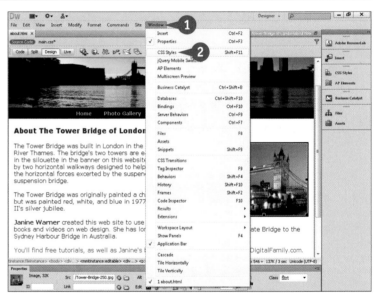

A The CSS Styles panel opens.

3 Double-click the name of a CSS style rule, such as `fltrt`.

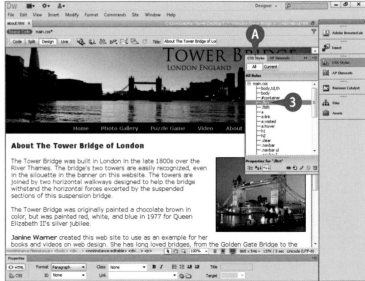

The rule opens in the CSS Rule Definition dialog box.

④ Click **Box**.

⑤ Type the amount of margin space that you want around the image in the **Margin** fields.

⑥ Click **OK**.

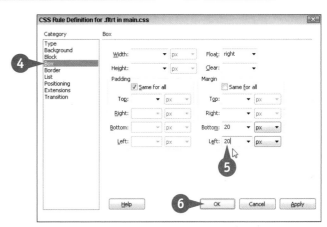

Ⓑ Extra space appears, creating a margin around the image in the size specified.

In this example, the margin space on the left and bottom of the image increased.

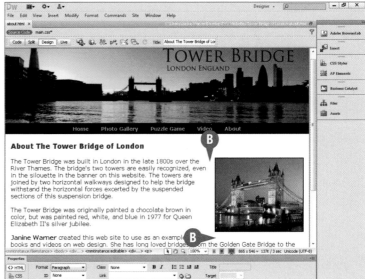

TIPS

How do I add a border around my image?

You can define a CSS rule to add a border around an image on any or all of the sides of the image. Using CSS, you can specify the size and color of the border. You learn more about CSS in Chapters 11 and 12.

How much space should I add around my image?

You can also add space around an image in a CSS rule by defining the margin property. In general, 8 to 10 pixels of margin space creates a visually appealing distance between an image and any text or other elements that wrap around it, but the amount of space that works best in your pages will depend on the rest of the design. If you like a lot of white space in your designs, add more margin space between elements. You learn more about creating margins with CSS in Chapters 11 and 12.

Crop an Image

You can trim, or *crop,* an image by using the Crop tool in the Property inspector. You can then drag the crop handles to adjust how much of the image you want to delete. The Dreamweaver cropping tool is useful for quick edits without using an external image-editing program, such as Photoshop. Be careful when you use the cropping tool in Dreamweaver, however, because it actually crops the image file — not just zooms in. When you save a page with an image you have cropped, the size of the image is permanently changed.

Crop an Image

1 Click the image to select it.

2 Click the Crop tool button (⊠).

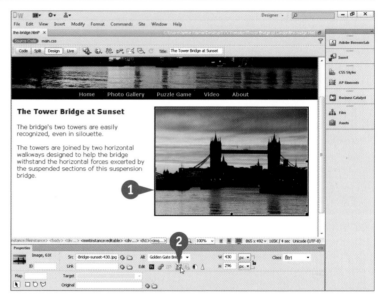

A warning dialog box appears.

Ⓐ You can turn off this warning by clicking the check box (☐ changes to ☑).

3 Click **OK**.

④ Click and drag the black square handles to define the area that you want to crop.

The part of the photo that appears grayed out will be deleted.

⑤ Double-click inside the crop box.

Ⓑ The image is trimmed to the size of the crop box.

Note: Keep in mind that when you save the page, the image is permanently cropped.

TIP

Should I edit images in Dreamweaver or use an external graphics program?
Adobe has added the Crop and other basic editing tools to make working on a web page faster and easier. If you need to do a simple crop, the Crop tool is faster than opening the image in an image-editing program such as Adobe Fireworks or Adobe Photoshop. However, if you want to save a copy of the original before you make the crop or do other image editing, then you need to use a dedicated image-editing program.

Resize an Image

You can change the display size of an image without changing its file size. You can do this by changing the pixel size in the Property inspector or by clicking and dragging a corner of the image. This technique is fine for making minor adjustments to the size of an image. However, if you want to change the size of an image significantly, you should do so in an image-editing program, such as Photoshop.

Pixels are tiny, solid-color squares that make up a digital image.

Resize an Image

Resize Using Pixel Dimensions

1 Click the image to select it.

A The dimensions of the image appear.

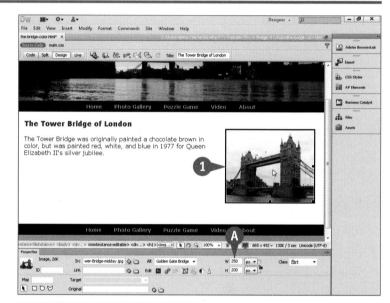

2 Type the width that you want in pixels.

3 Press Enter (Return).

4 Type the height that you want in pixels.

5 Press Enter (Return).

B The image is displayed with its new dimensions.

Click and Drag to Resize

1 Click the image to select it.

2 Drag one of the handles at the edge of the image (changes to).

To resize the image proportionally, press and hold down **Shift** as you drag a corner.

The image expands or contracts to the new size.

Reset the Image to Its Original Size

Note: You can reset any image to its original size.

1 Click the image to select it.

2 Click the Reset Size button (🔄) in the Property inspector.

The image returns to its original size.

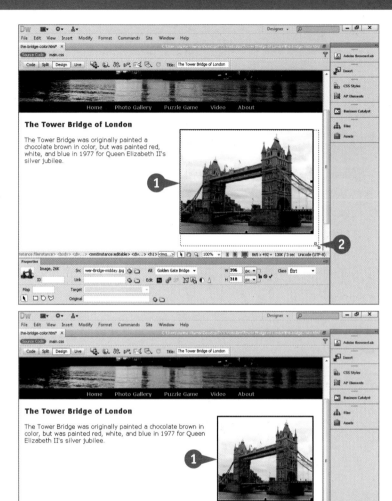

TIP

What is the best way to change the dimensions of an image on a web page?
Although you can quickly change the display size of an image by changing the pixel dimensions in the Property inspector or by clicking and dragging to stretch or shrink it on the web page, this does not actually resize the image's true dimensions. Enlarging the display size of an image by changing the pixel size in Dreamweaver may cause distortion or blurriness. Reducing the size of an image this way requires visitors to your site to download an image that is larger than necessary. A better way to resize an image is to open it in an image editor such as Adobe Fireworks or Photoshop and change its actual size.

Open an Image in an Image Editor

Adobe designed Dreamweaver to work with multiple image programs so that you can easily open and edit images while you are working on your web pages. Adobe Fireworks and Photoshop are sophisticated image-editing programs that you can use to make significant changes to the size, color balance, and other elements of an image.

Although you can use any image editor, Fireworks and Photoshop can be integrated into the program so that they can be launched from within Dreamweaver because Adobe makes all three programs.

Open an Image in an Image Editor

1 Click the image to select it in Dreamweaver.

Note: You can open any image in an external image editor from within Dreamweaver.

2 Click the Photoshop button (⬛) in the Property inspector.

You may have to wait a few moments while Photoshop opens.

Note: In Dreamweaver's preferences, you can associate other image editors, such as Adobe Fireworks.

The image opens in the Photoshop window.

You can now edit the image.

3 After making your changes, click **File**.

4 Click **Save As**.

5 Save the image with the same name and format, to replace the original image.

Your changes to the image become permanent.

Note: You can save a copy of the image with a new name, leaving the originally unchanged, but you will have to reinsert the image to replace it in your web page.

A Photoshop saves the image, and it is automatically updated in the Dreamweaver window.

To edit the image again or to edit another image, you can select the image and repeat steps **2** to **5**.

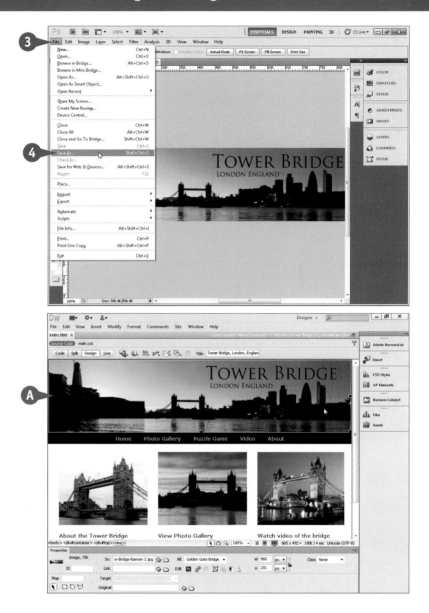

TIP

What can you do in an image-editing program?
A program such as Adobe Fireworks or Photoshop enables you to edit and combine images to create almost anything that you can imagine. In Dreamweaver's preferences, you can associate Adobe Fireworks, Photoshop, or any other editor on your computer. If you use Fireworks, you can open it to edit an image directly from Dreamweaver by clicking the **Edit/Fireworks Logo** button (or ◰ if you use Photoshop).

Add a Background Image

You can insert an image into the background of a web page to add texture and depth to your design. Background images appear behind any text or images that are on your web page. This means that you can use background images behind other images to create a layered effect in the design. By default, background images are repeated across and down the web browser window unless you use the settings in the Property inspector to set the image not to repeat.

Add a Background Image

1 Click **Page Properties** in the Property inspector.

The Page Properties dialog box appears.

2 Click **Appearance (CSS)**.

3 Click **Browse**.

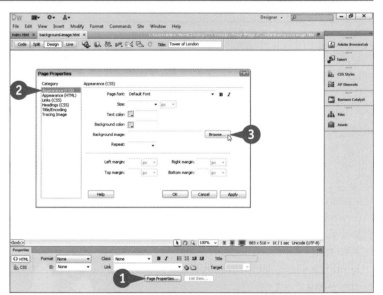

The Select Image Source dialog box appears.

4 Click ▾ and select the folder that contains the background image file.

5 Click the background image that you want to insert.

Ⓐ A preview image appears.

6 Click **OK**.

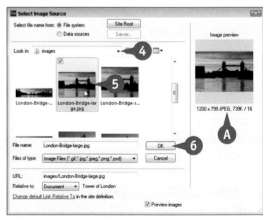

You are returned to the Page Properties dialog box.

B The image filename and path appear in the Background Image text field.

7 Click ▼ and choose an option to specify whether or not the image should repeat across and down the page.

8 Click **OK**.

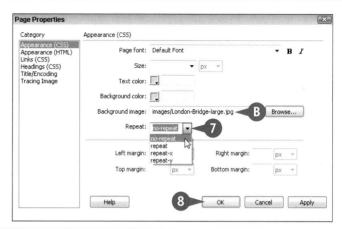

The image appears as a background on the web page.

Note: In this example, I defined the rule with **no-repeat** selected in step 7 because the image fills the entire design area. By default, if the image is smaller than the display area, it tiles horizontally and vertically to fill the entire window. As you can see in step 7, you can define the rule so that the image repeats only on the x-axis (horizontally) or the y-axis (vertically).

TIPS

What types of images make good backgrounds?
Textures, subtle patterns, and photos with large open areas all make good background images. It is important to make sure that the image does not clash with the text and other content in the foreground or overwhelm the rest of the page. Using an image that tiles seamlessly is also a good idea so that your background appears to be one large image that covers the entire page. Fireworks and

Photoshop include a number of features that can help you create background images.

Are backgrounds typically patterns?
That depends on the overall design of your website. Using CSS, you can alter the way an image appears in the background of a page so that it does not repeat — or so that it repeats only vertically or horizontally.

Change the Background Color

You can add interest and depth to your design by changing the background color of your web page. When you use the color well in the Page Properties dialog box in Dreamweaver, you can choose from a collection of color swatches, or you can select almost any color that you can imagine using the Color Picker. Adding color to your designs can make your pages look richer and more vibrant. Make sure that the color you use for your text has enough contrast with the background color so that your pages are readable on a computer monitor.

Change the Background Color

1 Click **Page Properties** in the Property inspector.

The Page Properties dialog box appears.

2 Click **Appearance (CSS)**.

3 Click the **Background color** ■ to open the color palette (⬚ changes to 🖊).

4 Click a color using the Eyedropper tool (🖊).

5 Click **OK**.

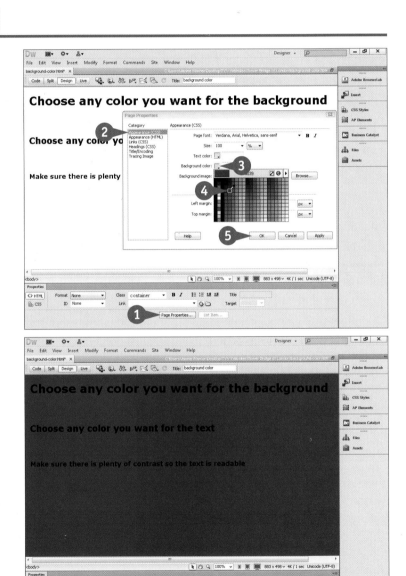

The background of your web page is displayed in the color that you selected.

Note: For additional information about web color, see Chapter 11, "Creating and Applying Cascading Style Sheets."

Change Text Colors

You can change the text color for the entire page using Dreamweaver's Page Properties dialog box. When you use the color well in the Page Properties dialog box in Dreamweaver, you can choose from a collection of color swatches, or you can select almost any color you can imagine using the Color Picker. When you alter page and text colors, make sure that the text is still readable. In general, light text colors work best against a dark background, and dark text colors work best against a light background.

Change Text Colors

1 Click **Page Properties** in the Property inspector.

The Page Properties dialog box appears.

2 Click **Appearance (CSS)**.

3 Click the **Text color** ■ to open the color palette (⟨⟩ changes to ✐).

4 Click a color using the Eyedropper tool (✐).

5 Click **OK**.

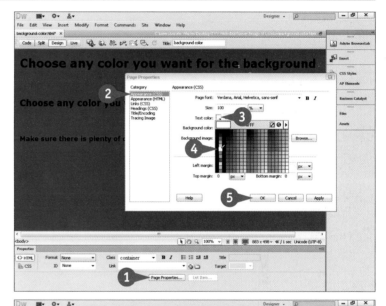

Any text on your web page is displayed in the color that you selected.

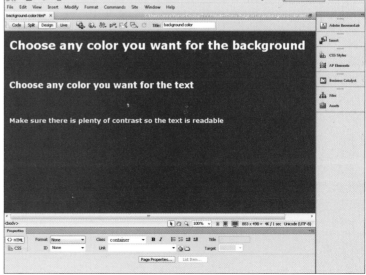

Insert a Flash File

You can add life to your web page by adding Flash animations and slide shows. A *Flash file* is a multimedia file that is created with Adobe Flash or other software that supports the Flash format with the .swf extension. Flash files are ideal for animated banners, cartoons, slide shows, interactive animations, and online games. Flash is well supported by browsers on most Windows and Mac computers, but Flash files do not display in web pages viewed on an iPhone or iPad.

Insert a Flash File

1 Position ⬚ where you want to insert a Flash file.

2 Click **Insert**.

3 Click **Media**.

4 Click **SWF**.

The Select SWF dialog box appears.

5 Click ▼ and select the folder that contains the Flash file.

Note: Flash filenames end with an .swf file extension.

6 Click the file that you want to insert into your web page.

7 Click **OK**.

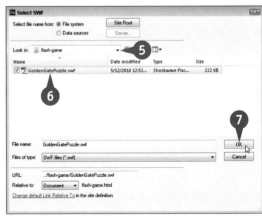

A A gray box representing the Flash file appears in the Document window.

B You can change the size of the Flash movie by clicking and dragging a corner or by entering a width and height in the Property inspector.

8 Click **Play** in the Property inspector to test the Flash file.

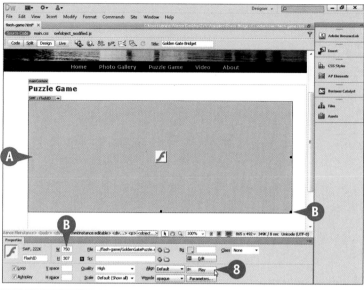

C The Flash file is displayed in your Dreamweaver document.

D You can click the **Quality** ▼ and select the level of quality at which you want your movie to play.

Note: The higher the quality, the better it is displayed, but then it takes longer to download.

Note: When you save a page after inserting a Flash file, Dreamweaver automatically creates special scripts to help the Flash file play in a web browser. See the Tip below for more details.

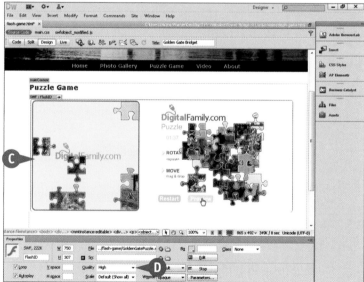

TIP

Why do I need scripts to play a Flash file?
When you insert a Flash file into a web page, Dreamweaver automatically inserts a special script into the code of the page and creates two files that are saved in your main site folder in a folder called *Scripts*. These scripts must be uploaded to your web server for the Flash file to play properly in a web browser. Make sure that you upload the entire Scripts folder, as well as the web page and the Flash file itself, when you publish the site on a web server. You learn how to publish your site with Dreamweaver's FTP features in Chapter 13, "Publishing a Website."

Insert a Flash Video File

You can add audio and video files to web pages in a variety of formats, including Windows Media Audio and Video, MP4, and QuickTime. When you insert video and audio files in the Flash format, Dreamweaver provides more options for how the files play in your web pages than when you insert videos files in other formats. Flash Video files have the .flv extension.

Note: You must have the Flash Player on your computer to play a Flash Video file. If the Flash Player is not installed, the browser displays a dialog box with instructions for downloading the player.

Insert a Flash Video File

1 Position ⌖ where you want to insert the Flash Video file in the Document window.

2 Click **Insert**.

3 Click **Media**.

4 Click **FLV**.

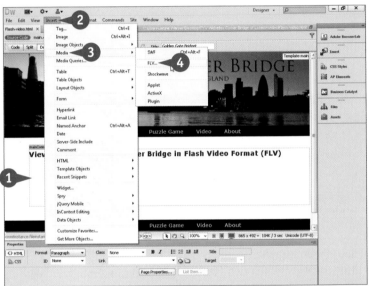

The Insert FLV dialog box appears.

5 Click **Browse** and select the Flash Video file.

Note: Flash Video filenames end with the .flv file extension.

6 Click **Detect Size** to automatically enter the height and width.

7 Click **OK**.

Note: The other settings are optional and can be left at the defaults.

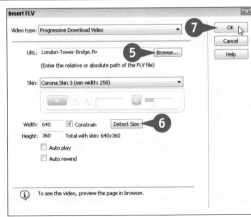

Ⓐ A gray Flash Video box appears in the Document window.

⑧ You can change the Flash Video settings in the Property inspector.

⑨ Click 🖳 to view the page in a web browser and play the video.

⑩ Click a browser.

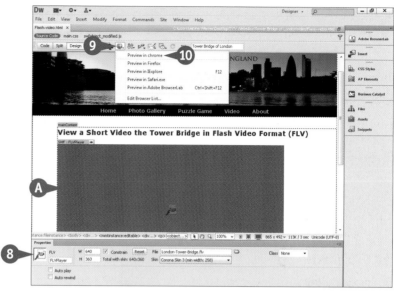

Ⓑ The selected web browser opens and displays the web page.

Ⓒ When a cursor is rolled over the video, the Flash Player controls are displayed.

Note: When you insert Flash Video, Dreamweaver automatically creates two Flash SWF files for the player controls. For the video to play properly, these files must be uploaded to the server when you upload the video file to your web server.

TIP

What should I consider when adding multimedia content to my website?
Remember that although you may have the latest computer software and a fast connection, some of your visitors may not have the necessary multimedia players or bandwidth for your multimedia files. You can add Flash, video, sound, and other multimedia files to jazz up a website, but if your visitors do not have the right programs, they cannot view them. Therefore, it is very important to use compression and other techniques to keep file sizes small and to offer links to players for any multimedia that you use.

Create a Rollover Image

You can use rollover images to add interactivity and surprise to your web pages. When a visitor rolls a cursor over a rollover image, the first image is replaced by a second image. A rollover effect can feature a dramatic change, such as the example in the figures in this section of an image taken in daylight to another taken at sunset, or it can be more subtle, depending on the differences between the two images that you use in the rollover. For the best results, both images must be the same size.

Create a Rollover Image

1 Position ⓘ where you want to insert the rollover image.

2 Click **Insert**.

3 Click **Image Objects**.

4 Click **Rollover Image**.

The Insert Rollover Image dialog box appears.

5 Type an identifying name for scripting purposes.

6 Click **Browse** and select the first image.

7 Click **Browse** and select the second image.

8 Type a description of the images.

9 Type a URL if you want the rollover to serve as a link.

10 Click **OK**.

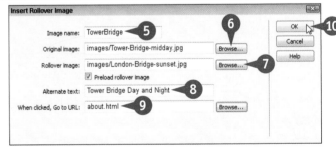

Dreamweaver automatically inserts the scripting that you need to make the rollover effect work.

(A) The first image in the rollover is displayed on the page.

(11) Click [⟳] to view the page in a web browser and test the rollover effect.

(12) Click a browser.

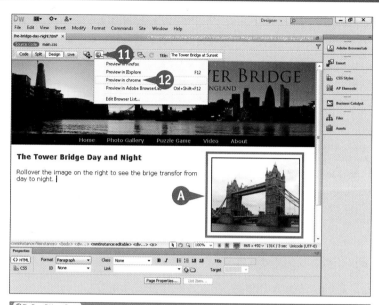

(B) When you roll your cursor over the first rollover image in a web browser, the second image appears.

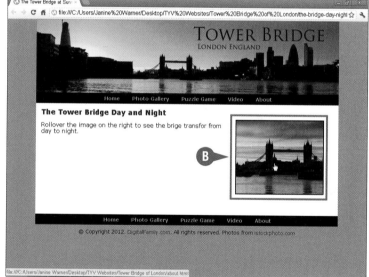

© Copyright 2012. DigitalFamily.com. All rights reserved. Photos from istockphoto.com

---

TIP

How does the rollover image work?
The interactive effect of a rollover image requires more than HTML. Dreamweaver creates this effect by using a scripting language called *JavaScript*. JavaScript is used for many kinds of interactivity, from image swaps to pop-up windows. JavaScript is more complex than HTML code. Dreamweaver includes many other JavaScript features in the Behaviors panel. To see what other kinds of behaviors are available, click **Window** and then click **Behaviors**.

Insert a YouTube Video

One of the easiest ways to add video to your web pages is to embed a video from the popular video site YouTube, www.youtube.com. You can upload your own videos to YouTube and then embed them into your pages, or you can embed almost any video already on YouTube into your website by copying and pasting a little code from YouTube into your site. When using videos from YouTube, be sure to follow the posted copyright rules. Many videos on YouTube can be used for personal or educational purposes, but most cannot be used for commercial websites without special permission.

Insert a YouTube Video

1 In a web browser, go to the YouTube website, www.youtube.com.

2 Type keywords into the Search field to find a video that you want to use.

3 Click the Search button.

Videos that match your search criteria appear.

4 Select the one that you want to insert into your web page.

5 Click **Share**.

The Share options appear.

6 Click **Embed**.

7 Copy the code from the Embed field.

8 In Dreamweaver, open the web page into which you want to insert the video.

9 Click **Split** to open the Code and Design views.

10 Click to place your cursor in the code where you want the video to appear in the page.

11 Paste the code that you copied from YouTube.

Ⓐ A gray box appears in the design area.

12 Click 🖥️ and select a browser to view the page in a web browser.

Ⓑ The video is displayed in your web page in the browser window.

13 Click the Play button to play the video.

Note: You must be connected to the Internet for the video to load from the YouTube site into your web page.

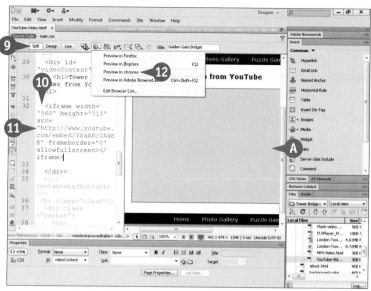

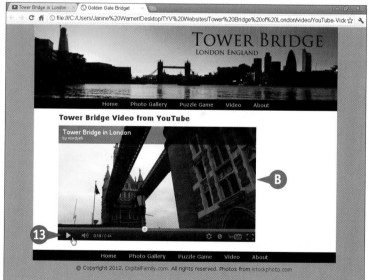

TIP

Is YouTube the only place I can host my videos?

YouTube is the most popular video-hosting site on the Internet, but there are now many websites that host video and make it easy for you to embed them in your web pages. Another popular site is Vimeo, www.vimeo.com, which many web designers prefer over YouTube because you can use Vimeo to host videos without making them visible to the public. Similarly, when you embed videos from Vimeo, you can choose not to have links to any other videos appear after your video is displayed.

CHAPTER 7

Creating Hyperlinks

Links, also called *hyperlinks,* are used to add references to web pages that take users to another page and trigger some other action, such as launching an email program to send a message. Using Dreamweaver, you can create links from one page to another page in your website or to other websites on the Internet, and you can also create email links and image maps. This chapter shows you how to create these kinds of links using both text and images.

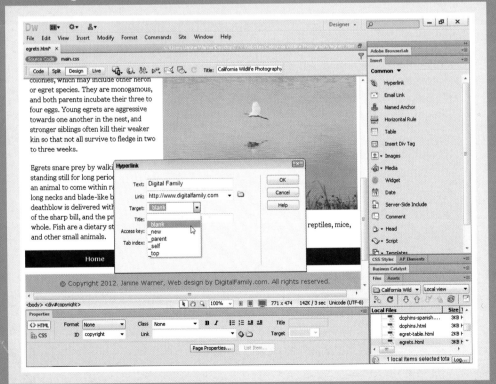

Link to Other Pages in Your Website

Links make the web go around by creating connections between related ideas and information. You can link from one page in your website to another in the site, and you can link to the same page multiple times in multiple places within the same website. Dreamweaver makes it easy to create these types of links and provides multiple options and tools for creating links. Links are a fundamental part of any website because they allow your visitors to navigate from one page to another.

Link to Other Pages in Your Website

Create a Link

1 Click and drag to select the text that you want to turn into a link.

2 Click ▼ and choose **Common**.

3 Click the **Hyperlink** 🔗.

The Hyperlink dialog box appears.

🅐 The selected text is automatically entered in the Text field.

4 Click 🖿 and select the HTML file to which you want to link.

Note: The other settings in the Hyperlink dialog box are optional.

5 Click **OK**.

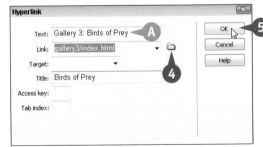

B The new link appears in color and underlined using Cascading Style Sheets (CSS), unless you have changed the link style to remove the underline.

Note: To change the appearance of links, see the section "Change the Color of Links on a Page" at the end of this chapter.

C The filename and path appear in the Link field.

Note: Links are not clickable in the Document window.

D You can click 🖳 to test the link by previewing the file in a web browser.

Open and Edit a Linked Page

1 Click anywhere in the text of the link whose destination you want to open.

2 Click **Modify**.

3 Click **Open Linked Page**.

The link destination opens in a Document window, allowing you to edit that document.

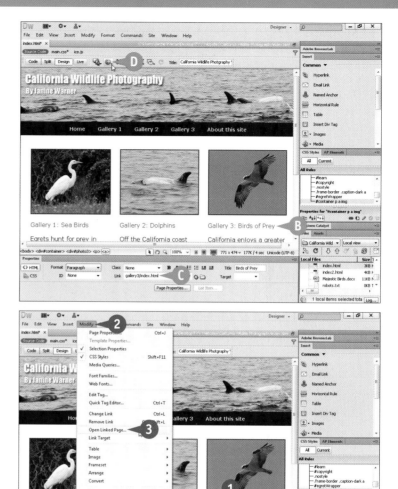

TIP

How should I organize the files that make up my website?
You should keep all the pages, images, and other files that make up your website in one main folder that you define as your local site root folder. This enables you to easily find pages and images and create links between your pages. It also ensures that all the links work correctly when you transfer the files to a web server. If you have many pages in one section, you can create subfolders in the Files panel to further divide your site's file structure. You may also want to create a separate folder for images. For more information on setting up your website, see Chapter 2, "Setting Up Your Website." For more information on transferring files to a web server, see Chapter 13, "Publishing a Website."

Link to Another Website

In addition to links within your website, you can link from your website to any other website on the Internet. Linking to other sites is a great way to build connections and give your visitors access to additional information that complements the information on your website. Adding links to other websites can help you provide access to valuable references, resources, and related information. When you set links to other websites, email the site owners and ask them to reciprocate with a link back to your site. Trading links is a great way to boost credibility and ranking with search engines.

Link to Another Website

Create a Link

1. Click and drag to select the text that you want to turn into a link.

2. Click ▼ and choose **Common**.

3. Click the **Hyperlink** 🖹.

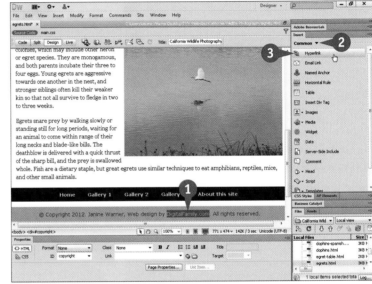

The Hyperlink dialog box appears.

Ⓐ The selected text is automatically entered in the Text field.

4. Type the web address of the destination page in the **Link** field.

Note: You must type **http://** before the web address.

5. Click ▼.

6. Click **_blank** to create a link that will open in a new browser window or tab.

7. Click **OK**.

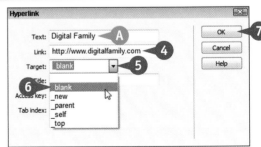

B The new link appears in a color and underlined, unless you have changed the link style.

Note: To change the appearance of links using CSS, see the section "Change the Color of Links on a Page."

C The URL appears here.

Note: Links are not clickable in the Document window.

D You can click [image] to test the link by previewing the file in a web browser.

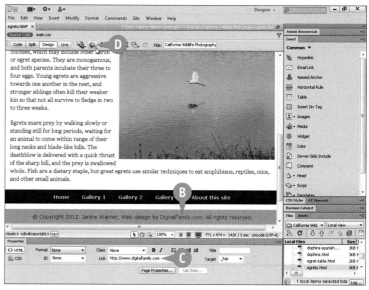

Remove a Link

1 Click to place ⃝ anywhere in the text of the link that you want to remove.

2 Click **Modify**.

3 Click **Remove Link**.

Dreamweaver removes the link, and the text no longer appears in a color (or underlined).

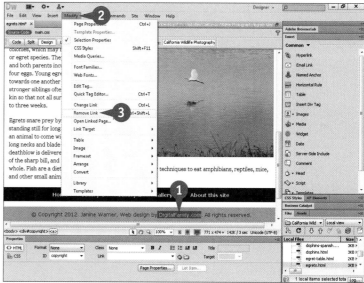

TIP

How do I ensure that my links to other websites always work?

If you have linked to a web page whose file is later renamed or taken offline, your viewers receive an error message when they click the link on your website. Although you cannot always control the sites to which you link, you can maintain your website by periodically viewing your own site in a web browser and checking to make sure that your links to other sites still work properly. You can also use online services, such as the W3C Link Checker, at http://validator.w3.org/checklink, to perform this check for you. Although neither method can bring back a web page that no longer exists, you can identify which links you need to remove or update.

Using an Image As a Link

Using an image as a link can make your links more interesting, eye-catching, and informative. You can turn any image in a web page into a link, and you can use images to link to pages on your own website, as well as pages on another website, in much the same way that you create links with text. Using images as links provides a visual alternative to text links and gives visitors to your site a different way to move from page to page.

Using an Image As a Link

1 Click the image that you want to turn into a link.

2 Click the **Link** 🔲.

Ⓐ You can also use the Hyperlink dialog box, which is available by clicking 🖉 in the Common Insert panel and was used in the first two sections of this chapter.

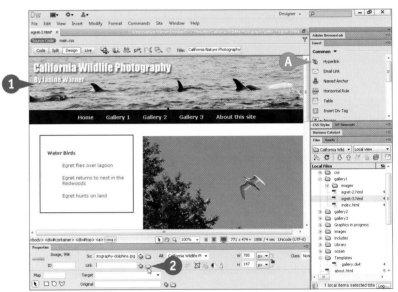

The Select File dialog box appears.

3 Click ▾ and select the folder that contains the destination page.

4 Click the HTML file to which you want to link.

5 Click **OK**.

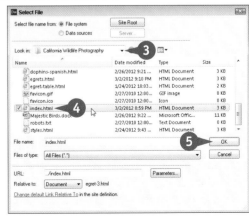

Your image becomes a link.

B Dreamweaver automatically inserts the filename and path to the linked page.

6 Click 🖳 and select a browser to test the link.

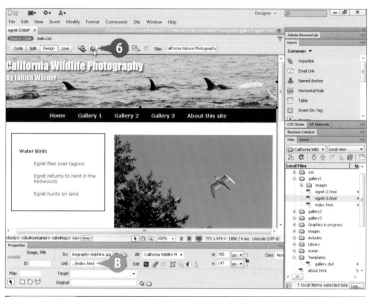

7 Click the linked image.

C The page the image links to opens in the browser, even when the website is viewed on your local computer.

© Copyright 2012. Janine Warner, DigitalFamily.com. All rights reserved.

TIPS

How do I create a navigation bar for my web page?
Many websites include a list of links to the main pages or sections of a website. This collection of links is commonly called a *navigation bar*. The best place to create these links is at the top, side, or bottom of each page. Including links to the main pages of your site on every page in your site makes it easier for viewers to navigate.

How will visitors to my website know to click an image?
When a visitor rolls the cursor over an image that serves as a link, the cursor turns into a hand. You can make it clearer which images are linked by putting links in context with other content and by grouping links to let visitors know that images are clickable.

Create a Jump Link within a Page

S ame-page links, often called *jump links* or *anchor links,* are commonly used on long pages when you want to provide an easy way to navigate to relevant information lower on the page. You can create a link to a specific place within the same page, and you can use jump links to link to a specific place on another web page in your site.

You create a jump link by first placing a named anchor where you want the link to go to and then linking from the text or image to the named anchor point.

Create a Jump Link within a Page

1. Position ⌖ where you want to insert the named anchor.

2. Click ▾ and choose **Common**.

3. Click the **Named Anchor** 🔖.

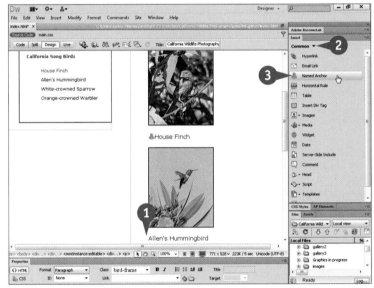

The Named Anchor dialog box appears.

4. Type a name for the anchor.

5. Click **OK**.

Ⓐ An anchor appears in the Document window.

⑥ Click and drag to select the text that you want to link to the anchor.

⑦ Click 🖾 in the Common Insert panel.

The Hyperlink dialog box appears.

⑧ Click the **Link** 🔽.

⑨ Click the anchor name.

⑩ Click **OK**.

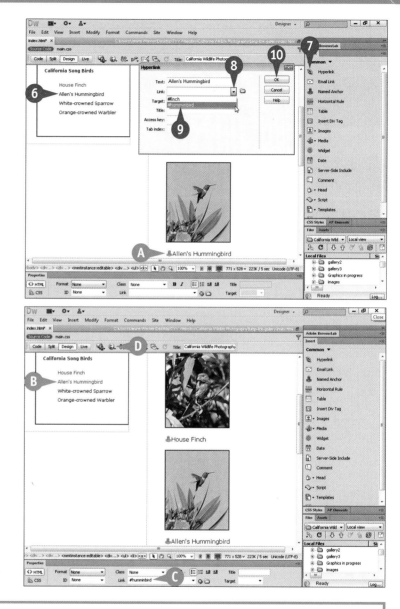

Ⓑ The text appears as a link on the page.

Ⓒ The anchor name appears in the Link field, preceded by a pound (#) sign.

Note: Links are not clickable in the Document window.

Ⓓ You can click 🖾 to test the link by previewing the file in a web browser.

Note: For more information about previewing a page in a web browser, see Chapter 2.

TIP

Why would you create a jump link to something on the same page?

Web designers use jump links to make it easier to find text that appears lower on a page. These links are frequently used on very long pages to give visitors an easy way to return to the top of a page by clicking a jump link lower on the page. Similarly, if you have a web page that has many sections of information, jump links enable you to link to each section from a link menu at the top of the page. A frequently asked questions (FAQ) page is another example of when to use same-page links; you can list all your questions at the top of the page and link to the answers lower on the page.

Create a Link to Another File Type

In addition to creating links to other web pages, you can create links to other types of files. You can link to image files, word-processing documents, PDF files, and multimedia files, including video and audio files. Many of these file types require their own players or viewers, but as long as your visitor has the required program, the file opens automatically when the user clicks the link. Some file types, such as PDFs, have become so popular that the viewer is built into most web browsers.

Create a Link to Another File Type

1. Click and drag to select the text that you want to turn into a link.

2. Click ▼ and choose **Common**.

3. Click the **Hyperlink** 🖾.

The Hyperlink dialog box appears.

Ⓐ The selected text is automatically entered in the Text field.

4. To link to a file on another website, type the web address, or copy and paste the URL of the file on the destination site.

OR

4. To link to a file on your own site, click 🖿 and select the file to which you want to link.

Note: The rest of the settings are optional.

5. Click **OK**.

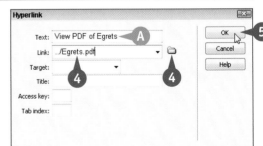

B The text appears as a link on the page.

Note: Links are not clickable in the Document window.

6 Click 🖳 and select a web browser.

The page opens in the browser that you selected.

7 Click the link.

C The linked file opens.

In this example, a PDF document opens in the web browser window.

TIP

How do users view files that are not HTML documents?

What users see when they click links to other types of files depends on how they have configured their web browsers and what plug-ins or other applications they have installed on their computers. For example, if you link to a QuickTime movie (which has an .mov file extension), your visitors need to have a player that can display QuickTime movies. It is always a good practice to include a link to the player for any special file type to make it easy for users to find and download the player if they choose.

Create an Image Map

Creating an image map makes it possible to link different areas of one image to different web pages. For example, you could add one big map of the United States to your page and then link each state to a separate page with information about that state. When you create an image map, you first define areas of the image, called *hotspots,* using Dreamweaver's image-mapping tools, and then you turn each area, or hotspot, into a link. You can use image maps to link to pages on your own site, as well as to pages on other websites.

Create an Image Map

1 Click the image.

2 Type a name for the image map.

Note: You cannot use spaces or special characters.

3 Click a drawing tool.

Note: You can create rectangular shapes with the Rectangular Hotspot tool (▭), oval shapes with the Oval Hotspot tool (◯), and irregular shapes with the Polygon Hotspot tool (▧).

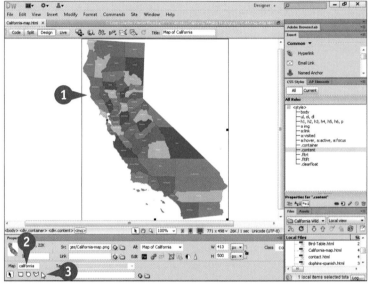

4 Draw an area on the image that will serve as a hotspot for a link.

Ⓐ If a message appears instructing you to describe the image map in the Alt field, click **OK** to close the dialog box, type a description in the **Alt** field, and then resume drawing the hotspot area over the image.

Ⓑ To link to another website, type the URL into the **Link** field.

5 Click ▭.

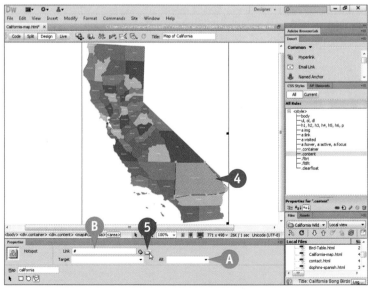

The Select File dialog box appears.

6 Click ⏷ and select the folder that contains the destination file.

7 Click the file to which you want to link.

8 Click **OK**.

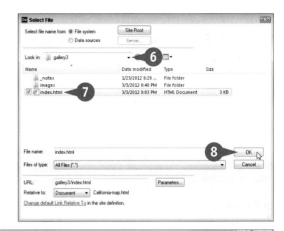

C The hotspot area defined by the selected shape is linked to the selected file, and the name and path to the file are displayed when the hotspot is selected.

To delete a hotspot, you can select it and then press `Del`.

You can repeat steps **3** to **8** to add other linked areas to your image.

Note: The image-map shapes do not appear when you open the page in a browser, but clicking anywhere in a hotspot area will trigger the corresponding link.

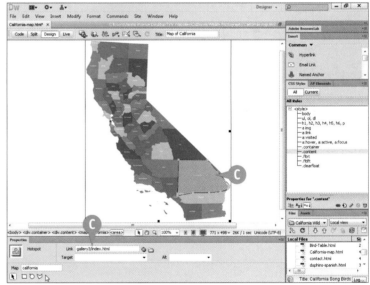

TIP

Can image maps be used for geographical maps that link to multiple locations?
Yes. An interactive geographical map, such as a map of Latin America, is a common place to see hotspots in action. You can create one by adding a graphic image of a map to your web page and then defining a hotspot over each location to which you want to link. Use the Polygon tool (✉) to draw around boundaries that do not follow a square or circular shape. Then link each hotspot to a page with information about the corresponding geographic region.

Create a Link Using the Files Panel

If you are creating multiple links from one page in your site to other pages in your site, the Point to File link option can save time because it enables you to create links quickly and easily. First you highlight the text or image you want to serve as a link and then use the Point to File button in the Property inspector to select any file in the Files panel.

Your web pages are displayed in the Files panel only if you have set up your website in Dreamweaver, an important first step that is covered in Chapter 2.

Create a Link Using the Files Panel

Note: Make sure that both the Document window and the Files panel are visible and that **HTML** is selected in the Property inspector.

1. Click and drag to select the text that you want to turn into a link.

2. Click the Point to File button (⊕).

3. Drag the cursor until it is over the file that you want to link to in the Files panel.

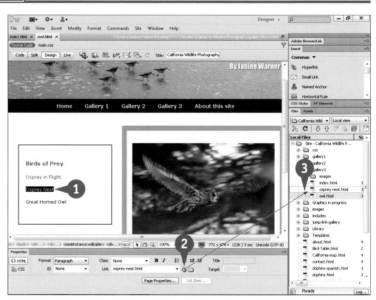

Ⓐ The text appears as a link on the page.

Note: You can change the appearance of links by following the steps in the section "Change the Color of Links on a Page."

Ⓑ The name and path to the file you linked to are displayed in the Link field in the Property inspector.

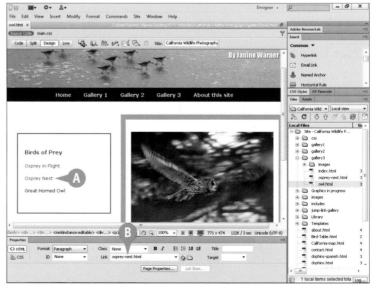

You can create a link that, when clicked, opens a new web browser window to display the destination page. Opening a new browser window allows a user to keep the previous web page open. This is a useful technique when you want to make related information available without taking a site visitor off the page he or she is viewing. For example, you might use the open-a-new-browser-window technique to provide the definition to a term in a long document, or to display a video, while keeping the main page visible behind it.

Open a Linked Page in a New Browser Window

1 Click and drag to select the link that you want to open in a new browser window.

2 Click the **Target** ▼.

3 Click **_blank**.

4 Click 🖳 and select a web browser to preview the page.

The page opens in the browser that you selected.

5 Click the link.

Ⓐ The link destination appears in a new browser window, and the page with the link remains open behind the linked page.

Note: If the user's browser window is set to fill the entire screen, the original web page will not be visible when the linked page is opened.

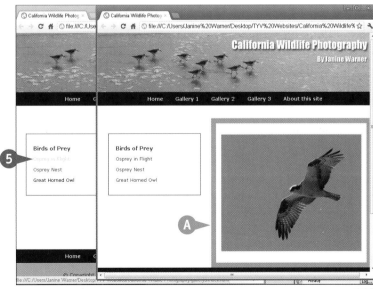

115

Create an Email Link

Another common link type is an email link. You can create an email link on your web page to make it easy for site visitors to send you email messages. When a user clicks the link, it launches the email program on the user's computer, creates a new message, and inserts the email address that you used in your link into the Address field. Email links are a useful shortcut for site visitors who want to send messages, but they only work if the user has an email program set up to work on the computer he or she is using.

Create an Email Link

1 Click to select the text or image that you want to turn into an email link.

2 Click the **Email Link** ▣.

Note: If ▣ is not visible, choose **Common** from the drop-down list.

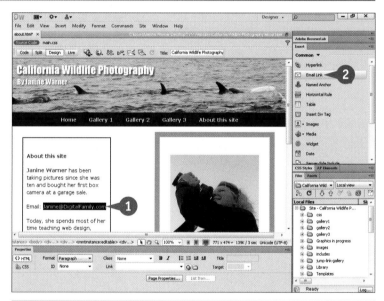

Ⓐ The Email Link dialog box appears, with the selected text in the Text field.

3 Type the email address to which you want to link.

4 Click **OK**.

Dreamweaver creates your email link, and the selected text is displayed as a link.

Ⓑ To test the link, you can click ▣ and select a web browser to preview the page.

116

Check Links

Broken links are one of the most common, and problematic, mistakes in web design. There are many ways that links can become broken. Fortunately, Dreamweaver not only helps you create links, but it also can help you find and fix broken links. You can automatically check all the links in a website using Dreamweaver's link-testing features. When you use these features, Dreamweaver generates a report that lists any links that are broken within the site, as well as links to other websites that you should test in a browser.

Check Links

1 Click **Site**.

2 Click **Check Links Sitewide**.

A Dreamweaver checks all the links and lists all broken links, external links, and orphaned files.

3 Click ▼ and select the type of links that you want displayed.

Note: Dreamweaver cannot verify links to web pages on external sites.

B To correct a broken link, double-click the file to open it, select the linked item, and click the **Browse** 🗀 to reset the link correctly.

Change the Color of Links on a Page

By default, links on web pages are blue and then turn to red after a user has clicked them. However, you can change the color of the links on your web page to make them any color that you want. Most web designers alter link colors so that they match the visual style of the other text and images on their web pages. You can also remove the underline under linked text, which many designers find distracting. Adding a third, contrasting color for the rollover state creates a nice visual effect when a visitor rolls a cursor over a link.

Change the Color of Links on a Page

① Click **Modify**.

② Click **Page Properties**.

Ⓐ You can also click **Page Properties** in the Property inspector.

The Page Properties dialog box appears.

③ Click **Links (CSS)**.

④ Click the **Link Color** ▣ (⌖ changes to ✐).

⑤ Click a color from the menu using the ✐ tool.

⑥ Repeat steps **4** and **5** to specify colors for Visited, Rollover, and Active links.

Ⓑ You can click the Color Picker (◉) to select a custom color.

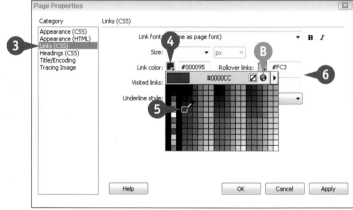

⑦ Click the **Underline Style** ▼.

⑧ Click **Show Underline Only on Rollover** to remove the underline from active links and display the underline only when a visitor rolls a cursor over the link.

⑨ Click **OK**.

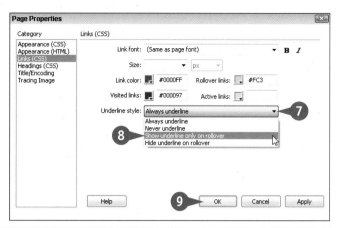

Ⓒ All links are displayed in the specified link color and underline option.

TIPS

What color will my links be if I do not choose colors for them?

Blue is the default link color in the Dreamweaver Document window. What viewers see when the page opens in a web browser depends on their browser settings. By default, most web browsers display unvisited links as blue, visited links as purple, and rollover links as red.

What do each of the link options in the Page Properties dialog box represent?

Link color represents the display color for a link that has not yet been clicked by a site visitor; **Visited links** represents the color a link changes to after it has been clicked; **Rollover links** represents the display color a link changes to as a visitor rolls a cursor over it; and **Active links** represents the display color a link changes to when a visitor is actively clicking it.

CHAPTER 8

Adding and Editing Tables

Tables are an ideal way to format tabular data, such as the information that you find in a spreadsheet. You can also use tables to create designs with multiple columns, even within the constraints of HTML. This chapter shows you how to create and format tables.

Insert a Table into a Web Page

Tables are ideal for formatting tabular data, the kind that you find in a spreadsheet or database. You can use tables to organize and design pages that contain financial data, text, images, and multimedia. Dreamweaver's layout features enable you to create tables with as many rows, columns, and cells as you want to create, and you can easily add or remove columns and rows after you insert a table. You can merge and split cells within a table. You can even insert tables inside other tables.

Insert a Table into a Web Page

Insert a Table

1 Position ⌖ where you want to insert a table.

By default, the cursor snaps to the left margin, although you can change the table alignment.

2 Click the **Table** ▦ in the Common Insert panel.

Ⓐ You can also click **Insert** and then click **Table**.

The Table dialog box appears.

3 Type the number of rows and columns that you want in your table.

4 Type the width of your table.

Ⓑ You can set the width in pixels or as a percentage of the page by clicking ▾ and selecting your choice of measurements.

5 Click to select a table **Header** option.

6 Click **OK**.

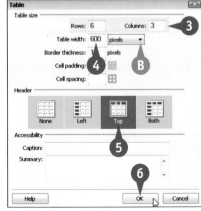

C An empty table appears, aligned to the left by default.

7 Click ▾.

8 Click an alignment option.

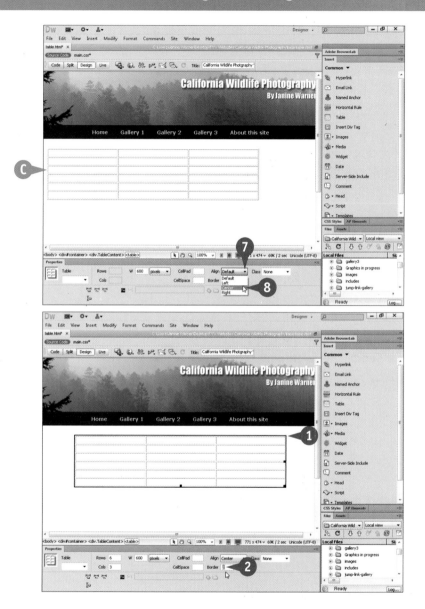

The table aligns on the page.

Edit the Table Border

1 Click any corner of the table to select the entire table.

The Property inspector changes to display the Table properties.

2 Type the number of pixels of border thickness you want in the **Border** field.

3 Press Enter (Return).

Note: If you set the border to 0, Dreamweaver will replace the visible border with a dashed line to show you the borders in the workspace. When you view the page in a web browser, the dashed table border disappears.

TIPS

Why are table headers important for accessibility?
The Table Header setting designates a row or column as the content that describes the information in the table. Its text is bold and centered. The setting also provides information about the header content that can be read aloud by *screen readers,* special web browsers that are used by the blind or visually impaired.

Can I change or remove the table borders?
You can set the table border to one pixel for a slim border or try five or ten pixels if you want a thick border. If you set the border to zero, it becomes invisible.

Insert Content into a Table

After you insert a table into a web page, you can add content to any or all of the table cells. You can fill the cells of your table with text, images, multimedia files, form elements, and even other tables, just as you would add them anywhere else on a web page. You can then format the text, images, and other content in table cells, just as you would format any other content on the page using the text and image settings in the Property inspector and menus.

Insert Content into a Table

Insert Text

1 Click to place your cursor inside the table cell.

2 Type text into the cell.

Note: To format your text, see Chapter 5, "Formatting and Styling Text."

Insert an Image

1 Click inside the table cell.

2 Click the **Images** 🖼.

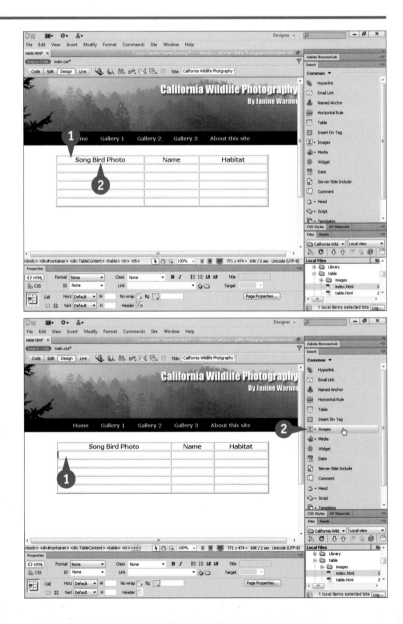

The Select Image Source dialog box appears.

③ Click ▼ and select the folder that contains your image.

④ Click the image file.

⑤ Click **OK**.

If the Image Tag Accessibility Attributes dialog box opens, enter a description of the image in the **Alt** field. The Accessibility Attributes dialog box can be turned on and off in the program's preferences.

Ⓐ The image appears in the table cell.

Ⓑ If the image is larger than the cell, the cell expands to accommodate the image.

Ⓒ You can click to select the image, and the image settings will be displayed in the Property inspector.

Note: To edit your image, see Chapter 6, "Working with Images and Multimedia."

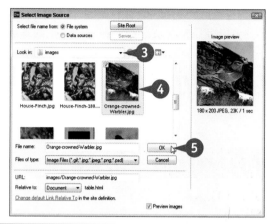

TIP

How do I change the appearance of the content inside my table?
You can specify the size, style, and color of text inside a table in the same way that you format text on a web page. Similarly, you can control the appearance of an image inside a table in the same way that you can control it outside a table. For more information on formatting text, see Chapter 5; for more information on images, see Chapter 6.

Change the Background Color of a Table

You can change the background color of an entire table or change the background color of only a single cell, a row, a column, or any selected set of cells, rows, or columns. Adding background colors is a great way to enhance the design of a table, make rows or columns easier to distinguish from one another, or to call attention to a specific section of a table. For more information on setting background colors for an entire page, see Chapter 6.

Change the Background Color of a Table

Using the Color Palette

1 Click any corner of a table to select the entire table, or click an individual cell, or click and drag to select a row or column of cells.

2 Click the **Bg** ■.

3 Click a color.

Ⓐ You can click the Color Picker button (◉) to select a custom color.

Ⓑ Click the Default Color button (▨) to remove a specified color.

Ⓒ The color fills the background of the selected cells.

Ⓓ You can also type a color name or hexadecimal color code in the color field.

Note: To change the font color on a web page, see Chapter 11, "Creating and Applying Cascading Style Sheets."

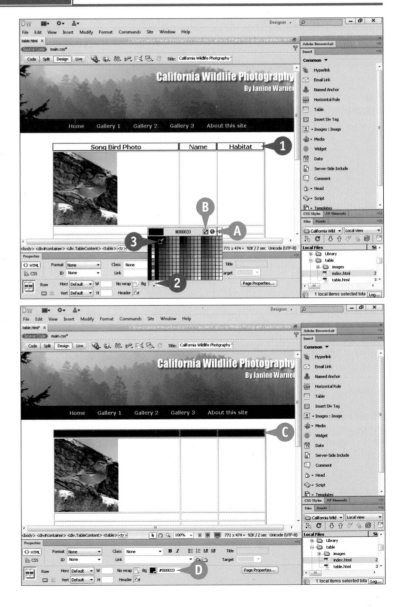

Using a Color from Your Web Page

1. Click any corner of a table to select the entire table, or click an individual cell, or click and drag to select a row or column of cells.

2. Click the **Bg** ▣ to open the color palette (◊ changes to ✐).

3. Click a color anywhere on the screen to select it.

Ⓔ The selected table cells' background fills with the color that you clicked.

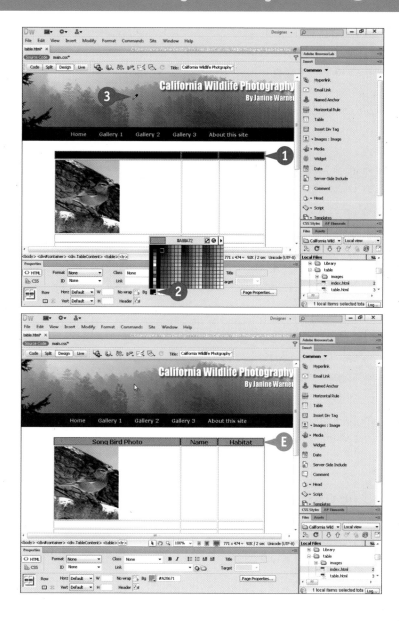

TIP

How can I change the background of an entire table?
To change the color of an entire table, you can click to select all the cells in a table and then choose a background color that will apply to all the cells. A better way is to create a style rule for the Table tag using Cascading Style Sheets (CSS) and specify a background image or color as part of that style. You find out how to create styles in Chapter 11.

Change the Cell Padding in a Table

The contents of a table can get a little crowded unless you add *padding*, or margin space. You can add cell padding to increase the space between a table's content and its borders. Adding cell padding can make the contents of a table easier to read and improve the design by adding white space between elements. The higher the number you enter into the CellPad field in the Property inspector, the more cell padding is added. To reduce the padding, simply lower the number you enter into the CellPad field.

Change the Cell Padding in a Table

1 Click any corner of the table to select the entire table.

Ⓐ The Property inspector changes to display the Table properties.

2 In the **CellPad** field in the Property inspector, type the amount of padding that you want in pixels.

3 Press Enter (Return).

Ⓑ The space changes between the table content and the table borders.

Note: Adjusting the cell padding affects all the cells in a table. You cannot adjust the padding of individual cells by using the CellPad field.

Change the Cell Spacing in a Table

You can enhance the design of your table and make table contents easier to read by adding cell spacing. Use cell spacing to adjust the distance that cells are from each other. The higher the number you enter into the CellSpace field in the Property inspector, the more cell spacing is added. To reduce the spacing, simply lower the number you enter into the CellSpace field in the Property inspector. Experiment with your table designs by increasing and decreasing cell padding and cell spacing until you are happy with the results.

Change the Cell Spacing in a Table

1 Click any corner of the table to select the entire table.

A The Property inspector changes to display the Table properties.

2 In the **CellSpace** field, type the amount of spacing that you want in pixels.

3 Press **Enter** (**Return**).

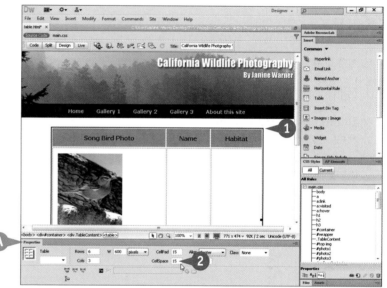

The cell spacing changes.

B You can change the width of the table or a column by clicking and dragging the cell borders.

Note: Adjusting the cell spacing affects all the cell borders in the table. You cannot adjust the spacing of individual cell borders by using the CellSpace field.

Insert a Table inside a Table Cell

For more complex table layouts, you can insert a new table inside any cell of an existing table. You insert a table into the cell of another table the same way you insert a table into a web page. Using tables inside of tables can help you to create designs with complex amounts of data. However, it is generally not recommended that you create tables inside of tables that are already inside of tables because creating tables with three or more levels requires highly complex code that can take longer to load in a web browser.

Insert a Table inside a Table Cell

1 Click inside the table cell.

2 Click the **Table** 🖼.

The Table dialog box appears.

3 Type values in the fields to define the characteristics of the table.

4 Click **OK**.

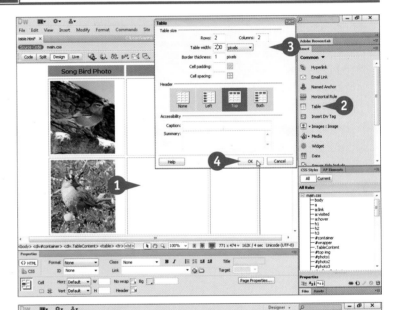

A The new table appears within the table cell.

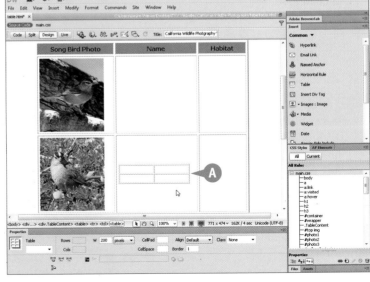

Change the Alignment of Cell Content

You can align the content in your table cells horizontally and vertically using the table alignment options. For example, you can align all the elements in a row or column to the top or bottom of their respective cells. This is useful for creating a more uniform look in a table row or column. If you are working with numbers that include a decimal point, aligning the contents of each cell to the right can help line up the decimal points. You can also center elements in a row or column.

Change the Alignment of Cell Content

1 Click and drag to select an entire column or row.

You can press **Shift** + click, or click and drag, to select multiple cells.

2 Click the **Horz** ▾ to change the alignment horizontally.

3 Click an alignment.

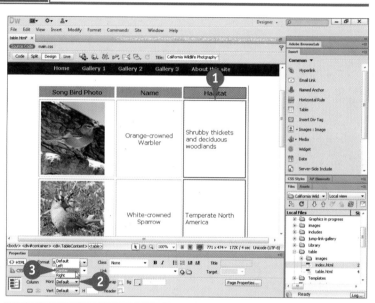

To change the vertical alignment, repeat steps **1** to **3**, clicking the **Vert** ▾ in step **2**.

Ⓐ The content aligns within the cells.

In this example, horizontal alignment is used to align the text in these cells in the center.

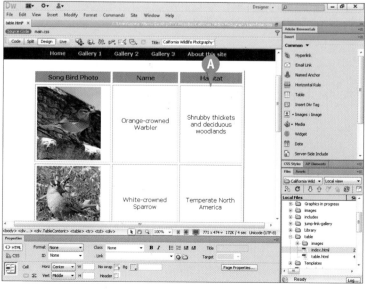

Insert or Delete a Row or Column

You can insert a row or column into your table to accommodate additional content or to create space between elements. You can also delete rows or columns to remove them when they are no longer needed. When you create a table, you specify the number of columns and rows. The ability to add or remove cells after you create a table makes it easy to adjust the design of your pages as you add or remove content.

Insert or Delete a Row or Column

Insert a Row or Column

1 Click any corner of the table to select the entire table.

A The Property inspector changes to display the Table properties.

2 Type the number of rows or columns that you want to insert in the Property inspector.

3 Press **Enter** (**Return**).

B Empty rows or columns appear in the table.

To add a row or column in the middle of a table, you can right-click inside an existing cell, click **Table**, and then click **Insert Row** or **Insert Column** from the menu that appears.

C You can also click **Modify**, click **Table**, and then click **Insert Row** or **Insert Column**.

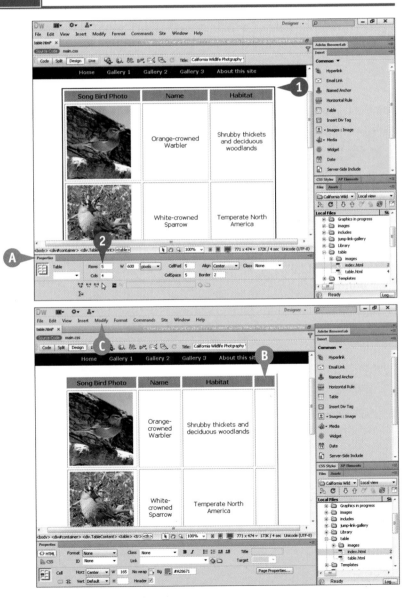

Delete a Row or Column

1 Select the cells that you want to delete by pressing Shift + clicking or clicking and dragging over them.

2 Press Del.

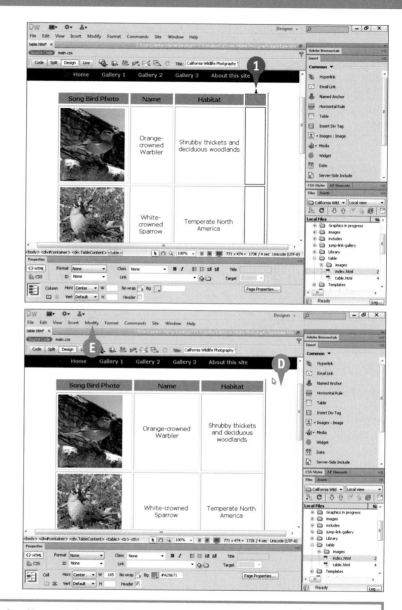

D The selected table cells disappear.

Note: The content of a cell is deleted when you delete the cell.

You can also delete cells by right-clicking inside the cells, clicking **Table**, and then clicking either **Delete Row** or **Delete Column** from the menu.

E You can also click **Modify**, click **Table**, and then click either **Delete Row** or **Delete Column**.

TIPS

Does Dreamweaver warn me if a deleted cell contains content?

No, Dreamweaver does not warn you if the cells that you are deleting in a table contain content. This is because Dreamweaver assumes that you also want to delete the cell content. If you accidentally remove content when deleting rows or columns, you can click **Edit** and then click **Undo** to undo your last action.

How do I move content around a table?

You can move the contents of a table cell by clicking to select any image, text, or element in the cell and then dragging it out of the table or into another cell. You can also use the Copy and Paste commands to move content from one cell to another or to another part of a page.

Split or Merge Table Cells

In addition to adding and removing entire rows and columns, you can split one cell into two cells or merge two or more individual cells into one larger cell. By splitting or merging cells in a table, you can create more elaborate designs. You might want to turn one large cell into two smaller ones to accommodate smaller data, or you might want to merge one or more cells to create larger cells adjacent to smaller ones. You can then insert text, images, audio and video files, and other content into the cells.

Split or Merge Table Cells

Split a Table Cell

1. Click to place your cursor in the cell that you want to split.

2. Click the Split Cell button (⌗) in the Property inspector.

   The Split Cell dialog box appears.

3. Click **Rows** or **Columns**, depending on which you want to use to split the cell (◎ changes to ◉).

4. Type the number of rows or columns.

5. Click **OK**.

   Ⓐ The table cell splits.

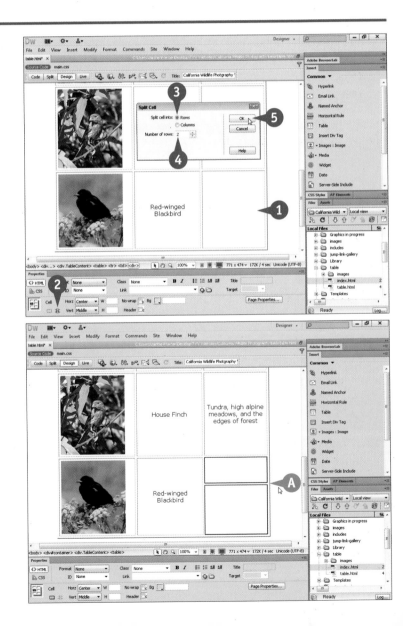

Merge Table Cells

1 Click and drag to select the cells that you want to merge.

2 Click the Merge button (▣) in the Property inspector.

B You can also merge cells by clicking **Modify**, clicking **Table**, and then clicking **Merge Cells**.

You can also merge cells by right-clicking inside the cells, clicking **Table**, and then clicking **Merge Cells**.

C The table cells merge.

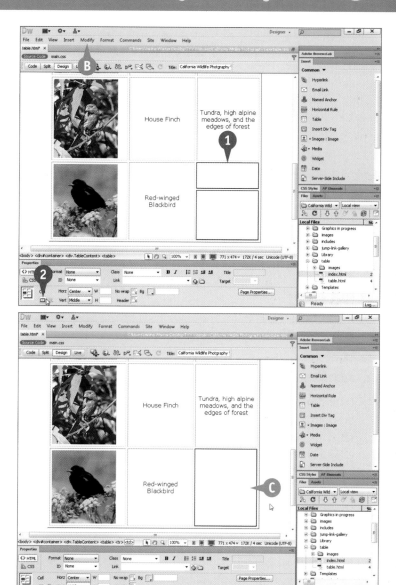

TIPS

Can I merge any combination of table cells?

No. The cells must have a rectangular arrangement. For example, you can merge all the cells in a two-row-by-two-column table. However, you cannot select three cells that form an L shape and merge them into one cell.

Can I add as many cells as I want?

Yes, just make sure that your final table design is displayed well on a computer monitor. For example, although it is common to design web pages that are long and require visitors to scroll down, it can be confusing to create overly wide pages that require scrolling right or left. For the best results, most web designers keep the overall page width under 960 pixels wide to ensure that it displays well on 1024 x 768 resolution computer displays.

Change the Dimensions of a Cell

You can change the dimensions of individual table cells to better accommodate their content. You can change the size of cells by entering a size in the Property inspector, or you can simply click and drag the side of any cell to enlarge or reduce it. You can also click and drag to enlarge or reduce an entire row or column. As you enlarge and reduce cells, you can create more complex tables for more precise design control.

Change the Dimensions of a Cell

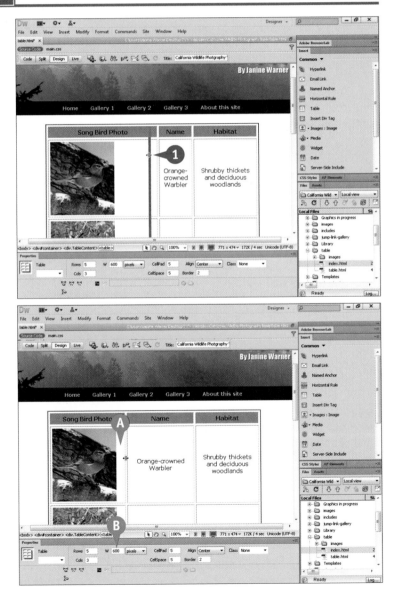

1 Click to select the edge of a cell and drag to adjust the size.

A The cell and its contents readjust to the new dimensions.

B You can also click to place your cursor inside any cell and then enter a size in the **W** (width) field in the Property inspector.

Note: Cell dimensions may be constrained by content. For example, Dreamweaver cannot shrink a cell smaller than the size of the content that it contains.

Change the Dimensions of a Table

You can change the dimensions of your entire table by enlarging or reducing the width and height. Most designers specify a width to ensure that the table fits well within the overall width of a web page. Be careful when you set the total width of all the cells in a table that their combined width does not exceed the total width of the table, or your content may be cut off. Similarly, it is a good practice to leave the height of a table unspecified because then the table will adjust automatically to accommodate the contents of the cells.

Change the Dimensions of a Table

1 Click any corner of the table to select the entire table.

Ⓐ The Property inspector changes to display the Table properties.

2 Type a width.

3 Click ▾ and select the width setting in pixels or a percentage of the screen.

4 Press **Enter** (**Return**).

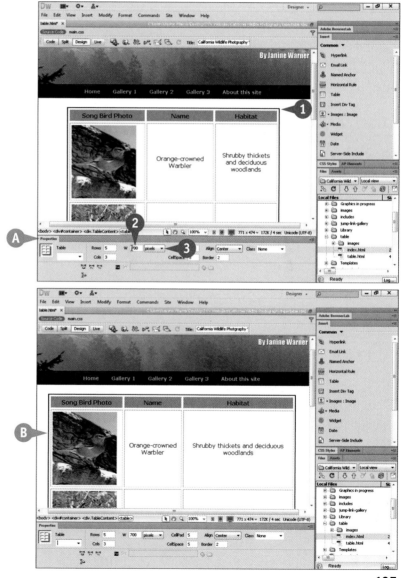

Ⓑ The table readjusts to its new dimensions.

Note: Table dimensions may be constrained by content. For example, Dreamweaver cannot shrink a table smaller than the size of an image that it contains.

If you do not specify a height or width, the table automatically adjusts to fit the space that is available on the user's screen.

137

Using Percentages for Table Width

You can specify the size of a table using pixels to create a fixed width or using percentages to create a table that automatically adjusts to fit the size of a user's browser window. Using a percentage enables you to create an adaptable design, one that will appear more narrow in a browser on a small monitor than on a larger one. Be careful, however, to test the results on different-sized monitors to make sure that the text and other elements on the page look good at varying sizes.

Using Percentages for Table Width

Set Table Width As a Percentage

1. Position ▷ where you want to insert the table.

    By default, the cursor snaps to the left margin, although you can change the table alignment.

    Note: For instructions on creating a table, see the section "Insert a Table into a Web Page."

2. Click **Insert**.

3. Click **Table**.

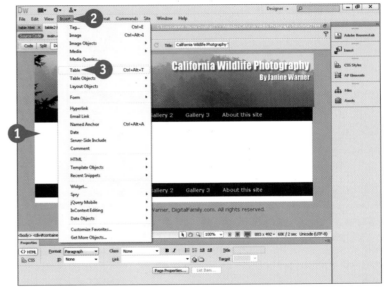

    The Table dialog box appears.

4. Type the number of rows and columns that you want in your table.

5. Type the percentage width you want your table to fill in the browser window.

6. Click ▾ and select **percent**.

7. Click **OK**.

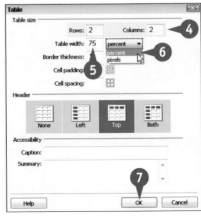

A An empty table appears, aligned to the left by default, and fills the available window based on the percentage width that you specified.

B You can click here and enter a different percentage.

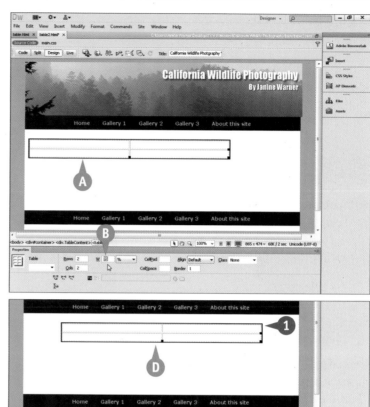

Center a Table

1 Click any corner of the table to select the entire table.

C The Property inspector changes to display the Table properties.

2 Click the **Align** ▼.

3 Click **Center**.

D The table aligns in the center of the page.

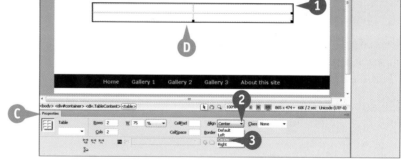

TIPS

What is a spacer image?

A *spacer image* is a transparent GIF image file that is used as a filler to ensure that blank spaces on your page remain consistent. You insert it into a table cell and use the height and width attributes to control its size. This is important because web browsers sometimes display elements closer together if there is no text or image to maintain consistent spacing within the design.

How can I make a spacer image?

You can create your own spacer image in an image-editing program, such as Adobe Photoshop or Fireworks. Create a new image and set the background color to transparent. Save it as a GIF file in your website folder. An ideal size for a spacer image is 10 pixels by 10 pixels; however, it can be any size. You can resize it in Dreamweaver to fit the space that you want to fill.

Format a Table with CSS

Although you can use table attributes to adjust the formatting and alignment of tables and table cells as shown earlier in this chapter, many web designers find it advantageous to create style rules to format a table instead. Cascading Style Sheets offer many advantages, including the ability to style all your tables with one rule instead of changing the settings on each table in your site. Although working with styles is more complex at first, using styles instead of table attributes creates cleaner, more efficient code and makes it easier to change the table formatting later.

Format a Table with CSS

1 Click **Format**.

2 Click **CSS Styles**.

3 Click **New**.

The New CSS Rule dialog box appears.

4 Click ▼.

5 Click **Tag**.

6 Type **table**.

Ⓐ Alternatively, you can click ▼ and choose the tag name **table** from the drop-down list.

7 Click **OK**.

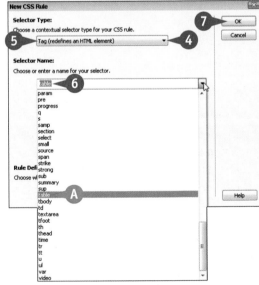

The CSS Rule Definition dialog box appears.

⑧ Click **Border**.

⑨ Specify the border settings that you want.

Ⓑ You can specify many other formatting settings in this dialog box by selecting other categories, such as **Type**.

⑩ Click **OK**.

Ⓒ The style is automatically applied to the table in the page.

In this example, the border turns brown.

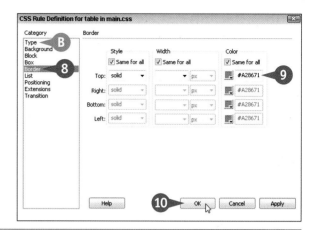

TIP

Can I do all my table formatting with CSS?
You can create rules using Cascading Style Sheets to redefine all the table tags. The table tags include `<table>`, the main tag; `<th>` for table header; `<tr>` for table row; and `<td>` for table data cell. By defining rules in CSS for each of these table tags, you can change the size, alignment, background and text colors, and other formatting options for the entire table. The advantage? You can use the same styles for all the tables in your site, making formatting quicker and easier and your code cleaner and faster to download.

Creating Web-Based Forms

You can make it easy for your website visitors to send you information by creating forms on your web pages. This chapter shows you how to create forms with different types of fields, buttons, and menus.

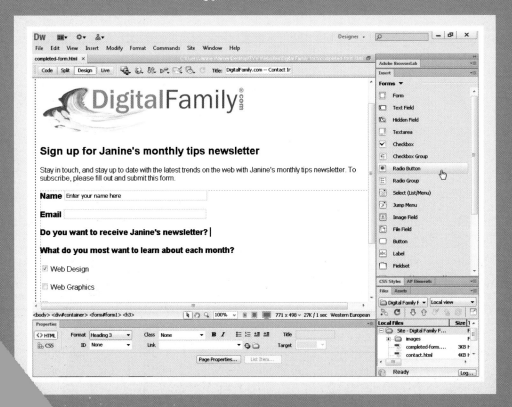

Introducing Forms

You can add forms to your website to make it more interactive, thus allowing viewers to enter and submit information to you through your web pages. However, in order for a form to function, you need to have a script on your web server to process the form information. Contact your web-hosting service to learn more about the unique requirements of your web server and see if they offer scripts that you can use to process forms. Most form scripts are written in a programming language such as Perl, PHP, ASP.NET, or Java.

Create a Form

You can use Dreamweaver to construct a form by inserting text fields, drop-down menus, check boxes, and other interactive elements into your page. You can also enter the web address of a form handler, or script, in Dreamweaver so that the information can be processed. Visitors to your web page fill out the form and send the information to the script on your server by clicking a Submit button.

Process Form Information

Form handlers or *scripts* are programs that process form information or execute an action, such as forwarding the contents of a form to an email address. Many ready-made form handlers are available for free on the web, but some require customization and special installation on your web server. Some web-hosting companies offer form services that you can use on your site. You may also want to consider using Adobe's form service, FormsCentral, available at www.acrobat.com/formscentral.

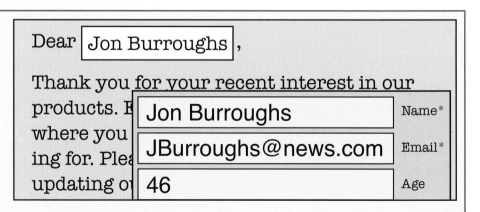

Define a Form Area

When you create a form, you begin by creating a form container. The `form` tag defines the area of the form. You then place any text fields, menus, or other form elements inside the `form` tags. If you do not create a `form` tag before you insert a form element, such as a radio button, Dreamweaver automatically inserts the `form` tag for you. To make the form function, you select the `form` tag and enter the name of a script or form handler that is on a web server into the Action field in the Property inspector.

Define a Form Area

1. Click where you want to insert your form.

2. Click **Insert**.

3. Click **Form**.

4. Click **Form**.

Ⓐ A red box appears, indicating that the form container is set up. To build the form, add elements inside the box.

5. Type the form address, using the name of the script and its location on your web server.

6. Click ▾.

7. Click either **POST** or **GET**.

Note: Use the command required by your script or form handler.

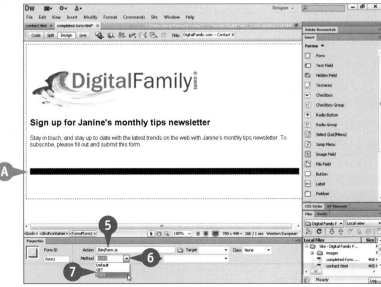

Add a Text Field to a Form

You can add a text field to enable viewers to submit text through your form. Text fields are probably the most common form element, enabling users to enter names, addresses, brief answers to questions, and other short pieces of text. You can include a message in a text field to encourage people to fill in the information that you want and provide additional instructions. You can also adjust the size of a text field to make it longer or more narrow.

Add a Text Field to a Form

1. Click inside the form container where you want to insert the text field.

2. Click ▾.

3. Click **Forms**.

4. Click the **Text Field** 🔲 on the Forms Insert panel.

The Input Tag Accessibility Attributes dialog box appears.

5. Type a one-word ID.

6. Type the text that you want for the label.

Note: This text will appear on the web page.

Ⓐ You can select the **Style** and **Position** attributes that you want (◎ changes to ◉).

Ⓑ Entering an access key and tab index can make your site more accessible.

7. Click **OK**.

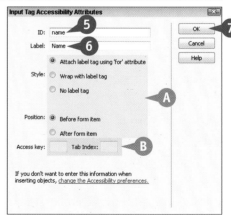

146

C A text field appears.

D Your label text appears.

E You can click **Multi line** if you want more than one line available for text.

F You can change the assigned ID of the text field.

8 Type an initial value for the text field.

9 Type a character width to change the size of the text box.

G You can type a maximum number of characters to limit what a user can enter.

H The initial value appears in the text field.

I The width of the text field changes based on the value that you entered in the Char Width field.

10 Click and drag to select the label text.

11 Select any of the label formatting options in the Property inspector.

Dreamweaver applies the formatting to the label text.

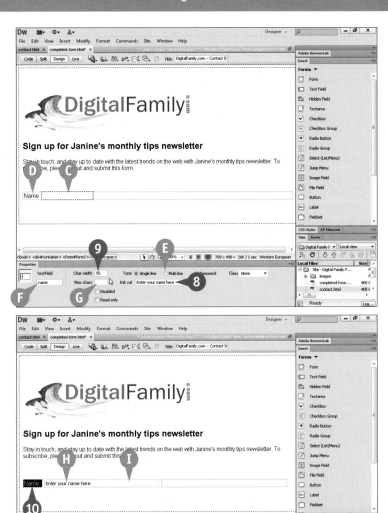

TIPS

Can I define the style of text that appears in the text field?

By default, the browser determines what style of text appears in form fields. It is not possible to format this type of text with plain HTML. You can use style sheets to manipulate the way the text in the form fields appears. You can find more information about style sheets in Chapters 11 and 12.

Can I create a text field with multiple lines?

Yes. You can create a text field and use the Property inspector options to make it a field with multiple lines. You can also create a text area, which has multiple lines by default. You can insert a text area just as you insert a text field, by clicking the **Textarea** ▤ in the Forms Insert panel.

Add a Check Box to a Form

Check boxes enable you to present multiple options in a form. When you use check boxes, you can give visitors the option of selecting one, several, or none of the options. That makes check boxes an ideal choice when you want to ask a question that can be answered multiple different ways. For example, if you want to gauge the interest of your audience in the topics you cover in a newsletter, you can use check boxes, and visitors can choose any or all of the options.

Add a Check Box to a Form

1 Click inside the form container where you want to insert the check box.

2 Click ▾.

3 Click **Forms**.

4 Click the **Checkbox** ☑ on the Forms Insert panel.

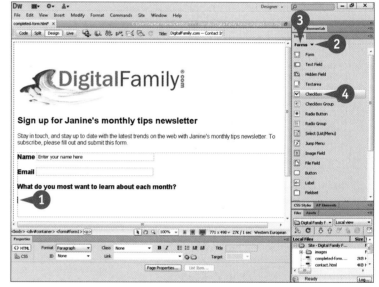

The Input Tag Accessibility Attributes dialog box appears.

5 Type a one-word ID.

6 Type the text that you want for the label.

Ⓐ You can select the **Style** and **Position** attributes that you want (◉ changes to ◉).

Ⓑ Entering an access key and tab index can make your site more accessible.

7 Click **OK**.

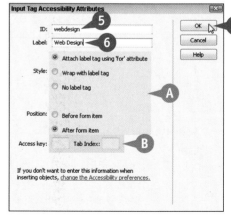

C The check box and label appear on the page.

8 Repeat steps **4** to **7** until you have the number of check boxes that you want on your form.

9 Click a check box to select it.

10 Click to select an **Initial state** option (◎ changes to ◉).

D You can specify other attributes, such as the class, ID, or checked value.

E You can click to select the other check boxes, one at a time, and specify the attributes of each separately.

F You can format the label text using the Property inspector.

TIP

When should I use check boxes, and when should I use radio buttons?

Check boxes are the perfect choice when you want visitors to be able to select more than one option. For these, you may want to include the message "Check all that apply."

On the other hand, when you want visitors to select only one option from a list of two or more options, radio buttons are the best choice. You can set up your radio buttons so that it is not possible to select more than one option.

Add a Radio Button to a Form

You can allow visitors to select one of several options by adding a set of radio buttons to your form. With radio buttons, a user cannot select more than one option from a set. The restriction to only one option makes radio buttons the best choice when you want to force users to choose only one response. For example, when you want to ask a yes or no question, radio buttons are ideal, but you can also use radio buttons when you want to offer more than two options but still want visitors to select only one of them.

Add a Radio Button to a Form

1 Click inside the form container where you want to insert a radio button.

2 Click ▾.

3 Click **Forms**.

4 Click the **Radio Button** ◉ on the Forms Insert panel.

The Input Tag Accessibility Attributes dialog box appears.

5 Type a one-word ID.

6 Type a label.

A You can select the **Style** and **Position** attributes that you want (◎ changes to ◉).

B Entering an access key and tab index can make your site more accessible.

7 Click **OK**.

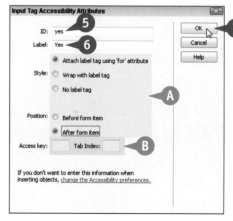

C A radio button and a label appear on the page.

8 Repeat steps **4** to **7** until you have the number of radio buttons that you want on your form.

9 Click a radio button.

10 Click to select an **Initial state** option(◯ changes to ◉).

D You can specify other attributes, such as the checked value, ID, and class.

11 Click to select the other radio buttons one at a time and specify attributes for each individually.

E You can format the label text using the Property inspector.

Are there alternatives to using check boxes or radio buttons?

Yes, there are many alternatives to simple check boxes and radio buttons. In the Forms Insert panel, you will also find the options Checkbox Group and Radio Group. Grouping check boxes and radio buttons makes it easier to organize them in your page designs and to track the results when data is submitted. When you have limited space in your page designs or an especially long list of options, such as a list of the 50 American states, you may prefer to use a list or menu. The List/Menu option in the Forms Insert panel enables you to create a drop-down menu that site visitors can use to select one or more items from a list. See the following section, "Add a List/Menu to a Form," for more information.

Add a List/Menu to a Form

List/menu form elements enable users to choose from a predefined list of choices. List/menus, sometimes called *drop-down boxes,* are similar to check boxes in that users can choose one or more options. Because list/menu elements are displayed as drop-down lists on web pages, they are an ideal way to present a long list of options without taking up a lot of space on a page. For example, if you want users to choose from a list of states or countries, a list/menu is a great choice.

Add a List/Menu to a Form

1 Click inside the form container where you want a menu or list.

2 Click ▼.

3 Click **Forms**.

4 Click the **List/Menu** 📰 on the Forms Insert panel.

The Input Tag Accessibility Attributes dialog box appears.

5 Type a one-word ID.

6 Type a label.

Ⓐ You can select the **Style** and **Position** attributes that you want (◎ changes to ◉).

Ⓑ Entering an access key and tab index can make your site more accessible.

7 Click **OK**.

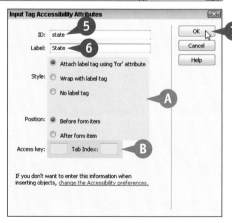

A blank menu appears in your form.

⑧ Click the menu to select it.

⑨ Click **List Values**.

The List Values dialog box appears.

⑩ Type an item label and a value for each menu item.

ⓒ You can click ⊞ or ⊟ to add or delete entries.

ⓓ You can select an item and click ▲ or ▼ to reposition the item in the list.

⑪ Click **OK**.

The entered values appear in the list box.

⑫ Click the item that you want to appear preselected when the page loads.

Dreamweaver applies your specifications to the menu.

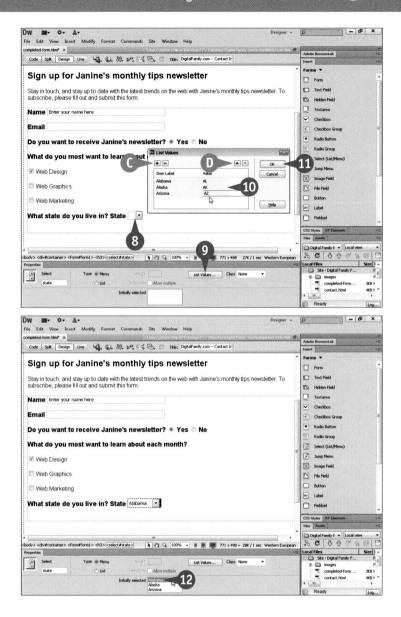

TIPS

What determines the height and width of a menu or list?
The widest item determines the width of your menu or list. To change the width of the menu, you can change the length of your item descriptions. You can set the height greater than 1 so that visitors to your site can see more of your list items.

Can I choose more than one item from a menu?
You can select only one item from a menu because of its design. If you want more than one selection, use a list and set it to allow multiple selections.

Add a Button to a Form

You can use a form button for many things, but its most common use is to add a Submit button at the end of a form. You need a Submit button to enable users to send the information that they have entered in the form to the specified script or form handler. Although the word *submit* is included on the button by default, you can change the text by editing it in the **Value** field in the Property inspector. You can also add a Reset button to clear the contents of a form.

Add a Button to a Form

Add a Submit Button

1. Click inside the form container where you want to add the Submit button.

2. Click ▼.

3. Click **Forms**.

4. Click the **Button** □ in the Forms Insert panel.

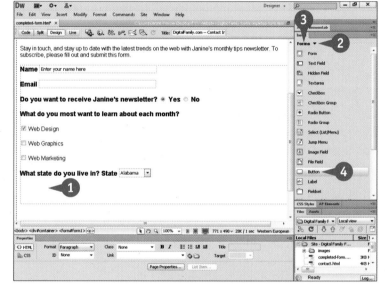

The Input Tag Accessibility Attributes dialog box appears.

5. Type a one-word ID.

Note: Most Submit buttons do not include a label.

Ⓐ You can select the **Style** and **Position** attributes that you want (◎ changes to ◉).

Ⓑ Entering an access key and tab index can make your site more accessible.

6. Click **OK**.

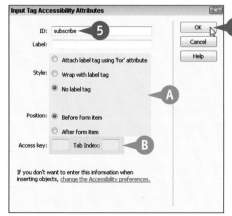

A Submit button appears in the form.

7 Click the button to select it.

8 Type a value for the button.

C The text on the button changes from **Submit** to the value that you entered.

Add a Reset Button

1 Repeat steps **1** to **8**, using a different ID in step **5**.

2 Click **Reset form** in the Property inspector (◎ changes to ◉).

TIPS

What happens to the data when a user clicks the Submit button?

Think of the Submit button at the end of a form as an activation button. When the user clicks Submit, you generally want it to trigger an action, such as emailing the contents of the form to you or starting a search across the pages of your website. The Submit button is only as good as the script or form handler that it triggers. For more information about processing forms, check out Adobe's form service, FormsCentral, at www.acrobat.com/formscentral.

Why would I add a Reset button to a form on a web page?

Including a Reset button is a common practice on the web. Reset buttons make it easy for visitors to your site to clear the contents of a form if they have made an error and want to redo the form.

Using Library Items and Templates

You can save time by storing frequently used web page elements as library items. You can create sites even more efficiently by saving complete page layouts as templates. These features help with consistency and can be updated automatically.

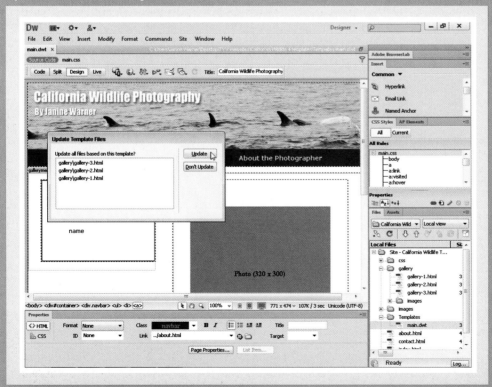

Introducing Library Items and Templates

The library items and templates features in Dreamweaver can help you work faster and smarter. You can streamline tasks by saving frequently used items as library items, and you can create entire pages faster and more efficiently by saving layouts as templates. After you create web pages from templates, you can then update all of those pages at once by editing the original template, which can save you loads of time. Library items can also be used to update multiple pages at once. Both features are accessible through the Assets panel or from the Modify menu.

Library Items

You can define parts of your web pages that are repeated in your website as library items. This saves you time because whenever you need a library item, you can just insert it from the Assets panel instead of re-creating it. If you make changes to a library item, Dreamweaver automatically updates all instances of the item across your website. Good candidates for library items include advertising banners, company slogans, copyright messages, and any other feature that appears many times across your website.

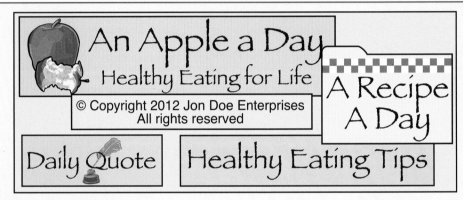

Templates

You can define entire web pages as templates and then save them to use later when you build new pages. Templates can help you maintain a consistent page design throughout a website. When you make changes to a template, Dreamweaver automatically updates all the pages in your website that were created from that template. The ability to make global updates to common areas of a template, such as a navigation bar, makes it faster to make changes to a site.

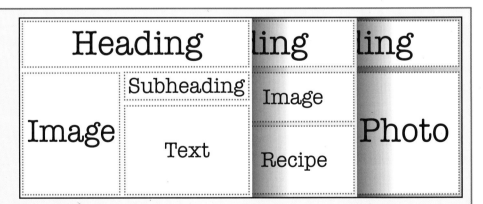

View Library Items and Templates

You can create and insert library items and templates using the Modify menu, but the simplest option is to use the Assets panel. You open templates and library items by double-clicking them in the Assets panel, and you insert library items by dragging them from the panel on to a web page.

Note: You must define a site in Dreamweaver before you can use these features. The site-definition process is covered in Chapter 2, "Setting Up Your Website."

View Library Items and Templates

View the Library

1 Click **Window**.

2 Click **Assets**.

Ⓐ The Assets panel opens.

3 Click the Library button (📖).

Ⓑ The Library window opens in the Assets panel.

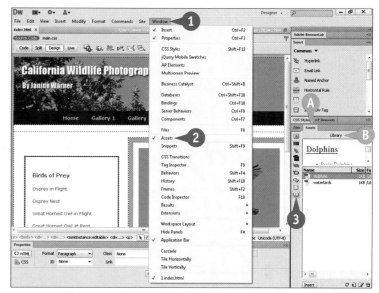

View Templates

1 Click **Window**.

2 Click **Assets**.

Ⓒ The Assets panel opens.

3 Click the Template button (📄) to view the templates.

Ⓓ The Templates window opens in the Assets panel.

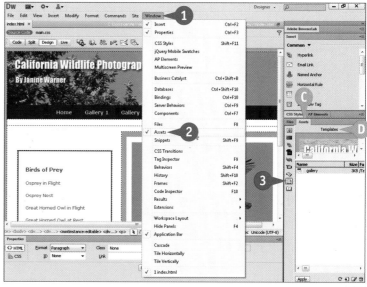

Create a Library Item

Dreamweaver's library item feature is ideal for elements that are used on more than one page in your site, such as a copyright message that you want to place in the footer of every page. You can save text, links, images, and other elements as library items, and you can insert the same item into any or all of the pages in your site, but the most time-saving feature of library items is the ability to automatically update the contents of a library item in all pages in which it appears.

Create a Library Item

1 Click and drag to select an element or collection of elements that you want to define as a library item.

Note: Before you can use the library item feature in Dreamweaver, you must first set up and define your local site. To set up a local site, see Chapter 2.

2 Click **Modify**.

3 Click **Library**.

4 Click **Add Object to Library**.

Ⓐ A new, untitled library item appears in the Library window.

❺ Type a name for the library item.

❻ Press **Enter** (**Return**).

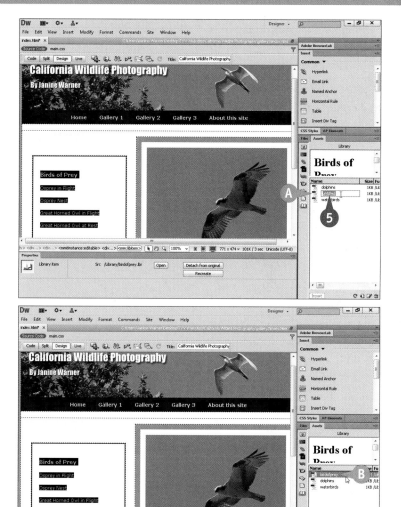

Ⓑ The named library item appears in the Assets panel.

Note: Defining an element as a library item prevents you from editing it in the Document window.

TIPS

What page elements should I make into library items?
Anything that appears multiple times in a website is a good candidate to become a library item. These elements include navigation menus, contact information, and disclaimers. Any element that appears in the body of an HTML document, including text, images, tables, forms, layers, and multimedia, may be defined as a library item.

Can I use multiple library items on the same HTML page?
There is no limit to the number of library items that you can use on a page. For example, you can create a library item for the logo at the top of the page and another for the copyright at the bottom.

Insert a Library Item

You can insert library items into any or all of the pages in a website. This makes creating new pages more efficient because you do not have to re-create the contents of the library item for each page. Using a library item also ensures that the element is identical, which can help you create a consistent look and feel throughout your site. In addition, all the pages to which you add a library item can be automatically updated throughout your site if you make changes to the library item later.

Insert a Library Item

① Click **Window**.

② Click **Assets**.

The Assets panel opens.

Ⓐ If the Library window is not open in the Assets panel, you can click 📖 to view it.

③ Click the name of the library item.

Ⓑ A preview of the library item appears at the top of the Library window.

④ Click and drag the library item on to the page in the place that you want it to appear.

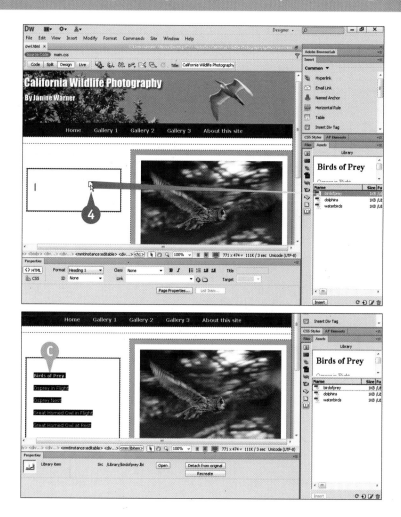

ⓒ Dreamweaver inserts the library item into the Document window.

TIPS

How do I edit a library item that has been inserted into a page?

Instances of library items on your page are locked and cannot be edited within the page. To edit a library item, you must either edit the original version of that item from the library or detach the library item from the library to edit it within the page. However, if you detach the library item from the library, the item is no longer a part of the library, and it is not updated when you change the library item.

Can I make an element a library item after I have used it on a few pages?

Yes. You can save any item to the library at any time. If you want to make sure that all instances of the item are attached to the library item, simply open any pages where you have already applied the item, delete it, and then insert it from the library.

Edit and Update a Library Item on Your Pages

One of the greatest advantages of using library items is that you can edit a library item and when you save the changes, Dreamweaver automatically updates all the pages in your website that feature that library item. This ability to make global changes can help you save time when updating or redesigning a website. For example, if you add or edit text or change or create links in a library item, those changes are applied to all the pages where the text or links in the library item appear in your site.

Edit and Update a Library Item on Your Pages

1 Double-click the library item.

The library item opens in a new window.

2 Edit any element in the library item.

You can add or delete text, insert images, and make any other edits to a library item that you can make to a web page.

Note: In this example, a new link is added to a gallery page titled "Birds of Prey."

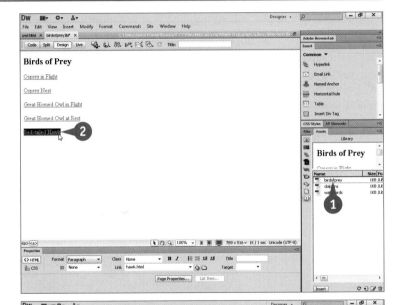

3 Click **File**.

4 Click **Save**.

You can also save the page with the key command Ctrl + S (⌘ + S).

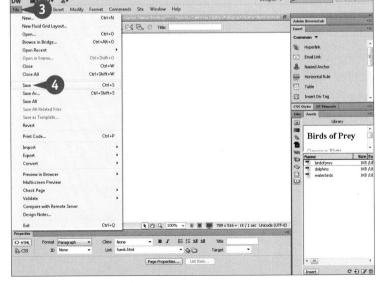

The Update Library Items dialog box appears, asking if you want to update all instances of the library item in the site.

5 Click **Update**.

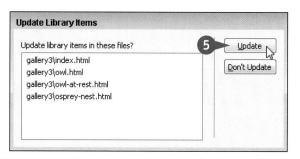

The Update Pages dialog box appears, showing the progress of the updates.

6 Click **Show log** to view the list of pages that were updated (☐ changes to ☑).

7 After Dreamweaver updates the site, click **Close**.

All pages in which the library item appears are updated.

Ⓐ Changes are also made to the stored library item and are visible in the Assets panel.

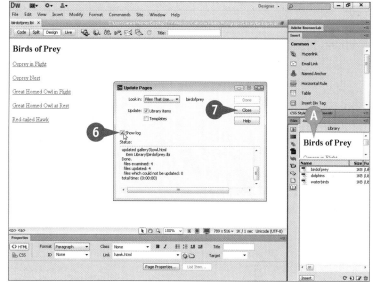

TIPS

What do my pages look like after I have edited a library item and updated my website?
When you edit a library item and choose to update any instances of the library item that are already inserted into your web pages, all those instances are replaced with the edited versions. By using the library feature, you can make a change to a single library item and have multiple web pages updated automatically.

Can I undo an update to a library item?
Technically, no. When you update pages with the library feature, the Undo command does not undo all the instances of these changes. However, you can go back to the Assets panel, open the library item, change it back to the way it was, and then apply those changes to all the pages again.

Detach Library Content for Editing

If you want to edit the contents of a library item without affecting all the pages in which you have inserted the library item, you can detach a single inserted library item from the original stored item. After the contents of a library item are detached from the original, you can then edit the text, images, and links of that library item as you would any other element on a web page. If you detach a library item, however, the contents of that library item will no longer be updated automatically when you change the original stored library item.

Detach Library Content for Editing

1 Click to select the library item that you want to edit independently.

2 Click **Detach from original**.

A warning dialog box appears.

Ⓐ You can prevent the warning from appearing each time that you perform this action by clicking **Don't warn me again** (☐ changes to ☑).

3 Click **OK**.

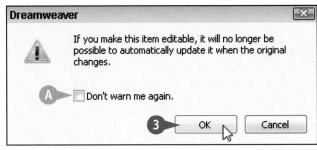

The element is no longer a library item and has no distinctive highlighting.

4 Click where you want to edit the library item and make any edits that you want.

B You can add, delete, and format text. In this example, the text in the last section is edited.

5 Press `Ctrl` + `S` (`⌘` + `S`) to save the page.

C Dreamweaver applies the editing only to the page you are working on.

Note: Editing a detached library item has no effect on library items that are used on other pages.

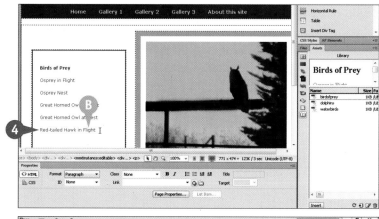

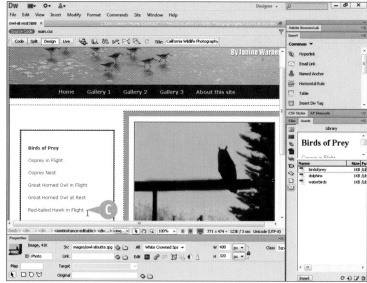

TIPS

When would I use the Detach from Original command?

This command is useful when you want to create an element in a page that will be similar to an element that you have saved as a library item. For example, if you use a copyright line that includes the photographer's name on every page of a 20-page photo gallery and then you decide to add one page with a photo taken by a different photographer, you could detach the library item so that you could change only that instance of the copyright line.

Can I reattach a library item?

Not exactly, but you can always reinsert a library item into a page and then delete the unattached library item. As a result, any changes that you make to the stored version are applied to the newly inserted version. Inserting a library item again may be faster than making the updates manually.

167

...items are useful for short text elements, such as copyright messages, or collections of links in a gallery. However, templates are an even more powerful and timesaving feature in Dreamweaver because they enable you to create entire page designs that can be reused over and over again. Templates can help you create more consistent designs for your pages, and just as with library items, you can make changes automatically to all the pages that you create from a template.

Create a Template

Note: To create templates for your web pages, you must already have defined a local website. To set up a local website, see Chapter 2.

1. Click **File**.
2. Click **New**.

The New Document dialog box appears.

3. Click **Blank Template**.
4. Click **HTML template**.

You can choose another template type if you are working on a site that uses another technology.

5. Click a **Layout** option.
6. Click **Create**.

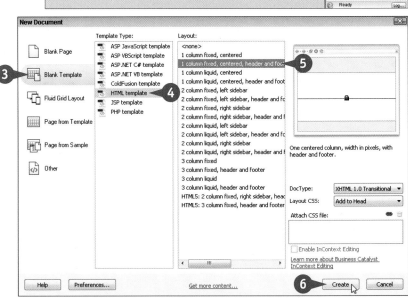

7 Design a new page as you would for any other web page, using the features that you want for your template.

Ⓐ You can add placeholder images and text to indicate where content is to be added to the pages created from the template.

8 Click **File**.

9 Click **Save as Template**.

If a Dreamweaver error dialog box appears with the warning "This template doesn't have any editable regions," click **OK**.

The Save As Template dialog box appears.

10 Click ▼ and select your site name.

11 Type a name for the template.

12 Click **Save**.

Ⓑ The new template is saved in the Templates folder.

If a Templates folder does not already exist, Dreamweaver automatically creates one, and it appears in the Files panel.

Note: To make the template functional, define editable regions to modify content, as you learn in the next section, "Set an Editable Region in a Template."

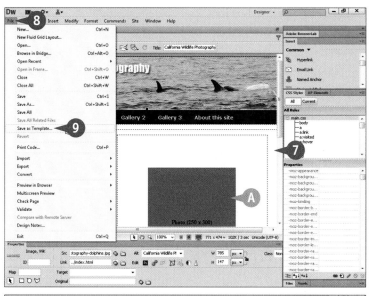

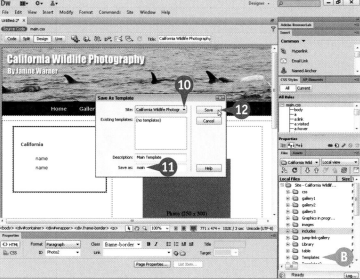

TIPS

Can I create as many pages as I want from a template?

Yes. There is no limit to the number of pages that you can create from one template. In fact, the more pages that you plan to create using the same design, the more reason you have to save that design as a template, so it does not have to be re-created each time.

How do I edit a page that is created with a template?

After you create a new web page from a template, you can change only the parts of the new page that are defined as editable. To change locked content, you must edit the original template file. For more information about creating editable regions in a template, see the following section.

Set an Editable Region in a Template

After you create a web page template, you must define which regions of the template are editable. Editable regions can be altered in every page created from a template. When you create a page from the template, you can add or edit the text, images, and other elements in editable regions. In contrast, any areas of the template that are not set as editable regions cannot be changed in pages that you create from the template. These uneditable regions can then be used to make global updates to all the pages created from the template.

Set an Editable Region in a Template

1 Click **Window**.

2 Click **Files**.

The Files panel appears.

3 Click the **Templates** + (+ turns to –).

4 Double-click a template name to open it.

You can also open a template by double-clicking the template name in the Assets panel.

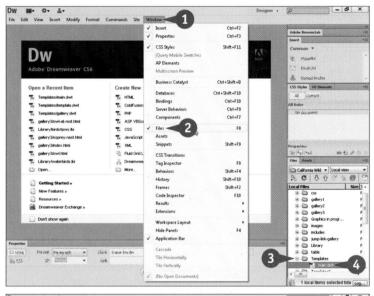

The template opens in the work area.

5 Click to select an image, `div` tag, or other element that you want to define as editable.

Note: In this example, a `div` tag is selected.

6 Click **Insert**.

7 Click **Template Objects**.

8 Click **Editable Region**.

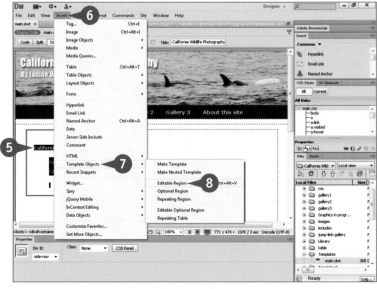

The New Editable Region dialog box appears.

9 Type a name for the editable region that distinguishes it from other editable regions on the page.

Note: You cannot use special characters, such as punctuation marks, in the name of an editable region.

10 Click **OK**.

Ⓐ A light-blue box with the region name indicates the editable region.

11 Repeat steps **5** to **10** for all the regions on the page that you want to be editable.

Ⓑ Each new editable region is indicated by a light-blue box with the region name.

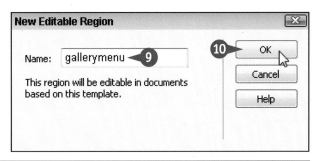

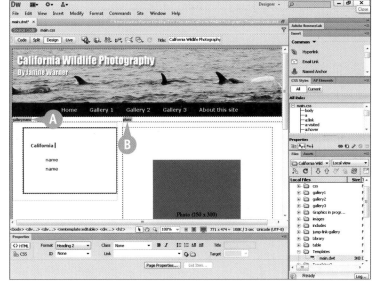

TIPS

What parts of a template should be defined as editable?

You should define as editable any part of your template that you want to change from page to page. This can include headlines, stories, images, and captions. In contrast, you should lock site navigation, disclaimers, and copyright information, which should be the same on all pages.

Can I use library items in my template pages?

Yes, you can use library items in templates. This is useful when you want to insert an item on pages that are made from the template. When you edit them, the library items are updated in the actual templates — and then in all the pages that are created from those templates.

Create a Page from a Template

After you create a template, you can create new web pages from that template. This step saves you from having to rebuild all the structure of each page and re-add all the common elements that appear on your pages. When you create a new page from a template, common elements that you have saved in areas of the template that are not editable, such as the main navigation links, logo, and copyright information, are already in place, giving you a great head start as you create each new page in your site.

Create a Page from a Template

1 Click **File**.

2 Click **New**.

The New Document dialog box appears.

3 Click **Page from Template**.

4 Click the name of the website.

5 Click the template.

Ⓐ A preview of the template appears.

6 Click **Create**.

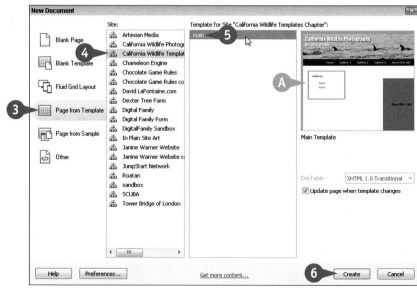

Dreamweaver generates a new page from the template.

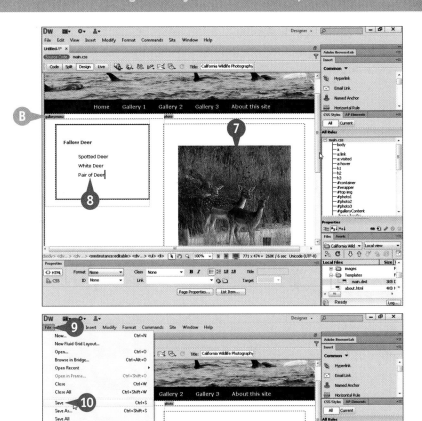

B The editable regions have blue labels and are surrounded by blue boxes.

7 Insert images as needed into the editable regions.

8 Type content as needed in the editable regions.

Note: Only editable areas can be altered in a page created from a template.

9 Click **File**.

10 Click **Save**.

Dreamweaver saves the new page based on the template.

TIP

How do I detach a page from a template?

1 Click **Modify**.

2 Click **Templates**.

3 Click **Detach from Template**.

The page becomes a regular document with previously locked regions now fully editable. Edits to the original template no longer update the page.

Edit a Template and Update Web Pages Created with It

After you create pages in your site from a template, you can make changes to all those pages at once by editing the regions of the original template file that are not editable in each page created from the template. That is why it is best to keep common elements, such as the main navigation links, logo, and copyright information, as uneditable regions because that allows you to edit those elements in the template and then update all the pages created from the template at once.

Edit a Template and Update Web Pages Created with It

1 Click **Window**.

2 Click **Files**.

The Files panel appears.

3 Click the **Templates** + (+ turns to –).

4 Double-click the template name to open it.

You can also open a template by double-clicking the template name in the Assets panel.

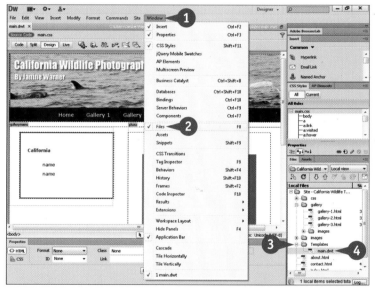

5 Click an area of the template that is not an editable region.

Note: Only locked regions of a template can be used to make updates to pages created from the template.

Ⓐ In this example, a navigation menu link is edited.

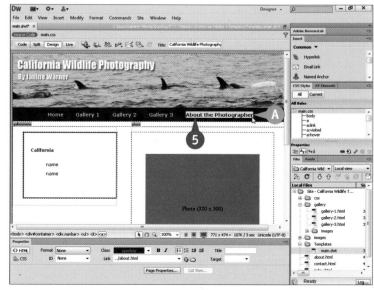

6 Press `Ctrl` + `S` (`⌘` + `S`) to save the page.

The Update Template Files dialog box appears, listing all files based on the selected template that will be updated.

7 Click **Update**.

The Update Pages dialog box appears.

8 Click **Show log** (☐ changes to ☑).

Ⓑ The results of the update process appear in the Status pane.

9 After Dreamweaver updates the website, click **Close**.

All the pages that use the template are updated to reflect the changes.

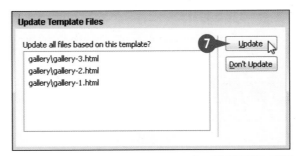

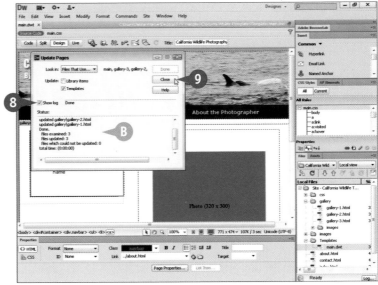

TIPS

How does Dreamweaver store page templates?
Dreamweaver stores page templates in a folder called *Templates* inside the local site folder. You can open the templates by clicking **File** and then clicking **Open**. In the Open dialog box, click ▾ and click the **Templates** folder. You can click a template file to select it. You can also open templates from inside the Assets panel.

What are editable attributes?
Editable attributes enable you to change the attributes of an element in the Property inspector. For example, you can change image attributes, such as alternative text, alignment, or size. To use this feature, select an element, such as an image, click **Modify**, then click **Templates**, an[d] **Attribute Editable**.

Creating and Applying Cascading Style Sheets

This chapter shows you how to use Cascading Style Sheets (CSS) to create and apply formatting, which helps you create sites that conform to modern web design standards.

Introducing Cascading Style Sheets

You can apply many different types of formatting to your web pages with *Cascading Style Sheets,* or CSS. Often referred to simply as *style sheets,* or by the acronym, CSS makes it possible to define style rules that can then be applied to the text, images, and other elements on a web page. For example, you can define a style for the headlines in your website and then apply that same style to all your main headings, which makes it faster and easier to apply multiple formatting options at once and to make changes to styles later.

Format Text

CSS enables you to create as many different style sheets as you want. You can then use them to format text by applying multiple formatting options at once, such as the font face, size, and color.

Style Sheet

Comic Sans, 18 pt., green

Garamond, 9 pt., blue

A Day At The Racetrack

It was a chilly Saturday morning when I showed up for my first day at the racetrack. It was early, too; 6 A.M., and jockeys were leading their horses out to the track for a pre-breakfast workout. I recognized Sam, whose word had gotten me this job, and I waved. He waved back, and grinned, "How's the city boy doing? Wish you were still in your nice, warm bed with a soft desk job waiting for you?" I laughed; there was no place I'd rather be than here but still, it had been hard to leave my bed this morning. I hadn't woken so early since - well, I'd never woken this early. Ever. Still, I made my choice, and even good choices, the ones you know deep down are the right choices, have their trade-offs. I idly wondered how long it would take me to

Create Page Layouts

You can use styles for more than just formatting text. You can create styles to align and position elements on a web page. Using styles in this way, you can create complex page designs that display well on small and large computer screens. You can find more instructions for creating page layouts in Chapter 12, "Designing a Website with CSS."

Style Sheet

Alignment: Centered

Position: Top

Font: Garamond, 9 pt., blue

I Become an Exercise Jockey

Cascading Style Sheet Selectors

Dreamweaver includes four different style selector types: the tag selector to redefine existing HTML tags, the class selector to create new styles that can be applied to any element on a web page, the ID selector to create styles that can be used only once per page, and the compound selector, which can be used to combine style definitions.

Selectors

Tag	`<h1>`
Class	.caption
ID	#sidebar
Compound	#sidebar h1

Internal Style Sheets

A style sheet saved within the HTML code of a web page is called an *internal style sheet*. Internal style sheet rules apply only to the page in which they are included.

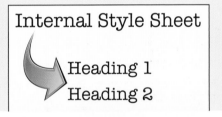

External Style Sheets

When you want your styles to apply to multiple pages on your website, you must save them in a separate file called an *external style sheet*. You can attach the same external style sheet to any or all of the pages in a website.

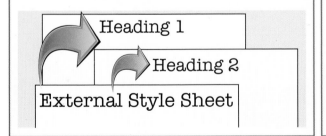

Style Sheets and Web Browsers

Some older web browsers do not support style sheet standards, and different web browsers display style sheets differently. Always test pages that use style sheets on different browsers to ensure that the content is displayed as you intend it to be for all your visitors.

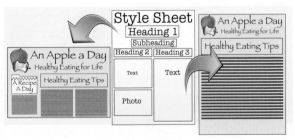

Edit Styles with the Property Inspector

CSS is the best way to format text, images, and other elements, but there are still times when you will want to use the HTML options. For example, it is a good practice to format headlines with the h1 HTML tag, but you can then alter the appearance using CSS. You can create and edit styles using the CSS Styles panel, covered later in this chapter. For quick edits to existing styles or to create new styles as you format elements, you can switch between the HTML options in the Property inspector and the CSS options.

Edit Styles with the Property Inspector

① Click an element on the page that you want to format.

In this example, a headline formatted with the h1 tag is selected.

② Click **CSS**.

Ⓐ If any CSS rules are already applied to your selected element, they are displayed in the Targeted Rule field.

③ Click ▾ and select any CSS rule from the list, or select **<New CSS Rule>** to create a new style rule.

④ Click **Edit Rule**.

The New CSS Rule dialog box appears.

⑤ Type a name for the style.

Note: If a style is already applied, changing the name or selector type is optional.

⑥ Click **OK**.

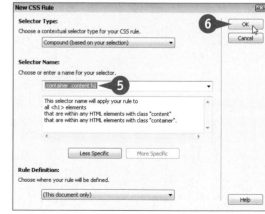

The CSS Rule Definition dialog box appears.

7 Click a style category.

8 Select the style settings that you want to define.

Ⓑ You can click **Apply** to see a preview of the style.

9 Click **OK**.

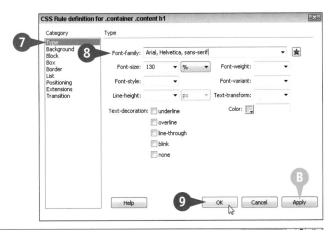

Ⓒ The selected element is formatted with the new style rule.

In this example, the font face and size are changed for the text formatted with the Heading 1 tag.

Ⓓ The CSS Styles panel displays the new style.

TIP

Why does Dreamweaver create compound styles in the Property inspector?

When you select an element on a page that is already formatted with HTML tags or styles, Dreamweaver gives you a head start by including that formatting information in the Targeted Rule field in the Property inspector. For example, if you select text formatted with an `h1` tag that is inside a `div` tag with the style `#mainContent`, the compound style looks like this: `#mainContent h1`. Compound styles are very specific styles, meaning that the style for an `h1` tag created as a compound style will apply only to text formatted with the `h1` tag if that text is contained within an `h1` tag that is contained in a `div` tag styled with `#mainContent`. This is useful when you want to apply formatting to a headline without changing all the text formatted with the `h1` tag. If you do want to redefine the `h1` tag in all the places that you have used it, remove the secondary style so that only `h1` appears in the **Targeted Rule** field.

Create a Class Style

You can create class styles that can be used to format text and other elements on a web page without affecting HTML tags. You can then apply those styles to any elements on your web page, much like you would apply an HTML tag. One of the advantages of class styles, in contrast with other style types, is that you can use them as many times as you like on the same page. That makes them ideal for formatting options that you are likely to use repeatedly, such as the text in the captions of all your images.

Create a Class Style

1 Click **Format**.

2 Click **CSS Styles**.

3 Click **New**.

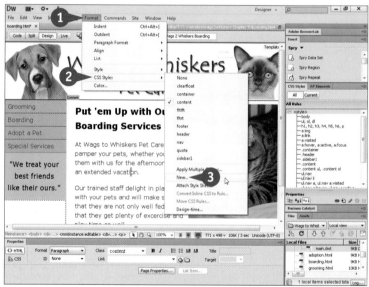

The New CSS Rule dialog box appears.

4 Click ▾ and select **Class**.

5 Type a name for the class style.

Note: Class style names must begin with a period (.). Dreamweaver adds one automatically.

6 Click ▾ and select **This document only**.

Note: To create style sheets for more than one document, see the section "Create an External Style Sheet."

7 Click **OK**.

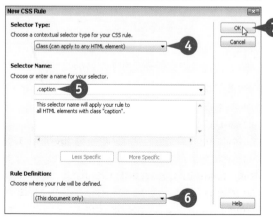

The CSS Rule Definition dialog box appears.

8 Click a style category.

9 Select the style settings that you want.

In this example, text style options are used to change the font weight and size.

10 Click **OK**.

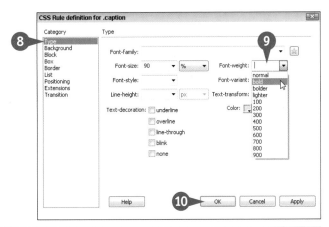

11 Click **CSS Styles**.

A You can also click **Window** and then click **CSS Styles**.

B The CSS Styles panel opens, displaying the new class style.

You can apply the class style to new or existing content using the Property inspector.

Note: To apply a new class style, see the following section, "Apply a Class Style."

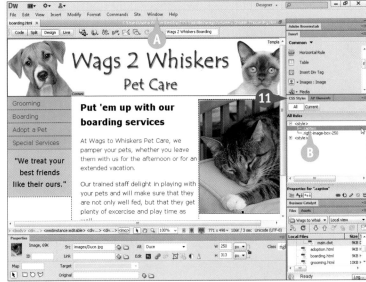

TIPS

Can the same styles be edited in the Property inspector and the CSS Styles panel?

Yes. You can create and edit styles using both the CSS Styles panel and the Property inspector, and styles created or edited in one place will automatically be updated in the other. The main difference is that the CSS Styles panel includes more features for editing and reviewing styles, and the Property inspector, in HTML mode, can also be used to apply class and ID styles.

Is it better to customize an HTML tag or create my own class styles?

One of the benefits of redefining existing HTML tags is that you can take advantage of recognized styles and hierarchies. This is especially true with heading tags. For example, if you change the way h1, h2, and h3 tags appear, it is best to maintain their relative size difference, keeping h1 as the largest and using it to format the most important heading on the page.

Apply a Class Style

Y ou can apply a class style to any element on your web page. Class styles enable you to change the color, font, size, alignment, and other characteristics. You can use the same class style multiple times on the same page, and you can use the same class style throughout a website. Thus, if you format all your image captions with the same style and then later decide to change the formatting options used in your captions, you can change the style rule — and all the captions formatted with that style will be automatically updated.

Apply a Class Style

Apply a Class Style to Text

Note: To create a new custom style, see the previous section, "Create a Class Style."

1 Click and drag to select the text to which you want to apply a style.

2 Click **HTML**.

3 Click the **Class** ⏷.

4 Click the name of the style.

Ⓐ Dreamweaver applies the style.

In this example, a font style is applied.

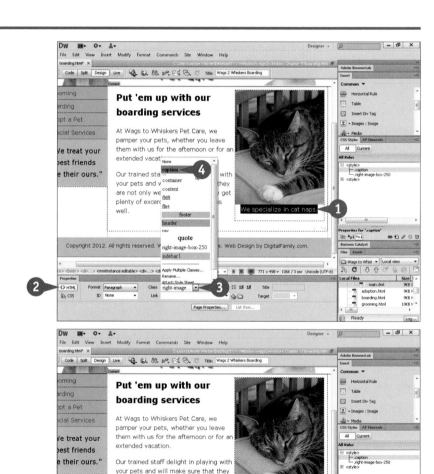

Apply a Class Style to an Image

Note: To create a new custom style, see the previous section, "Create a Class Style."

1 Click the image to select it.

2 In the Property inspector, click the **Class** ▼.

3 Click the name of the style.

B Dreamweaver applies the new style to the image in the Document window.

In this example, the image is aligned to the right, and 8 pixels of margin space are added to the left side of the image.

TIPS

What are some other options that I can use to define the formatting for text with a style sheet?

With style sheets, you can specify a numeric value for font weight. This enables you to apply varying degrees of boldness, instead of just a single boldness setting as with HTML. You can also define type size in absolute units, such as pixels, points, picas, inches, centimeters, or millimeters, or in relative units, such as ems, exes, or percentage.

Can I create as many styles as I want?

Yes. However, one of the goals of style sheets is to help you work more efficiently, so you should try to create styles that are as efficient as possible in the way they contain formatting options.

Edit a Style

Y ou can edit the settings in any style rule. When you change the settings in a style rule, the changes are automatically applied to all the text or other elements to which you have applied the style in your website. This ability to change the formatting of many elements at once by using the same style consistently throughout a website is one of the things that makes CSS so powerful. To use the same style on multiple pages, you must save the style in an external style sheet.

Note: To create style sheets for more than one document, see the section "Create an External Style Sheet."

Edit a Style

1 Click **Window**.

2 Click **CSS Styles**.

Ⓐ The CSS Styles panel opens.

3 Click **All** to display all the available styles.

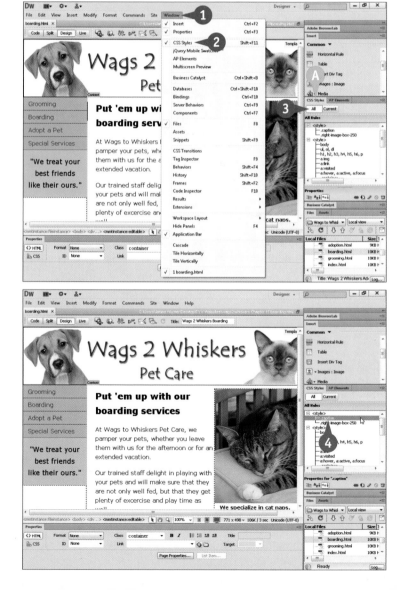

4 Double-click the name of a style that you want to edit.

The CSS Rule Definition dialog box opens.

5 Click a style category.

6 Select the style settings that you want.

In this example, the font color is changed.

7 Click **OK**.

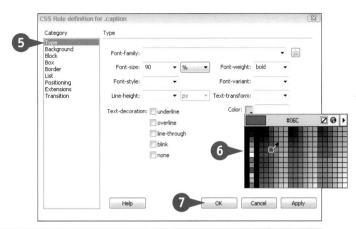

Dreamweaver saves the style sheet changes and automatically applies them anywhere that you have used the style.

B In this example, the font color changes automatically in the text where the style has already been applied.

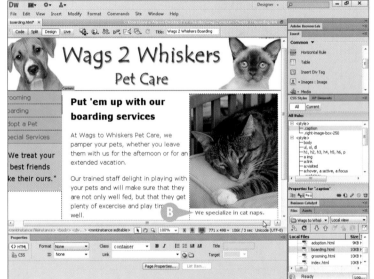

TIP

How many different kinds of styles are there?

You can create multiple kinds of style rules, but the main options are tag styles, class styles, ID styles, and compound styles. Tag styles are used to redefine HTML tags. Class styles are used to create new styles that can be applied to any element on a page and used multiple times. ID styles are commonly used with `<div>` tags to control the placement of elements on a page and create page layouts.

Customize an HTML Tag

In addition to creating new styles, you can use CSS to customize the style that an existing HTML tag applies. This enables you to apply special formatting whenever you use that tag to format text. For example, you can use the h1 tag to format all of your most important headlines and then create an HTML tag style rule for the h1 tag that changes the font, size, color, and other features wherever that tag is applied. This is a quick, easy way to apply multiple style options with one HTML tag.

Customize an HTML Tag

1 Click **Format**.

2 Click **CSS Styles**.

3 Click **New**.

The New CSS Rule dialog box appears.

4 Click ▼ and select **Tag**.

5 Click ▼ and select the HTML tag.

You can also type a tag name into the field.

6 Click ▼ and select **This document only** or choose an external style sheet.

Note: To create style sheets for more than one document, see the section "Create an External Style Sheet."

7 Click **OK**.

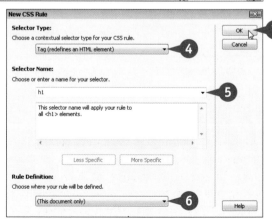

The CSS Rule Definition dialog box appears.

8 Click a style category.

9 Select the style settings that you want.

10 Click **OK**.

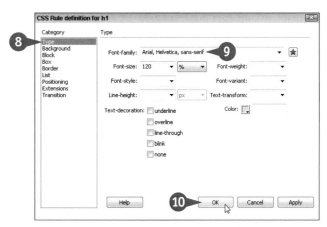

A Dreamweaver adds the new style to the CSS Styles panel.

B Any content that is formatted with the redefined tag is updated.

In this example, the h1 tag is redefined to use a different font face and size.

C In this example, you can also apply the style by selecting content on the page and selecting **Heading 1** from the **Format** drop-down list.

TIPS

Why should I redefine an HTML tag?
When you redefine an HTML tag, you can apply more than one style to the tag. As a result, you have to use only one HTML tag instead of several to apply multiple formatting options. For example, you can add center alignment to all your h1 tags to control the alignment of heading styles in one step. A special advantage of redefining HTML tags is that if a user's web browser does not support style sheets, the HTML tag still provides its basic formatting.

Does redefining an HTML tag change the format of any content that uses that tag?
Yes. When you redefine an HTML tag, you change the tag's formatting effect anywhere that you use the tag. You can limit the change to the page that you are working on, or you can include it in an external style sheet and apply it to an entire site. If you do not want to alter the style of an existing HTML tag, you should create class style sheets instead of redefining HTML tags. For more information on class style sheets, see the section "Create a Class Style."

Change the Font Face

You can change the font style of your text in a variety of ways in Dreamweaver, but all of them require using CSS. For example, you can create a new style rule using the font face that you want and define it with a class selector. You can then apply the class style to any text on the page. You can also change the font face settings with a CSS rule defined to format any existing HTML tag, such as the h1 or h2 tag, and any text formatted with that tag will be displayed in the specified font.

Change the Font Face

1 Click and drag to select the text.

2 Click **CSS** in the Property inspector.

3 Click the **Font** ⏷.

4 Click a font collection.

Note: Leave the Targeted Rule field set to <New CSS Rule>. In the section "Edit Styles with the Property Inspector," you can find instructions for editing CSS rules with the Property inspector.

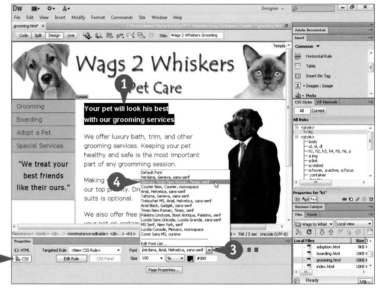

The New CSS Rule dialog box opens.

5 Type a name for the new style.

Note: Do not use spaces or special characters.

Ⓐ If the selected text is already formatted with an HTML tag, Dreamweaver inserts the tag name into the Selector Name field.

In this example, the headline is formatted with an h1 tag.

6 Click **OK**.

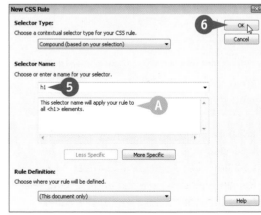

B The text changes to the first font in the collection that is available on your hard drive.

The new style can be applied to additional elements by using the Property inspector.

Note: To find out more about how to create and apply styles, see the sections "Create a Class Style" and "Apply a Class Style."

7 Click **CSS Styles**.

8 Click the name of the new style rule.

9 Use ▾ to change the font collection.

The font face is changed.

TIPS

How are fonts classified?

The two most common categories of fonts are serif and sans serif. Serif fonts are distinguished by the decorations, or *serifs,* that make the ends of their lines curly. Common serif fonts include Times New Roman, Palatino, and Garamond. Sans serif fonts lack these decorations and have straight edges. Common sans serif fonts include Arial, Verdana, and Helvetica.

Why are there so few fonts available from the Font menu?

Unless you link to a font, as discussed in the following section, "Using a Linked Font in a Style Rule," a font must be installed on the user's computer to be displayed in a web browser. Dreamweaver's default list of fonts specifies the common typefaces that are available on most computers, and alternative styles if the user does not have those fonts installed. If you want to use an unusual font, you should link to the font or convert the text to a graphic.

a Linked Font in a Style Rule

hanks to advances in HTML and CSS, you can now link to almost any font and use it to format text on your web pages. However, because different operating systems require different fonts, and not all browsers display fonts the same way, there are some complexities as to how a font needs to be hosted on a web server in order for it to be available to use on your web pages. For that reason, most web designers use one of the many font repositories online, such as the Google Web Fonts site, featured in this section.

Using a Linked Font in a Style Rule

Link to a Font Online

1 In a web browser, go to www. google.com/webfonts.

2 Click **Start choosing fonts** to search for a font that you want to use on your web page.

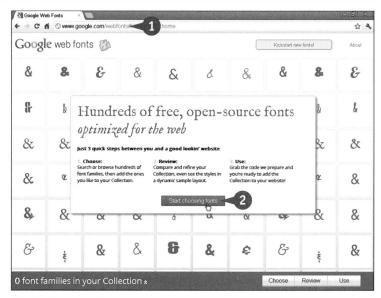

The Web Fonts page appears.

3 Scroll through the font names until you find one that you like.

A You can type text in the **Preview Text** field to see how it will be displayed in each font.

4 When you find a font that you want to use, click **Add to Collection**.

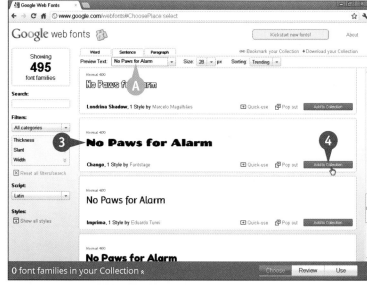

B The collection area opens at the bottom of the browser window.

5 Click **Use**.

The font collection page appears.

6 Scroll down and select the code in the **Add this code to your website** box.

7 Right-click (**Option** + click) and choose **Copy**.

TIP

Where can I find fonts that I can use on my website?

There are many sites on the web that offer fonts that you can use on your website. Some offer fonts for free, whereas others charge a fee.

These are some of the most popular font repositories online:

- **Google Web Fonts** (www.google.com/webfonts) has a limited list of fonts, but it is the simplest site to use. Just copy a little code from the Google site to yours, and you can use any of their fonts in your styles for free.

- **Typekit** (www.typekit.com) offers a wide range of professional-quality fonts for limited use for free, or for professional use for a fee. Typekit is owned by Adobe.

- **FontSquirrel** (www.fontsquirrel.com) provides a collection of free fonts and makes it easy to use them on your pages.

- **Fontspring** (www.fontspring.com) is a clearinghouse that sells fonts, ready for use in printed and digital materials.

continued ▶

A fter you link to a font hosted on a web server, as you did in the first half of this section, you can use that font in any of your CSS style rules. You can link to as many fonts as you want, but it is a good practice to limit your site to no more than a few fonts on your pages. You can link a font to a single page or to a Dreamweaver template to make it available to all the pages created from that template.

Using a Linked Font in a Style Rule (continued)

Using a Font in a Style

8 In Dreamweaver, click **Split**.

9 Click to place your cursor just before the closing `</head>` tag in the HTML code.

10 Right-click (**Option** + click) and paste the link that you copied in step **7** into the code.

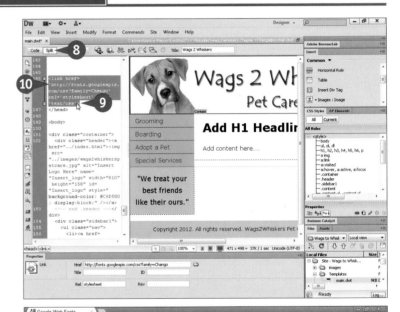

11 In a browser, return to the Google Web Fonts page where you copied the link in step **7**.

12 Scroll further down the same page and select just the name of the font from the text in the **Integrate the fonts into your CSS** section.

13 Right-click (**Option** + click) and choose **Copy**.

Note: If you plan to add the font as shown in the next step, you need to copy only the name of the font. Google provides more code in this field so that you can copy the entire code string directly into the CSS code in any web page.

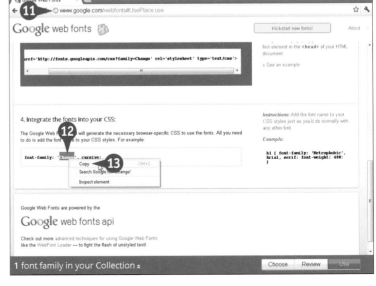

14 In Dreamweaver, create a new CSS style rule or double-click the name of an existing style.

The CSS Rule Definition dialog box appears.

15 Paste the name of the font into the **Font-family** field.

16 Click **OK**.

The font name is added to the CSS style rule definition.

17 Click **Live**.

A The font is displayed on the page.

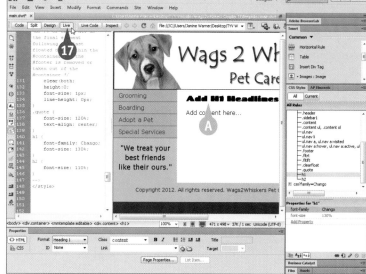

TIP

Can I use a linked font in my logo?
Yes, you can use any linked font anywhere in your site. However, when you are linking to a font on another web server, even when it is as reliable as Google's servers, there is always the risk that the connection can be broken and the font will not be displayed on your page. Also, keep in mind that not all web browsers support linked fonts; all the new browser versions support these font features, but older browsers will default to displaying only the fonts on your visitor's hard drive. Although you can expect your linked fonts to work most of the time, because they are not 100% reliable, many web designers prefer to save the font in their logo in a graphic to ensure that it always will be displayed properly.

Change the Font Size

You can change the size of your text by using the font size options in the CSS pane of the Property inspector. Unlike the heading tags, when you change the font size with the font size options in a CSS rule, you can alter the size of text within a paragraph, and Dreamweaver does not add a paragraph return. This is an ideal option when you want to make text stand out within a paragraph or want to increase the size of text in an address or other text block that does not include extra space between lines.

Change the Font Size

1 Click and drag to select the text.

2 Click **CSS**.

3 Click the **Targeted Rule** ▼.

4 Click the name of a style or choose **<New CSS Rule>**.

5 Type a number to specify the percentage that you want to increase or decrease the text size.

6 Click ▼ and select **%**.

A The size of the text changes.

B The CSS style rule changes to include the size setting.

You can change the color of text on all or part of your web page. Similarly to altering the font size, you can define a color in a style and then apply it to any selected text on your page. This is an ideal way to add emphasis and make specific text, such as the name of your company or organization, stand out on the page. When you alter the color of text on your page, just make sure that there is a good contrast with the background color so that the text is readable.

Change the Font Color with the Property Inspector

1 Click and drag to select the text that you want to change.

2 Click the **Targeted Rule** ▾.

3 Click the name of a style.

If you have not yet created a style, you can choose **<New CSS Rule>**.

4 Click ■.

The Color Palette appears.

5 Click a color.

Ⓐ The selected text appears in the new color.

Ⓑ The CSS style rule changes to include the color setting.

Change Font and Text Colors for an Entire Page

You can change the font face, color, and size, as well as other formatting options for the entire page, in the Page Properties dialog box. CSS is designed so that you can specify pagewide settings and then override them with more specific styles. Thus, you can specify the font face for the entire page, and it will be applied to all the text except text that is formatted with styles applied more specifically to a section of text, such as the headline styles created earlier in this chapter.

Note: You can change the properties for any HTML or template file in Dreamweaver.

Change Font and Text Colors for an Entire Page

1 Click **Modify**.

2 Click **Page Properties**.

A You can also click **Page Properties** in the Property inspector.

The Page Properties dialog box appears.

3 Click the **Page font** ▾.

4 Click any font collection to select it.

5 Click the **Size** ▾ and choose a preset size or type a number.

6 Click this ▾.

7 Click a font size option.

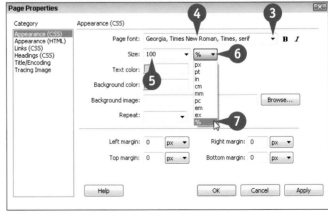

8 Click the **Text color** ▣.

The Color Palette appears.

9 Click any color to select it.

10 Click **Apply** to see the changes applied to the page.

11 Click **OK** to save the changes and close the dialog box.

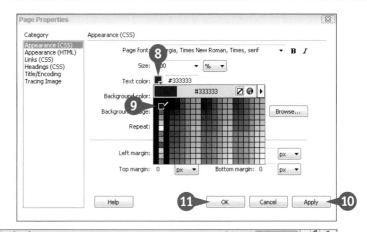

Your text appears in the new font, size, and color on your web page.

B Dreamweaver creates the corresponding styles, and they appear in the CSS Styles panel.

TIP

What are the letter and number combinations that appear in the color fields of Dreamweaver?
HTML represents colors using six-digit codes called *hexadecimal codes,* or hex codes. These codes start with a pound sign (#) and are followed by a series of numbers that represent the amount of red, green, and blue used to create a particular color. Instead of ranging from 0 to 9, hex-code digits range from 0 to F, with A equal to 10, B equal to 11, and so on through to F, which is equal to 15. The first two digits in the hex code specify the amount of red in the selected color. The second two digits specify the amount of green, and the third two specify the amount of blue. When you select a color from a color picker, Dreamweaver automatically generates the corresponding hex code.

Create Styles with the Page Properties Dialog Box

You can use Dreamweaver's Page Properties dialog box to define a variety of pagewide settings, including background colors, link styles, and text options. Using the link settings, you can remove the underline from your links and change the active, visited, and hover link colors. When you define text and other options in the Page Properties dialog box, Dreamweaver automatically creates the corresponding CSS style rules and adds them to the CSS Styles panel by defining a style for the `body` tag. When you define link colors, Dreamweaver creates the corresponding link styles.

Create Styles with the Page Properties Dialog Box

1 Click **Modify**.

2 Click **Page Properties**.

Ⓐ You can also click **Page Properties** in the Property inspector.

The Page Properties dialog box appears.

3 Click **Appearance (CSS)**.

4 Select a color for the background of the page or click **Browse** and specify a background image.

5 Set the page margins to **0** to remove the default indent in the left and top margins of the display area.

6 Click **Apply**.

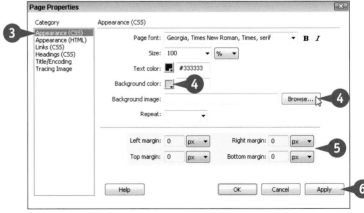

200

7 Click **Links (CSS)**.

8 Select the font, size, and link colors.

9 Click ▾ and select an underline style, such as **Show underline only on rollover** to remove the underline style from all links on the page.

10 Click **OK**.

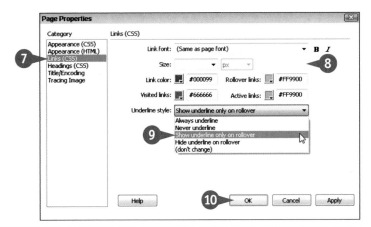

B Dreamweaver saves the corresponding styles in the CSS Styles panel.

C Dreamweaver automatically applies the new style information to the page.

In this example, the link style for the entire page is changed.

TIPS

What are some nontext-based features that I can implement with style sheets?

Probably the most exciting thing that you can do with style sheets is to position elements precisely on the page. Style sheets give you freedom from traditional, and imprecise, layout methods, such as HTML tables. Style sheets often use the `<div>` tag, which defines an area on the page where you can position an element with alignment attributes. You can also position elements more precisely by specifying margin and padding settings.

Do all web browsers support CSS in the same way?

No, unfortunately not all web browsers support CSS in the same way, and some do not support styles at all. However, styles have come a long way in the last few years, and so have browsers. Although some visitors may not be able to see your designs as you intend if you use CSS, the vast majority of people surfing the web these days have browsers that support CSS.

Create an External Style Sheet

External style sheets enable you to define a set of style sheet rules and then apply them to any or all of the pages in your website. You can even apply style rules in an external style sheet to pages on different websites. This enables you to keep a consistent appearance across many pages and to streamline formatting and style updates. When you change the definition of a style rule in an external style sheet, any formatting used in the style is automatically updated on all the pages in which the style is used.

Create an External Style Sheet

Note: Make sure that the CSS Styles panel is open. Click **Window** and then click **CSS Styles**.

1 Press **Ctrl** (**⌘**) + **N**.

The New Document dialog box appears.

2 Click **Blank Page**.

3 Click **CSS**.

4 Click **Create**.

A new blank CSS file appears.

5 Press **Ctrl** (**⌘**) + **S**.

The Save As dialog box appears.

6 Type a name.

7 Click **Save**.

Ⓐ The style sheet is displayed in the CSS Styles panel.

Ⓑ The name of the style sheet appears in the Files panel.

⑧ Click ⊠ to close the external style sheet.

The style sheet closes.

If you have another document open in the background, it becomes visible in the workspace.

Note: The external style sheet is created inside your local site folder. For this to work, you must have defined your site in Dreamweaver. To define a site and identify the local site folder, see Chapter 2, "Setting Up Your Website."

TIPS

How can I add more styles to an external style sheet?
When you create any new style, you have the option of selecting an existing style sheet from the **Rule Definition** field in the New CSS Rule dialog box. This applies when creating a class style or when customizing an HTML tag. When you define a new style in an external style sheet, it is automatically added to the selected CSS file.

Is it possible to add new styles later?
Yes. You can add styles to an external style sheet anytime, even months after the site was first published. You can make changes or additions while you work on any page attached to an external style sheet, and those styles will become available on any page to which the style sheet is attached.

Attach an External Style Sheet

After you have created a style sheet, you can attach it to any or all of the web pages in your site. You can even attach multiple style sheets to the same page. After you attach an external style sheet to a page, all the style rules in the style sheet become available, and you can apply the style rules to the text, images, and any other elements on the page just as you would apply styles from an internal style sheet.

Attach an External Style Sheet

1 With the page or template to which you want to attach a style sheet open, click **Format**.

2 Click **CSS Styles**.

3 Click **Attach Style Sheet**.

The Attach External Style Sheet dialog box appears.

4 Click **Browse**.

The Select Style Sheet File dialog box appears.

5 Click the name of the style sheet that you want to attach.

6 Click **OK**.

You are returned to the Attach External Style Sheet dialog box.

7 Click **OK**.

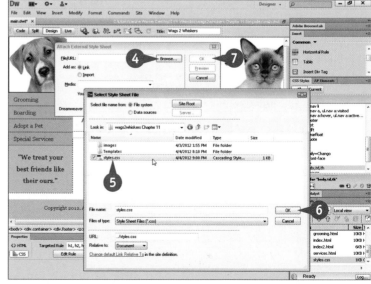

Ⓐ The external style sheet is linked to the page, and the style sheet is displayed in the CSS Styles panel.

Any styles in the external style sheet are automatically applied to the page.

Note: To apply styles to content in a document, see the section "Apply a Class Style."

⑧ Click and drag to move a style from the page's internal style sheet to the external style sheet.

Ⓑ You can move any or all of the styles from an internal style sheet to an external one.

To delete a style or to remove a style sheet from a file, click to select it and press Del.

TIP

How can I move multiple styles to an external style sheet simultaneously?

① Click here and attach an external style sheet.

② Click + to open the internal `<style>` list.

③ Click to select one or more internal styles and drag the cursor over the name of the external style sheet.

Ⓐ Dreamweaver moves the internal styles to the external style sheet.

Note: You must save the CSS file to save the newly moved styles.

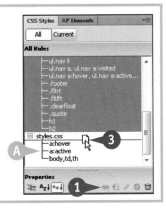

Edit an External Style Sheet

You can include hundreds of styles in a single external sheet, or you can create multiple style sheets and apply each one to any or all of the pages in your website. This enables you to organize and manage styles as your site grows and you add more style rules. You can also edit any or all of the individual style rules in any of your style sheets. When you edit a style rule in an external style sheet, the changes are automatically made anywhere that the style is applied.

Edit an External Style Sheet

1 Click **Window**.

2 Click **CSS Styles**.

A The CSS Styles panel appears.

B You can click here and drag to expand the CSS Styles panel.

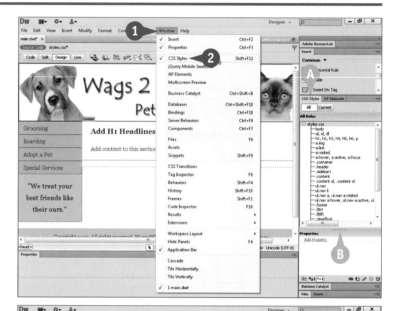

3 Double-click the name of the style that you want to modify.

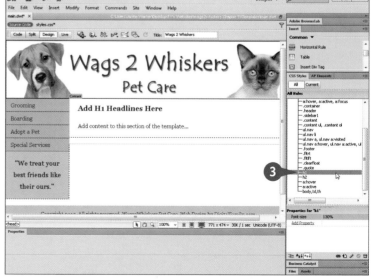

The CSS Rule Definition dialog box appears.

④ Click a style category.

⑤ Select the style settings that you want.

Ⓒ In this example, the font color is changed.

⑥ Click **OK**.

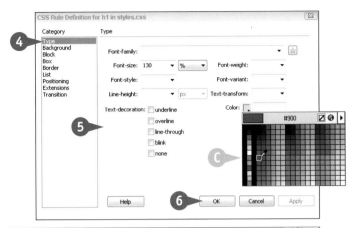

Ⓓ Dreamweaver saves the new style definition in the external style sheet.

Ⓔ The new style is automatically applied to any content formatted with that style on all pages to which the external style sheet is attached.

TIP

What problems can arise when I use CSS?
The benefits of using Cascading Style Sheets are enormous, and they mostly outweigh the challenges that come with their implementation. However, because CSS is not displayed the same way in all web browsers, pages designed with CSS may not appear the same on all computers. You should always test your pages to make sure that you like the results in all the browsers that you expect your visitors to use. For the best results, redefine existing HTML tags when possible and create your page designs so that they will be readable and will be displayed well even if the styles are not supported.

Designing a Website with CSS

In addition to creating styles for text, you can use CSS to create styles that position and align elements on a page. Using styles with `divs` and other HTML tags, you can create complex layouts in Dreamweaver that meet today's web standards.

Introducing CSS Layouts

You can use advanced Dreamweaver tools to create CSS layouts that are flexible, adapt well to different screen sizes and resolutions, and are accessible to all your site visitors. You can use Dreamweaver's CSS features to create completely custom designs, and you can get a great head start on your designs by selecting one of the CSS layouts available in the New Document window. Most CSS layouts, including the ones that come with Dreamweaver, are created by combining a series of `div` tags and other HTML elements with style rules.

The CSS Box Model

One of the most popular and recommended approaches to web design today is the CSS Box model. By combining a series of HTML `div` tags with CSS styles, it is possible to create designs that are complex in their appearance but simple in their construction. One of the advantages of this model is that web pages with CSS layouts display well on a variety of devices.

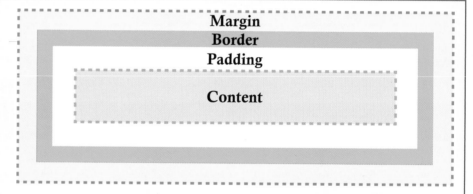

Alignment with Floats

Instead of using the familiar left and right alignment icons, the best approach to aligning images and other elements with CSS is to create styles that use floats. By floating elements to the right or left of a page, you can align them and cause any adjacent elements, such as text, to wrap around them.

Centering CSS Layouts

The Center attribute is no longer recommended in CSS, so how do you center a design? The trick is to set the margins on both the left and right of a `div` to "auto," or automatic. This causes a browser to automatically add the same amount of margin space to both sides of the element, effectively centering it on the page.

Dreamweaver's CSS Layouts

Dreamweaver includes a large collection of CSS layouts that are carefully designed and ready for you to use to create your own web pages. Although you will need to edit the CSS styles to customize these layouts, they can give you a great head start and help you avoid some of the common layout challenges of CSS.

AP Div Basics

AP Divs are discrete blocks of content that you can precisely position on the page, make moveable by the user, and even make invisible. Most significantly, you can stack AP Divs on top of each other. AP Divs can contain any kind of content, including text, graphics, tables, and even other AP Divs. Unfortunately, layouts created completely with AP Divs are not very flexible and thus not well-suited to the many different displays in use on the web. Use AP Divs sparingly and test to ensure that your pages work properly on a variety of screen sizes and web browsers.

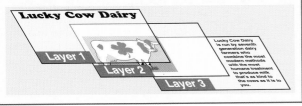

Nested AP Divs

AP Divs can contain nested AP Divs, which create areas of content that stay linked together on a page for better control during production of web pages. *Nested,* or child, AP Divs can inherit the properties of their parent `divs`, including visibility or invisibility. You can also nest AP Divs within `divs` that do not use absolute positioning.

Create a Web Page with a CSS Layout

Dreamweaver includes a collection of CSS layouts to make it easy to design pages using HTML `div` tags and styles. Creating a new page with a CSS layout is as easy as creating a new blank page, but with the advantage of already having many design elements in place. As you create a new page using the New Document dialog box, choose the CSS layout that most closely resembles the page design that you want to create. Then use the CSS Styles panel to edit or create as many new styles as you need for your design.

Create a Web Page with a CSS Layout

1 Click **File**.

2 Click **New**.

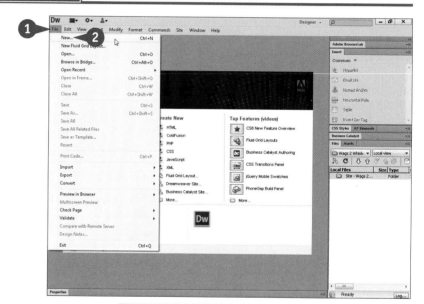

The New Document dialog box appears.

3 Click **Blank Page**.

4 Click **HTML**.

5 Click a layout option.

6 Click **Create**.

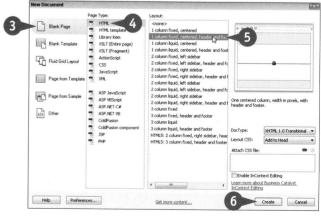

Dreamweaver creates a page with the selected layout.

7 Add a page title by changing the text here.

8 Press `Ctrl` + `S` (`⌘` + `S`) to save the page.

Note: Never use spaces or special characters in the name of a web page. Hyphens (–) and underscores (_) are okay.

9 Replace the placeholder text in the layout with your own text.

10 Press `Ctrl` + `S` (`⌘` + `S`) to save the page.

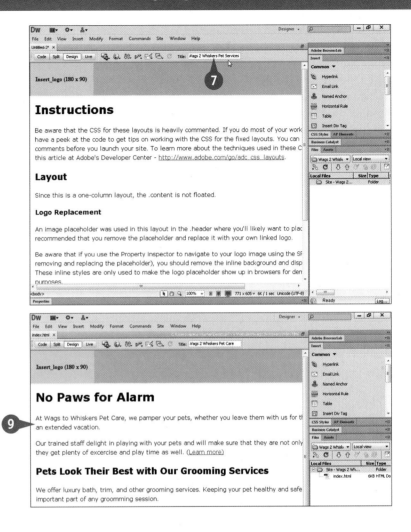

TIPS

How do I delete or change the text in a CSS layout?

All of the CSS layouts in Dreamweaver CS6 include text that describes how the layouts were created. This text makes it easy to see how your own text will appear in the layout. To remove or replace this text, select any or all of it and press `Del`. Then type to enter new text or use copy and paste to insert text from another page or program.

Can I save CSS layout styles to an external style sheet?

Yes. You can always move styles to an external style sheet. First, create a new CSS file, then attach it to the page, and finally click and drag the styles into the external style sheet in the CSS Styles panel. You can find more detailed instructions in the previous chapter, "Creating and Applying Cascading Style Sheets."

Edit a CSS Layout

After you create a new page with a CSS layout in Dreamweaver, you can change the colors, fonts, and other features to create your own designs. If you are not familiar with CSS, editing one of these page layouts can be confusing at first, but using Dreamweaver's CSS features, you can identify which style needs to be edited to change the colors, fonts, and other features in the design. You can create as many pages as you like from the same CSS layout. When you save a layout, you create a new page, leaving the original CSS layout unaffected.

Edit a CSS Layout

Ⓐ If the CSS Styles panel is not open, click **Window** and then click **CSS Styles** to open it.

❶ Double-click the name of the style that you want to change.

In this example, the `.footer` style is selected.

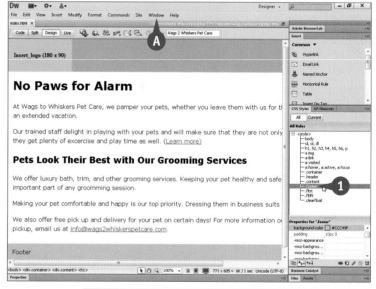

The CSS Rule Definition dialog box appears.

❷ Click a category.

❸ Edit the style.

Ⓑ In this example, the background color for the footer style is changed.

❹ Click **OK**.

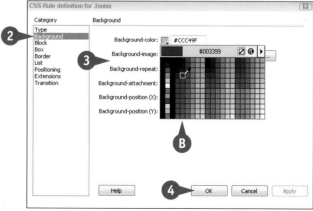

C The changes to the style are automatically applied in the workspace.

In this example, the background color in the footer area changes.

D The style is updated in the CSS Styles panel, and the new style option is displayed in the Properties pane.

E You can also edit CSS styles in the CSS Properties pane.

In this example, the text color in the footer is changed to white.

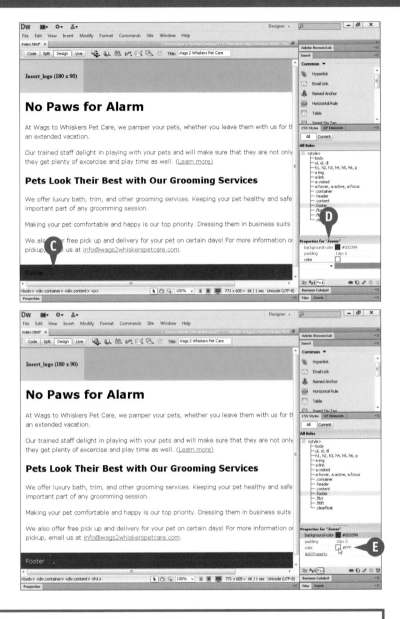

TIP

How do I know which style corresponds to which part of the layout?
To identify what style is controlling the design of any part of the page, place your cursor in the page where you want to change the style and look at the tag selector at the bottom of the design area — just above the Property inspector. In the tag selector, you see all the tags that surround whatever you have selected in the design area. Another way to identify styles is to view the HTML source code. Choose the Split view and select some text or an image that is in an area of the page that you want to edit. Then look in the code to see what style is applied to your selection.

Add an Image to the Header

All of Dreamweaver's CSS layouts include an area at the top of the page for a header. You can add images or text to the header area.

If you only want to add text, delete the image placeholder and type text as you would anywhere else on the page. If you want to use an image as your header, you can select the existing image and replace it using the image field in the Property inspector. You can also delete the placeholder image and insert a new image.

Add an Image to the Header

1 Click **CSS Styles**.

A Alternatively, if the CSS Styles panel is not open, click **Window** and then click **CSS Styles** to open it.

2 Double-click the name of the header ID style.

The CSS Rule Definition dialog box appears.

3 Click **Background**.

4 Click ▣ and change or delete the background color.

Note: If you delete the background color, the color will change to the color of the page.

5 Click **OK**.

B The color behind the banner image is changed.

In this example, the background color is deleted.

6 Double-click to select the green image placeholder in the banner.

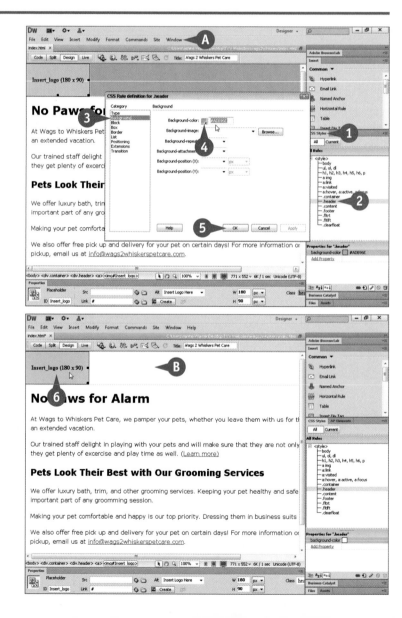

The Select Image Source dialog box appears.

7 Click ▼ and select the folder that contains the image.

8 Click the name of the image.

9 Click **OK**.

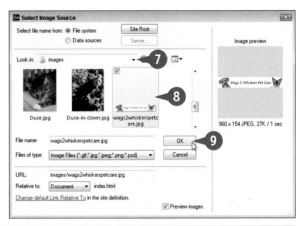

C The image appears in the header area of the layout.

10 Click the image.

11 Delete the text in the **Alt** field and type your own description of the image that you inserted.

12 Press Enter (Return).

The text in the Alt field is saved and will be visible in a browser if the image is not displayed.

TIPS

Can I change the width of a CSS layout?
Yes. The width setting for the CSS layouts in Dreamweaver is controlled by the style that includes the ID #container. Select the #container style name in the CSS Styles panel and then change the width setting to alter the width of the entire CSS layout. For more details, see the section "Change the Dimensions of a CSS Layout" later in this chapter.

What kinds of images should I use for the header area?
Most websites include a logo in the header area of the page. Although you can enter text in the header area and format it with almost any style, if you want to include a logo, it is generally best to use an image of the logo to ensure that the text will appear in the exact font used in the logo.

Add an Image to a CSS Layout

You can insert images into a CSS layout just as you would insert them into any other page in Dreamweaver. You can insert images into the header area of a CSS layout, and you can add images into the sidebars, main content areas, and footers. After you have inserted an image, you can format and align it using CSS. If you want text to wrap around an image, you can align the image to the right or left side of a content area using CSS floats, as shown in the following section, "Using Floats to Align Elements."

Add an Image to a CSS Layout

A If the CSS Styles panel is not open, click **Window** and then click **CSS Styles** to open it.

1 Click to place ⚲ where you want to add an image.

2 Click **Window**.

3 Click **Insert**.

4 Click the **Images** ▣.

The Select Image Source dialog box appears.

5 Click ▾ and select the folder that contains the image.

6 Click the name of the image.

7 Click **OK**.

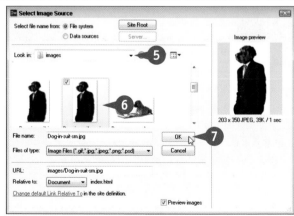

The Image Tag Accessibility
Attributes dialog box
appears.

⑧ Type a description of the
image.

Ⓑ A long description URL is
optional.

⑨ Click **OK**.

Ⓒ The image appears in the
layout.

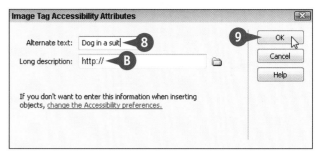

TIPS

Can I change the background color of the page?
Yes, you can change the background color of the
entire page in a CSS layout just like you would
change the background color on any page — by
using the Page Properties dialog box. Click **Window**
and then click **Page Properties** to open the dialog
box. Choose the **Background** category and use the
Background Color field to select a color.

**Can I change the background color of only a
section of the page?**
You can change or add color to any section of the
page by creating a rule that assigns a color to the
style that controls that part of the page. For
example, to change the background color of an
individual `div` tag in the design, you have to edit
the corresponding CSS style. To learn more, see the
section "Edit a CSS Layout."

Using Floats to Align Elements

You can use CSS styles to align images and other elements on a web page. Many designers create class styles that float elements to the right and left, an ideal way to wrap text around an image.

Many of Dreamweaver's CSS layouts include class styles for floats with the names `fltrt` to float elements to the right and `fltlft` to float elements to the left. In addition to the alignment settings, it is a good practice to include a little margin space in these types of styles so that text does not butt up against an image when it wraps.

Using Floats to Align Elements

Align to the Left

A If the CSS Styles panel is not open, click **Window** and then click **CSS Styles** to open it.

1 Click to select an image or other element that you want to align.

2 Click ▾ and select `fltlft`.

The image aligns to the left, and any text on the page wraps up around it.

Align to the Right

1 Click to select an image or other element that you want to align.

2 Click ▼ and select `fltrt`.

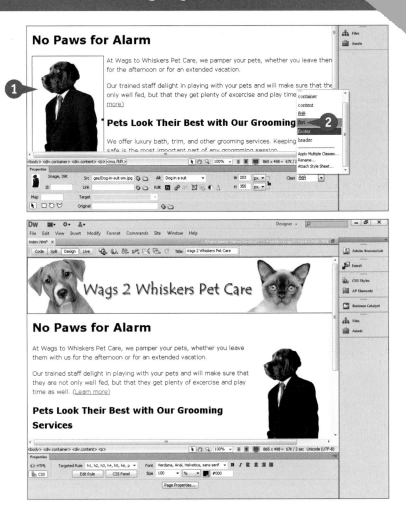

The image aligns to the right, and any text on the page wraps up around it on the left.

TIP

How do I align a caption and a photo together?

You can align an image by itself to wrap text around it, but if you want to include a caption with an image and align both, your best option is to use a `div` tag. First, insert both the image and the caption text into a `div` tag. Then define a style that aligns the `div` tag to the right or left of the page. Make sure that the rule includes a width setting that is the size of the image, or just slightly larger. You also can add margin space to keep the image from bumping up against the text that wraps around the `div` tag. To frame the image and caption together, add a border and include padding around the inside of the `div`. Also note that you should not combine styles that use floats to align elements. So if you insert an image into a `div` tag with a style that aligns the entire `div`, you should not align the image itself within the `div`.

...ange the overall width of any page design, and you can change the width of the sidebar and ... sections by changing the width settings in the corresponding CSS style. All the CSS layouts include a class style named `.container` that controls the width of the entire design area. As you adjust the width settings of different sections of the page, make sure that the combined width of all the elements in the design do not exceed the total width set for the `.container`.

Change the Dimensions of a CSS Layout

A If the CSS Styles panel is not open, click **Window** and then click **CSS Styles** to open it.

1 Double-click the `.container` style in the CSS Styles panel.

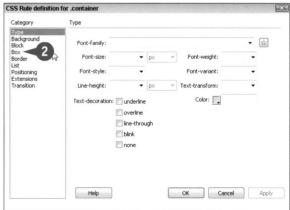

The CSS Rule Definition dialog box appears.

2 Click **Box**.

The Box category options are displayed.

3 Type a width setting.

In this example, the width is changed from 1000 px to 960 px.

4 Click **OK**.

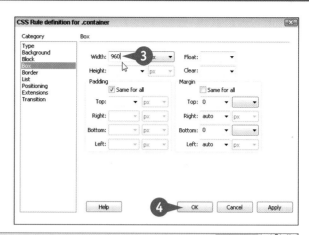

The width of the page design changes to the width entered.

B You can also change the width in the CSS Styles Properties pane.

TIPS

Why can I not drag the edge of a column to change the size?
You cannot change a CSS layout by simply clicking and dragging the border of a `div` tag. To edit the width or height of any of the `div`s in a Dreamweaver CSS layout, you have to edit the corresponding CSS style. In most CSS layouts on the web, that style is named `.container` or `.wrapper`.

How wide should I make my web page layout?
Most web designers create web page layouts that are 960 pixels wide because most computers today have monitors that support at least a 1024 x 768 screen resolution. The reason designers limit the size to 960 even though their pages will be displayed on a 1024 screen is to leave room for the browser scroll bars.

Change the Color of a Headline

You can change the color of a headline by creating a new style to control the appearance of the headline or by editing an existing style that is already applied to the headline text. For example, if you have formatted your text with the h1 tag, changing the h1 tag style will change the color of the headline automatically. If you create a new class or ID style for your headlines, you need to apply that style to the headline text before the color will be affected.

In this section, you create a new style to change the headline color.

Change the Color of a Headline

Ⓐ If the CSS Styles panel is not open, click **Window** and then click **CSS Styles** to open it.

① Click and drag to select the headline.

② Click the New CSS Rule button (⊞).

The New CSS Rule dialog box appears.

Ⓑ The selector type is already selected, based on the element highlighted in the Document window. Do not change this unless you want to create a different kind of style.

Ⓒ The name of the new style is already entered in the Selector Name field.

Note: If the name of the style is not there, close the dialog box, reselect the *entire headline,* including the h1 tag that surrounds the text, and try again.

③ Click **OK**.

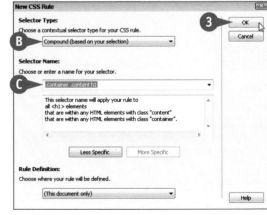

The CSS Rule Definition dialog box appears.

④ Click the **Color** ■.

⑤ Click to select a color.

⑥ Click **OK**.

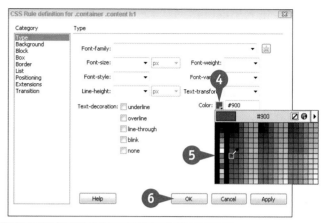

Ⓓ The new style appears in the CSS Styles panel.

Ⓔ The headline changes to the specified color.

Ⓕ You can edit the style in the CSS Styles Properties pane.

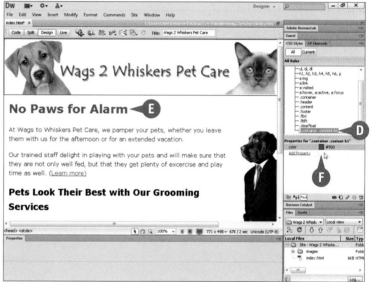

TIPS

How do I change the font face and size of a headline?
In this section, you change the color of the headline by creating a style that includes a rule to specify the color. Similarly, you can change the font face, font size, and other attributes by editing that same style. Just select the headline and then choose a font from the **Font** drop-down list in the Property inspector at the bottom of the workspace. You can change the size using the Property inspector's **Size** drop-down list.

Can I choose a color from my page to change the headline color?
Yes. When you click ■ in Dreamweaver to select a color, the cursor changes to the shape of an eyedropper. You can then use that eyedropper to select any color on the page, including colors in photos and other images.

Create a Compound Style

You can create styles using the class, tag, or ID selectors, or you can create a compound style that combines one or more styles to create a more specific style. Compound styles make it possible to change the formatting of an element in one part of a page without altering the formatting of other elements.

In the example shown in this section, a compound style is used to add a border to the image in the main area of the page without adding a border to the image in the header.

Create a Compound Style

Ⓐ If the CSS Styles panel is not open, click **Window** and then click **CSS Styles** to open it.

① Click to select the image in the main part of the page where you want to add a border.

② Click ▣.

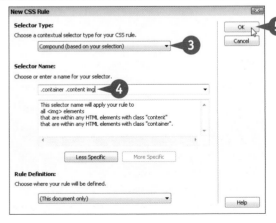

The New CSS Rule dialog box appears.

③ If it is not already selected, click ▼ and select **Compound**.

④ Make sure that the name is already entered in this field and ends with `img` for the image tag.

In this example, a style is being created that looks like this: `.container . content img`. This style will apply only to an image if it is contained within a style called `.content`, which is contained in a style called `.container`.

⑤ Click **OK**.

The CSS Rule Definition dialog box appears.

6 Click **Border**.

7 Click ▾ and select a border type.

8 Click ▾ and select a thickness.

9 Click ▣ and select a color.

In this example, a solid, thick, black border is added.

10 Click **OK**.

B The new style appears in the CSS Styles panel and the Property inspector.

C In this example, a border is added to the image in the main content area of the page.

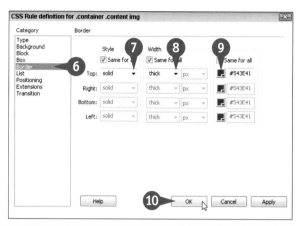

TIPS

Can I create a really think border, like a picture frame?

Yes, you can add a very thick border around an image by entering a size in pixels. The more pixels, the thicker the border. For example, a 1-pixel border will appear very thin, whereas a 50-pixel border would be much thicker. Experiment with different sizes to find the best border width for your designs.

Can I add space between an image and the border?

Yes, you can use the padding settings to add space, or *padding*, between an image and the border that surrounds it. The space created by the padding settings will be displayed in the same color as the background of the page.

Add a Drop Shadow

Drop shadows, which are created using the `box-shadow` rule in CSS, add depth to designs by creating the illusion that an image or other element is casting a shadow as it floats over the page. Drop shadows have been used on the web for years, but until recently, you had to save the shadow in an image. Thanks to the latest version of Cascading Style Sheets, CSS3, you can now add a box shadow with CSS code. You can define rules in CSS3 to add drop shadows to images, `divs`, and other box elements, and you can specify the size, color, and position of the shadow to create a wide variety of effects.

Add a Drop Shadow

① Click the name of the style to which you want to add a box shadow in the CSS Styles panel.

② Click **Add Property**.

③ Click ▼.

④ Click **box-shadow**.

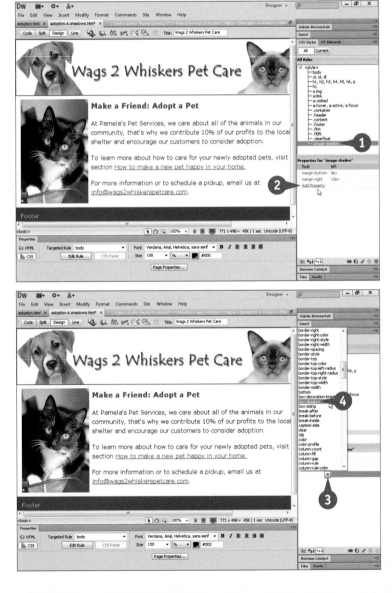

The Box Shadow options appear in the CSS Properties pane.

5 Click [▣].

6 Type a number in pixels to specify how far offset the shadow will be on the X- and Y-axis.

7 Type a number in pixels to specify the size of the shadow and the amount of blur.

8 Click the **Color** [▣] and select a color.

9 Press Enter (Return).

10 Press F12 on the keyboard to preview the page.

Ⓐ The box shadow is displayed on any box element to which the style is applied.

Note: Dreamweaver does not display CSS3 style features, such as box shadows, in Design view.

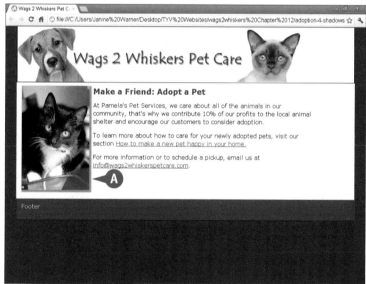

TIP

Why can I not see my box shadow in Dreamweaver?

The Design view features in Dreamweaver work like an older web browser. They do not support the latest version of CSS3. Although you can use the Live view option by clicking the **Live** button at the top left of the workspace in Dreamweaver to view some CSS3 features, you cannot see *all* the latest CSS3 options in Live view, but you can see many of them. The best way to test CSS3 features, such as box shadows, in your web page designs is to view them in the latest version of one of the popular web browsers, such as Google Chrome, Mozilla Firefox, or Apple Safari.

Add a Text Shadow

Text shadows help your words stand out from the page and can make text easier to read, especially against a busy background. Text shadows are also helpful when there is little contrast between the color of the text and the background color. You can define rules in CSS3 to add text shadows using class styles or by adding the rules to existing HTML tags, and you can specify the size, color, and position of the shadow to create a wide variety of effects.

Add a Text Shadow

① Click the name of the style to which you want to add a text shadow in the CSS Styles panel.

② Click **Add Property**.

③ Click ▼.

④ Click **text-shadow**.

The Text Shadow options appear in the CSS Properties pane.

5 Click ⬛.

6 Type a number in pixels to specify how far offset the shadow will be on the X- and Y-axis.

7 Type a number in pixels to specify the amount of blur.

8 Click the **Color** ⬛ and select a color.

9 Press **Enter** (**Return**).

10 Click **Live**.

Ⓐ The text shadow is displayed on any text to which the style rule is applied.

Note: Dreamweaver does not display CSS3 style features, such as text shadows, in Design view. You must click **Live** to see text shadows or preview the page in a recent version of a popular web browser.

TIPS

Why do my text shadows not line up properly?
If your text shadows do not line up where you want them in relation to your text, try making the X- and Y-axis offset values a little larger or smaller to adjust the placement. You can also raise the number in the **Blur radius** field to soften the blur of the shadow.

Can I create text shadows in any color?
Yes. Text shadows are most commonly created in a light gray color, but you can select any color that you want using the ⬛ text shadow option in the CSS Properties pane.

Create an AP Div with Content

AP Divs are scalable rectangles, inside of which you can place text, images, and just about anything else that you can include on a web page. Although they work similarly to the `divs` used in Dreamweaver's CSS layouts, AP Divs include an Absolute Positioning setting, which means that they maintain their position on a page irrespective of the browser size. Because they use absolute positioning, you can click and drag them to any position on the page, but they do not adjust to the size of a browser window like other elements without absolute positioning.

Create an AP Div with Content

Create an AP Div

1 Click ▾ and select **Layout** in the Insert panel.

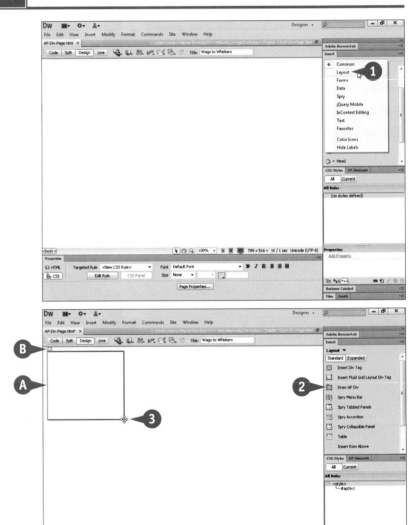

2 Click the **Draw AP Div** ▤.

3 Click and drag to create an AP Div on the page.

You can resize and reposition an AP Div after you create it.

Ⓐ The outline of the AP Div appears.

Ⓑ You can click the tab in the upper-left corner of the AP Div to select it.

Ⓒ When you select the AP Div, the Property inspector displays its properties.

232

Add Content to an AP Div

1 Click inside the AP Div.

2 Click to select an element in the Files panel and drag it into the AP Div.

D You can also insert an image by clicking **Insert** and then **Image** and selecting an image using the Insert Image dialog box.

You can add text by typing inside the AP Div.

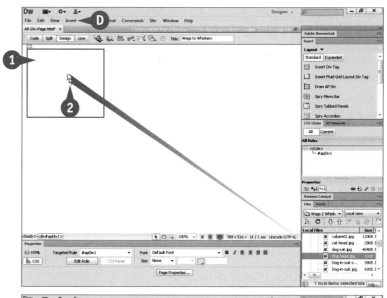

E The element is displayed inside the AP Div.

You can format text and images within an AP Div using the Property inspector, just as you would format text or images anywhere else on a page.

Note: To format text, see Chapter 5, "Formatting and Styling Text." For image options, see Chapter 6, "Working with Images and Multimedia."

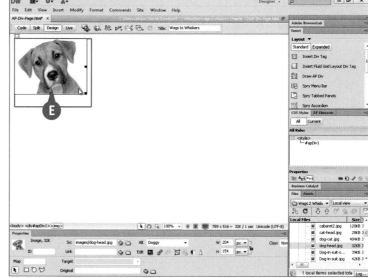

TIPS

Should I use AP Divs to create a page layout?
Although AP Divs are very powerful layout tools, they are not the best option for creating an entire page layout. AP Divs serve as a nice complement to other page layout options, but when used exclusively, they create very inflexible designs that can look very different in different browsers.

What happens if a browser does not display AP Divs properly?
Although the latest versions of Internet Explorer and Firefox support AP Divs consistently, older browsers that do not support AP Divs may not display them as you intended. Similarly, text can get cut off if the font size is displayed larger than you intended in a browser and the text exceeds the size of the AP Div.

Resize and Reposition AP Divs

When you create a new AP Div, you can adjust its position and dimensions to make it fit attractively within the rest of the content on your page. One of the advantages of AP Divs is that you can move them easily by clicking and dragging them. You can resize AP Divs precisely by entering the exact size in the height and width fields in the Property inspector. You can also position AP Divs by entering the distance that you want them to appear in pixels from the top and left of the page.

Resize and Reposition AP Divs

Click and Drag to Resize an AP Div

1 Click the tab in the upper-left corner of the AP Div to select it.

A Square, blue handles appear around the edges of the AP Div.

2 Click and drag one of the handles (☝ changes to ⬄).

Dreamweaver resizes the AP Div to the new size.

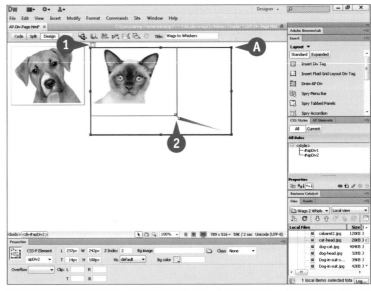

Resize with the Width and Height Attributes

1 Click this tab.

2 Type a new width in the **W** field.

3 Press Enter (Return).

Dreamweaver changes the AP Div's width.

4 Type a new height in the **H** field.

5 Press Enter (Return).

Dreamweaver changes the AP Div's height.

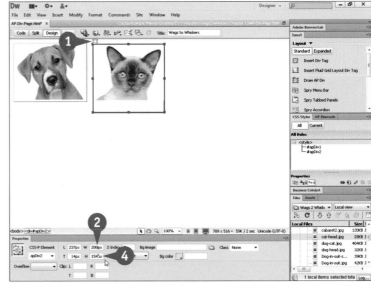

234

Reposition with the Cursor

1 Click and drag the tab in the upper-left corner of the AP Div to move it to a new position (⬚ changes to ⬚).

Dreamweaver moves the AP Div to the new location.

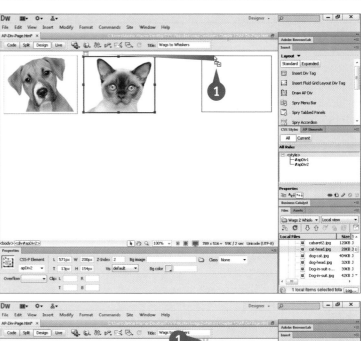

Reposition with the Left and Top Attributes

1 Click this tab.

2 Type the new distance from the left side of the window.

3 Press Enter (Return).

4 Type the new distance from the top of the window.

5 Press Enter (Return).

Dreamweaver applies the new positioning to the AP Div.

Note: Setting left and top positioning to 0 puts the `div` in the top-left corner of a page.

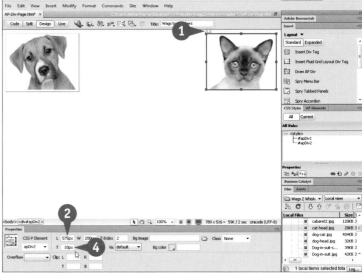

TIPS

How can I change the visibility of an AP Div?
To change an AP Div's visibility, select an AP Div and then click the **Vis** ▼ in the Property inspector. You can make an AP Div visible or invisible. If it is a nested AP Div, it can inherit its characteristics from its parent, which is the enclosing AP Div.

Can I create nested AP Divs?
Yes. A nested AP Div is often called a *child AP Div*, and the AP Div that contains the nested AP Div is called the *parent*. They act as a unit on the page; if the parent AP Div moves, the child goes with it. You can nest one AP Div inside another by clicking and dragging the name of the child AP Div over the name of the parent in the AP Elements panel.

235

Publishing a Website

After you are done building your web pages, you can publish your site on a server where anyone with an Internet connection can view them. This chapter shows you how to publish your website and keep it up to date with Dreamweaver.

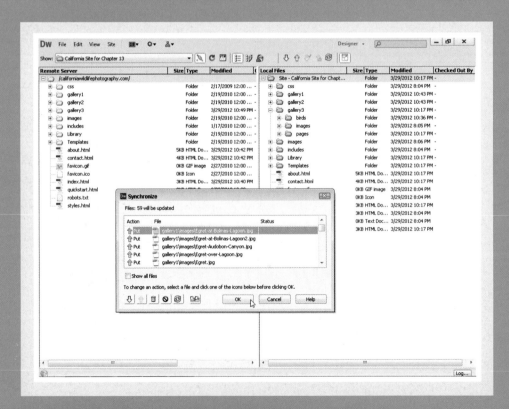

Publish Your Website

Most designers build and test their websites on their local computers and then transfer their sites to a web server when they are ready to publish them on the Internet for all the world to see. A *web server* is an Internet-connected computer running special software that enables the computer to serve files to web browsers. Dreamweaver includes tools that enable you to connect and transfer pages to a web server using FTP (File Transfer Protocol) as well as more advanced transfer options.

Publish Your Website

To publish your site files using Dreamweaver, follow these steps:

1 Identify the main folder on your computer where all your website files are kept.

Note: To define a local site, see Chapter 2, "Setting Up Your Website."

2 Enter the web server information to publish your files.

Note: To define a remote site, see the section "Set Up a Remote Site."

Most people publish their web pages on servers maintained by their Internet service provider (ISP), a web-hosting company, or their company or school.

3 Connect to the web server and transfer the files.

The Site window displays a user-friendly interface for organizing your files and transferring them to the remote site.

After uploading your site, you can update it by editing the copies of the site files on your computer (the local site) and then transferring those copies to the web server (the remote site).

Using the Site Window

When you expand the Files panel in Dreamweaver, you can view all the files and folders in your local folder and on your web server at once in the Site window. You can rename files and folders and drag files in and out of folders using the Site window, and you can upload local files to your web server and download remote files to your local site folder. You can access the Site window by clicking the Expand/Collapse button in the Files panel. For more information about the Files panel, see Chapter 3, "Exploring the Dreamweaver Interface."

Ⓐ Local files

The right pane displays all the files in the root folder of your local computer.

Ⓑ Remote site

The left pane displays all the files in your site that have been published to the remote web server.

Ⓒ File transfer

The 🖾 button connects to the remote site. The Put button (⬆) enables you to upload files to the remote server, and the Get button (⬇) enables you to download files from the remote server.

Ⓓ Site menu

This menu lists all the websites that you have set up in Dreamweaver and makes it easy to switch from working on one site to working on another. For more information about setting up sites in Dreamweaver, see Chapter 2.

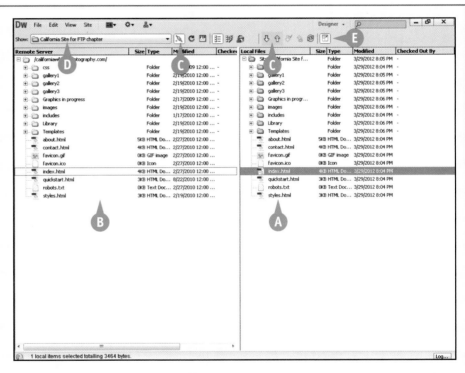

Ⓔ Expand/Collapse Files panel

You can click the Expand/Collapse button (🗗) to expand the Files panel to two panes. With the Files panel expanded, you can see the local and remote sites simultaneously, making it easier to upload and download files. To close the expanded view and return the Files panel to one column, click 🗗 again.

Add Web Browsers for Testing Pages

Because web pages do not always look the same in different web browsers, it is important to test your pages in more than one browser to make sure that they will look good to everyone who visits them.

Dreamweaver makes it easy to add browsers to the Preview in Browser menu, and I recommend that you test your site in the latest versions of Google Chrome, Internet Explorer, Mozilla Firefox, and Apple Safari, which is popular on Macintosh computers but is also available for Windows.

Add Web Browsers for Testing Pages

1 Click **File**.

2 Click **Preview in Browser**.

3 Click **Edit Browser List**.

The Preferences dialog box appears.

4 Click **Preview in Browser**.

5 Click ➕.

The Add Browser dialog box appears.

6 Click **Browse**.

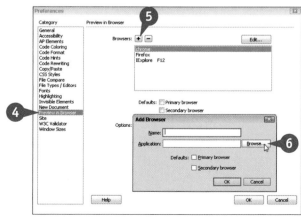

The Select Browser dialog box appears.

7 Click ▾ and select the folder that contains the browser program.

8 Click the browser that you want to add.

9 Click **Open**.

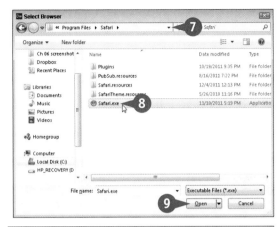

You are returned to the Add Browser dialog box.

10 Click **OK**.

You are returned to the Preferences dialog box.

11 Repeat steps **5** to **10** to add additional browsers.

12 Click **OK**.

The browsers are added to the Preview in Browser list.

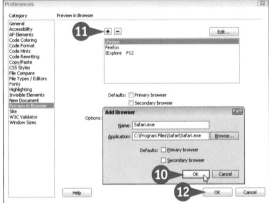

TIPS

Why do web pages look dissimilar in different browsers?
Over the years, web design has evolved. In the early days of the web, you could create sites only with simple HTML and images. As the technologies evolved to include more advanced options, such as CSS and multimedia, web browsers evolved as well. Unfortunately, many people still have older browsers that do not support all the latest design options in use on the web, and not all browser companies updated their programs in the same ways.

What is the most popular browser?
There are dozens of browsers in use on the web, but the most popular are Google Chrome, Mozilla Firefox, Microsoft Internet Explorer, Apple Safari, and Opera. There are also special browsers, called *screen readers,* that read web pages aloud to visually impaired users.

Preview Your Pages in Multiple Web Browsers

Before you publish your website, it is always a good practice to test your pages on your local computer first. You can preview an HTML page in any browser that is installed on your computer and set up for preview in Dreamweaver, as described in the preceding section, "Add Web Browsers for Testing Pages." When you preview web pages in a browser on your local computer, all your links and most other interactive features will work just as they would when published to a server on the Internet.

Preview Your Pages in Multiple Web Browsers

1 Click **File**.

2 Click **Preview in Browser**.

3 Click any of the web browsers.

You can also preview the page in the browser that you have designated as primary by pressing **F12**.

The web browser launches and displays the page.

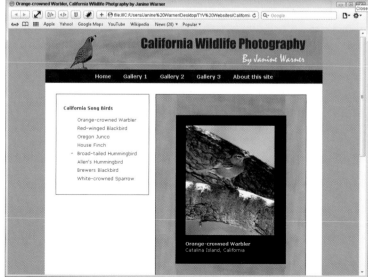

④ In Dreamweaver, click the Preview in Browser button (🖼).

⑤ Click a different web browser from the drop-down menu.

The web browser launches and displays the page.

Note: It is a good practice to test your pages in as many web browsers as possible.

TIP

What if I do not have all the web browsers that I should use to test my web pages?

In addition to testing your pages with multiple web browsers on your own computer, you can test your pages after they are published on a web server by using one of the many web browser tools that simulate the way different web browsers work. These tools are especially useful for testing your pages in older web browsers, which are harder to find for use on your own computer.

These are some of the most popular online web browser testing tools:

• Adobe BrowserLab: http://browserlab.adobe.com

• Browser Sandbox: http://spoon.net/browsers

• Browsershots: www.browsershots.org

• CrossBrowserTesting.com: www.crossbrowser testing.com

Organize Your Files and Folders

You can use the Files panel to organize the files and folders that make up your website. Creating subfolders to organize files of a similar type can be useful if you have a large website. You can use the Files panel to create and delete files and folders and to move files into and out of folders. The advantage of using the Files panel is that when you move or rename files and folders, Dreamweaver automatically updates any associated links and inserted images.

Organize Your Files and Folders

1 Click **Window**.

2 Click **Files**.

The Files panel is displayed.

3 Click ▾ to display the contents of the site.

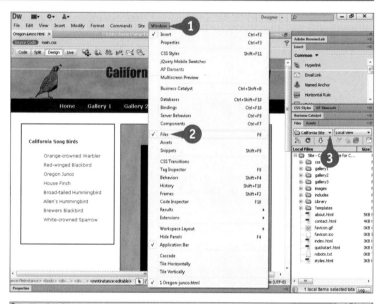

4 Click + to view the files in a subfolder (+ changes to –).

The folder contents are displayed.

Ⓐ You can click – to close the subfolder.

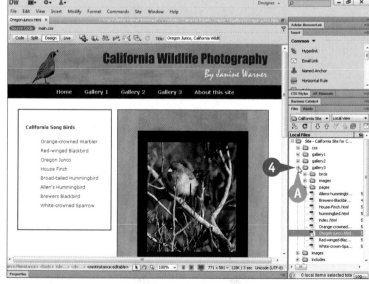

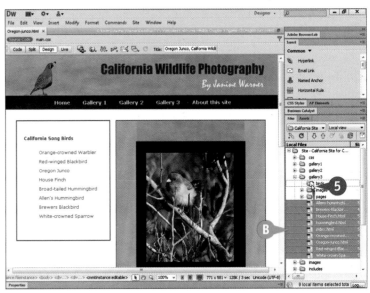

5 To move a file in your local site folder into a subfolder, click and drag it to the new subfolder (👆 changes to 👆).

Ⓑ To move multiple files at once, hold down **Shift** and click to select a group of files simultaneously.

The Update Files dialog box appears, asking if you want to update your links.

6 Click **Update** to keep your local site links from breaking.

Dreamweaver automatically makes any changes necessary to preserve the links.

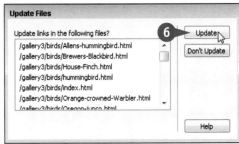

TIPS

What happens to links when I move files?

When you create a hyperlink from one page to another, Dreamweaver creates the necessary HTML code, which includes a reference to the name and location of the page to which you are linking. If you move or rename files after they are used in a link, the link code must be updated, or the link will be broken. When you use the Files panel to move or rename files or to move files into subfolders, Dreamweaver keeps track of any affected code and updates it automatically.

Should I use subfolders?

Organizing your text, image, and multimedia files in subfolders can help you keep track of the contents of your website. Although you can store all the files in your site in one main folder, most designers find it easier to find files when they are organized in subfolders.

Set Up a Remote Site

Before you can publish your website in Dreamweaver, you need to set up the remote site to create a connection to your web server. You set up a remote site by entering the FTP information, including your username and password, for your web server. You can then use Dreamweaver to transfer your files from your computer to the remote server.

Note: Before you can set up a remote site, you need to set up your local site and define it in Dreamweaver. To do so, see Chapter 2.

Set Up a Remote Site

1 Click **Site**.

2 Click **Manage Sites**.

The Manage Sites dialog box appears.

3 Click a site name from the list.

4 Click the Edit button (✎).

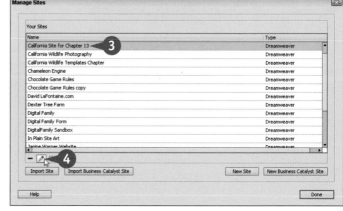

The Site Setup dialog box appears.

5 Click **Servers**.

6 Click ⊞.

A dialog box appears.

7 Type a name to identify the server setup.

8 Click ▾ and select **FTP**.

Note: FTP is the most common way to transfer a website to a web server.

9 Type the name of the FTP host (web server).

10 Type your login name and password.

11 Type the directory path of your site on the web server.

A You can click **Test** to confirm the web server information.

12 Click **Save**.

13 Click **Save**.

14 Click **Done** in the Manage Sites dialog box.

The remote site is now set up.

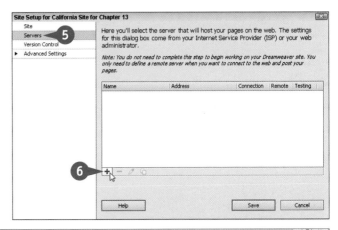

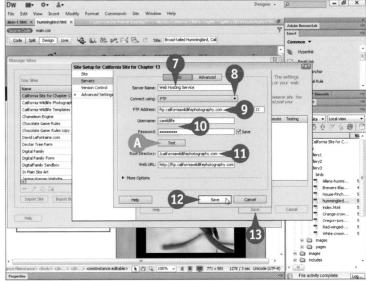

TIPS

What happens if I change my ISP and I need to move my site to a different server?
You need to change your remote site settings to enable Dreamweaver to connect to your new web server. Your local site settings can stay the same. Make sure that you keep your local files current and backed up before you change servers.

How do I register a domain name?
You can register a domain name at a number of domain-registration services on the Internet. Two of the most popular, and least expensive, are Go Daddy (www.godaddy.com) and 1&1 (www.1and1.com). As long as you pay the annual fee, which is less than $10 a year at these sites, the domain is yours. To direct the domain to your website, you need to specify where your web server is at the domain-registration service.

Connect to a Remote Site

You can connect to a web server using Dreamweaver and then use the built-in file transfer features to copy files between the remote web server and your local computer. Dreamweaver includes multiple ways to copy files to a web server, including the most popular process, which is known as *FTP*. Before you can connect to a remote server, you need to set up your remote site. For more information, see the preceding section, "Set Up a Remote Site."

Connect to a Remote Site

1 In the Files panel, click the Expand Site Panel button (⊡) to expand the remote and local site panels.

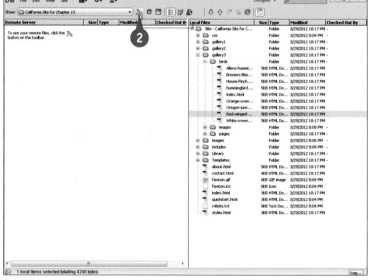

The Files panel expands to fill the screen.

2 Click the Connect button (⊡) to connect to the web server.

Note: Dreamweaver displays an alert dialog box if it cannot connect to the site. If you have trouble connecting, review the host information that you entered for the remote site.

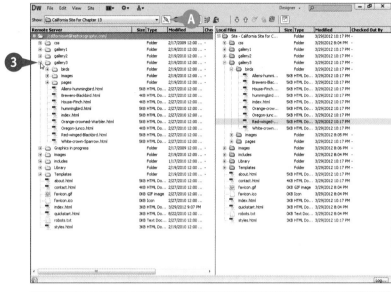

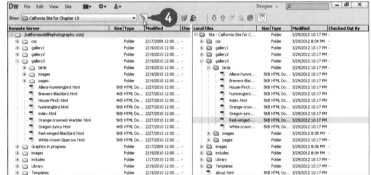

(A) When you are connected to the Internet, [icon] changes to [icon].

Dreamweaver displays the contents of the remote site's host directory.

③ Click + to view the contents of a directory on the web server (+ changes to –).

Dreamweaver displays the contents of the directory.

④ Click [icon] to disconnect.

Dreamweaver disconnects from the web server.

If you do not transfer any files for 30 minutes, Dreamweaver automatically disconnects from the web server.

TIPS

How do I keep Dreamweaver from prematurely disconnecting from the web server?

You can click **Edit**, then click **Preferences**, and then click **Site**. You can adjust the FTP transfer options to change the time that Dreamweaver allows to pass between commands before it logs you off the server; the default is 30 minutes. Note that web servers also have a similar setting on their end. Therefore, the server, not Dreamweaver, may sometimes log you off if you are inactive for more than the server's allotted time.

What can I do if the connection does not work?

If Dreamweaver fails to connect to your server, your Internet connection may be down. Make sure that your computer is connected to the Internet and try again. If you still cannot connect, you may have incorrectly entered the FTP settings. Check with your service provider or system administrator if you are not sure about your web server settings.

Upload Files to a Web Server

To make your web pages available to others on the Internet, you need to publish them to a web server where they can be viewed in a web browser over the Internet. You can use Dreamweaver's built-in FTP features to upload files from your local site folder to your web-hosting service or any other remote web server. You can also use Dreamweaver's file transfer features to download files from the remote server to your local computer.

Upload Files to a Web Server

Publish Files Online

1 Click 🔌 to connect to the web server through the Site window (🔌 changes to 🔌).

2 Click the file that you want to upload.

3 Click the Put button (⬆).

A You can also right-click the file and select **Put** from the menu that appears.

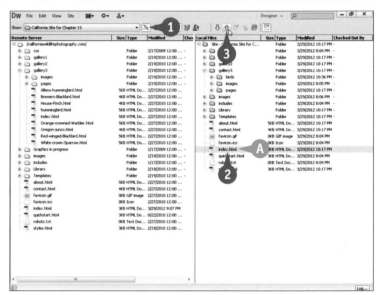

A dialog box appears, asking if you want to include dependent files.

Note: *Dependent files* are images and other files associated with a particular page.

4 Click **Yes** or **No**.

Note: If you do nothing, after 30 seconds, the file and related files will be transferred automatically.

B You can click here (☐ changes to ☑) to avoid seeing this dialog box again.

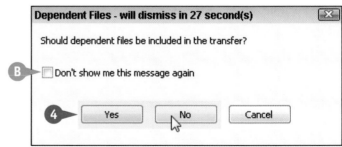

C The file transfers from your computer to the web, and the filename appears in the Remote files panel.

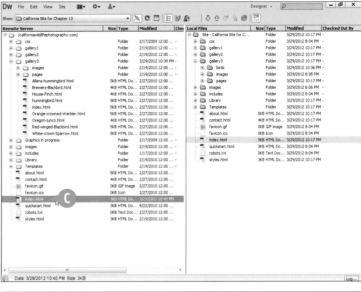

Upload a Folder

1 In the right pane, click the folder 📁 that you want to upload.

2 Click 🔼.

D You can also right-click the folder in the local site and select **Put** from the menu that appears.

Dreamweaver transfers the folder and its contents from your computer to the web server.

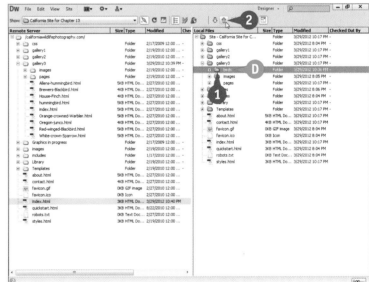

TIPS

How do I stop a file transfer in progress?

You can click **Cancel** in the Status dialog box that appears when a transfer is in progress. You can also press Esc to cancel a file transfer.

How can I delete a file from the web server?

With the Site window open, connect to the web server. When the list of files appears in the left pane, click the file that you want to delete and then press Del. A dialog box appears, asking if you really want to delete the selected file. Click **OK**. You can also delete multiple files and folders.

Download Files from a Web Server

Y ou can use Dreamweaver's file transfer features to download files from a remote server to your local computer. You can download files from your web server as easily as you upload files. After they are downloaded, you can make changes or updates to the pages in Dreamweaver and then put them back on the web server. If you are working on an existing website, you can start by downloading the entire site to your computer using these features.

Download Files from a Web Server

Download a File

1. Click 🔌 to connect to the web server (🔌 changes to 🔌).

2. Click the file that you want to download.

3. Click the Get button (⬇).

   Ⓐ You can also right-click the file on the remote site and select **Get** from the menu that appears.

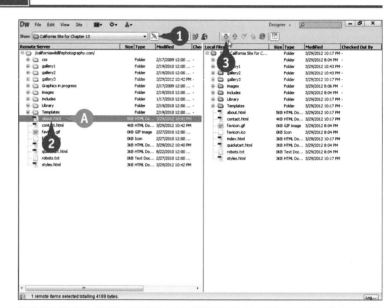

A dialog box appears, asking if you want to include dependent files.

Note: *Dependent files* are images and other files associated with a particular page.

4. Click **Yes** or **No**.

   Ⓑ You can click the check box (☐ changes to ☑) to avoid seeing this dialog box again.

   Ⓒ The Background Activity dialog box appears when Dreamweaver needs to reestablish a connection to the server to complete the upload or download process.

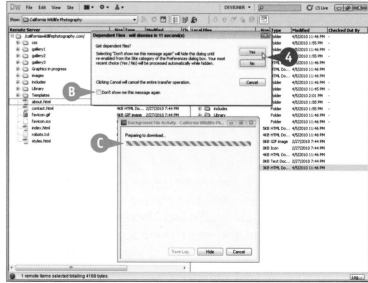

D The file transfers from the web server to your computer.

If the file already exists on your local computer, a dialog box appears, asking whether it is okay to overwrite it. Click **Yes** to do so.

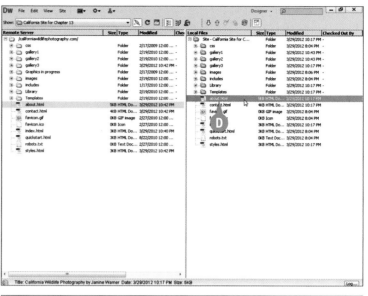

Download Multiple Files

1 Press and hold **Ctrl** (**Control**) and click to select the files that you want to download.

2 Click ⬇.

The files transfer from your web server to your computer.

E The downloaded files appear in the Local Files panel.

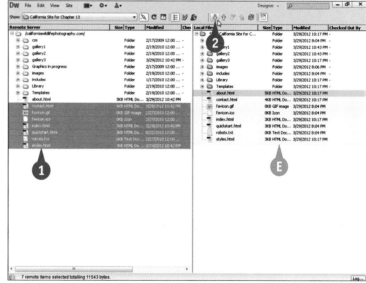

TIPS

Where does Dreamweaver log errors that occur during file transfer?

Dreamweaver logs all transfer activity, including errors, in a file-transfer log. You can view it by clicking **Window**, then clicking **Results**, and then clicking **FTP Log**. The FTP Log panel appears at the bottom of the screen.

Can I use my website to store files while I am still working on them?

If a file is on your web server, it can be viewed on the Internet. When pages are under construction and you do not want them to be seen, you should not put them up on your website, even temporarily. Even if the page is not linked to your site, someone may find it, or a search engine may even index and cache it.

Synchronize Your Local and Remote Sites

Dreamweaver can synchronize files between your local computer and your remote server so that both locations have an identical set of the most recent files. This ability to synchronize both versions of your site can be useful if other people are editing the files on the remote site and you need to update your local copies of those files. It is also handy if you edit pages and you do not remember all the pages that you need to upload after you have updated them.

Synchronize Your Local and Remote Sites

1. Click [icon] to connect to the web server ([icon] changes to [icon]).

2. Click the Synchronize button ([icon]).

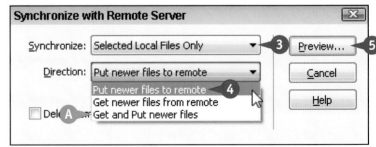

The Synchronize with Remote Server dialog box appears.

3. Click [▼] and select the files that you want to synchronize.

4. Click [▼] and select the direction that you want to copy the files.

A. You can place the newest copies on both the remote and local sites by selecting **Get and Put newer files**.

5. Click **Preview**.

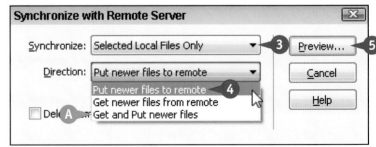

Dreamweaver compares the sites
and then lists the files for
transfer, based on your
selections in steps **3** and **4**.

⑥ Click to select the files that you
do not want to transfer.

⑦ With the files selected, click the
Trash button (🗑) to remove
them from the transfer list.

⑧ Click **OK**.

Dreamweaver transfers the files.

The local and remote sites are
now synchronized.

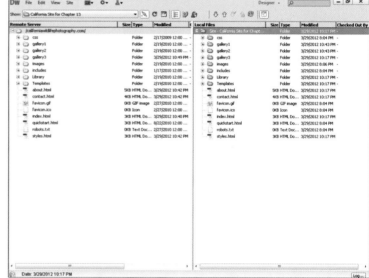

TIP

Are there other FTP tools besides those available in Dreamweaver?
Dreamweaver offers the convenience of transferring files without having to open other programs. However,
if you are transferring especially large files or you want to access a server with multiple programs, there are
many good alternatives available. For example, in Windows, you can use CuteFTP (www.globalscape.co.uk/
cuteftp), FileZilla (www.filezilla-project.org), and SmartFTP (www.smartftp.com). In Mac OS, you can use
FileZilla, Fetch (www.fetchsoftworks.com), or Cyberduck (www.cyberduck.ch). You can download evaluation
copies of these programs from the specified websites or from www.download.com.

Maintaining a Website

Maintaining a website and keeping its contents fresh can be as much work as creating the site. Dreamweaver's site-maintenance tools make updating your site faster and easier.

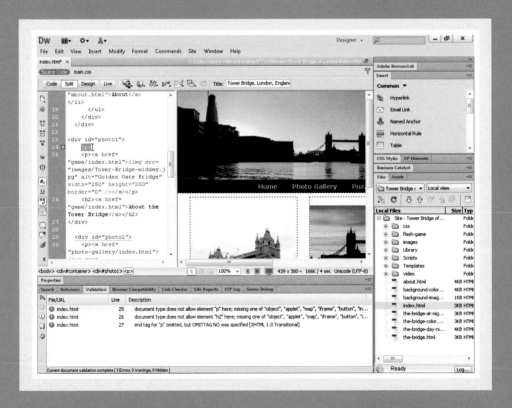

View Visual Aids

Dreamweaver's visual aids make it possible to see things that are not visible in a web browser, such as the outline of a `div` tag or the border of a table. These visual aids make it easier to manage the features of your site and to edit your page designs. Although visual aids are helpful, sometimes you may prefer to turn them off so that you can see how your designs will look in a web browser, without all the borders and outlines.

View Visual Aids

① Click the Visual Aids button (🖾).

② Click **CSS Layout Outlines**.

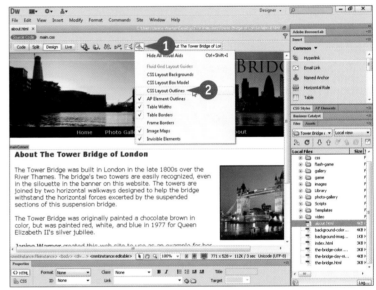

Ⓐ A dotted line appears around any `div` tags or other CSS layout elements.

③ Click 🖾 again.

④ Click **CSS Layout Outlines** again to remove the ☑.

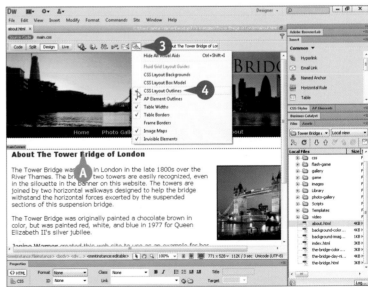

The dotted lines around CSS layout elements disappear.

5 Click  again.

6 Click **Hide All Visual Aids**.

All visual aids disappear.

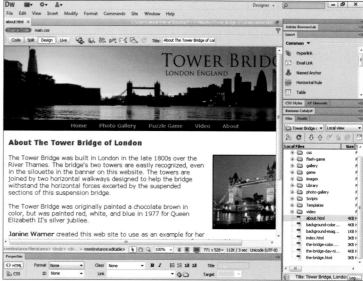

TIPS

Are visual aids displayed in a web browser?
No. Visual aids are visible only in the Dreamweaver workspace. Visual aids are designed to provide additional information and guides as you work on a page layout, but they will not be visible when your visitors to your site view your page designs in a web browser.

Is there a shortcut to hide all visual aids?
Yes. Like many features in Dreamweaver, you can use a keyboard shortcut instead of selecting an option from a menu or panel. To hide all visual aids at once, press Ctrl plus Shift plus the letter *I* (on a Windows computer). If you are using a Mac, press ⌘ + Shift + I. To turn visual aids back on, press the same keys in combination again.

Manage Site Assets

Y ou can view and manage elements that appear on the pages of your site with the Assets panel. The Assets panel provides an easy way to insert elements that you want to use more than once in your site. Using the Assets panel, you can keep track of many different kinds of assets, including images, links, library items, and templates. You can also create collections of favorite assets to make it easier to find commonly used elements, such as logos and links to popular websites.

Manage Site Assets

1 Click **Window**.

2 Click **Assets**.

A You can also click the **Assets** tab in the Files panel to open the Assets panel.

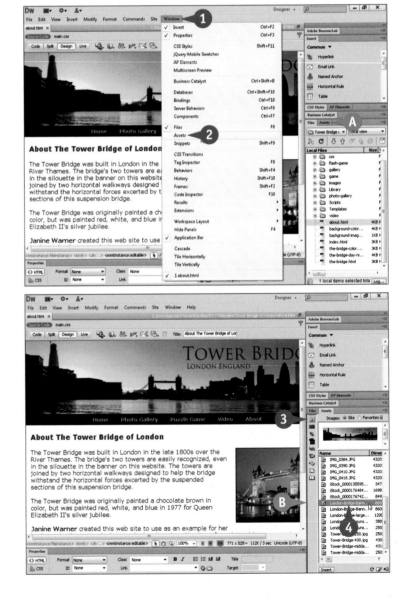

The Assets panel appears, displaying objects from the active collection.

3 Click an icon to display a collection of assets.

In this example, the Image assets are shown.

4 Click the name of any asset to preview it in the Assets panel.

B You can click and drag the side of the Assets panel to expand it.

C The Assets panel displays the preview of your selected asset.

5 Click a column heading.

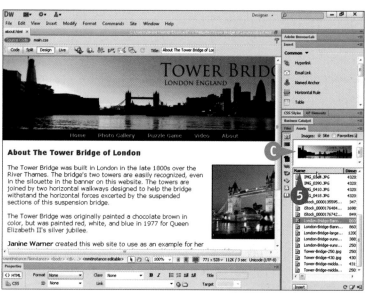

The assets are now sorted by the selected column heading in ascending order.

Note: If you click the name of the column that the assets are already sorted by, the asset order switches to descending order.

D To view other assets, you can click a different category button.

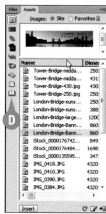

TIP

How are assets organized?

Items in the Assets panel are organized into the following categories:

Category	Description	Category	Description
Images	GIF, JPG, and PNG images	Movie	QuickTime and MPEG movies
Color	Text, background, link, and style-sheet colors	Scripts	External JavaScript or VBScript files
URLs	Universal Resource Locators (external web addresses used in the site)	Templates	Dreamweaver templates (.dwt files)
Flash	Flash-based multimedia	Library	Library items (reusable page elements)
Shockwave	Shockwave-based multimedia		

Add Content with the Assets Panel

You can add frequently used content to your site directly from the Assets panel. This technique can be more efficient than using a menu command or the Insert panel. For example, to add an image from the Image assets, you simply click to select the image that you want in the panel and then drag it onto the page where you want the image to appear, and Dreamweaver automatically inserts the image for you. You can also drag and drop library items into your web pages.

Add Content with the Assets Panel

1. Click the **Assets** tab to open the Assets panel.

2. Click a category.

3. Click an asset.

4. Drag the asset onto the page.

If the asset is an image, the Image Tag Accessibility Attributes dialog box appears.

5. Type a description of the image.

Ⓐ Entering a long description URL is optional.

6. Click **OK**.

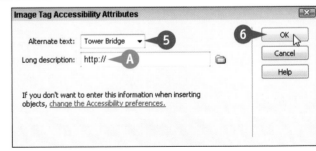

Dreamweaver inserts the asset into your Document window.

In this example, an image is added to the page.

7 Click to select the image or other asset.

8 Edit the asset as you would any other asset.

In this example, an image alignment option is applied.

Dreamweaver applies your changes to the asset in the Document window.

B In this example, the image is aligned to the right.

TIPS

How do I copy assets from one site to another?
Click one or more items in the Assets panel, and then right-click (Control + click) the selected assets. From the menu that appears, click **Copy to Site** and then click a site to which you want to copy the assets. The assets appear in the Favorites list under the same category in the other site.

Are all my links saved in the Assets panel?
Only links to external websites and email addresses are saved in the Assets panel. Links to internal pages in your site are not saved in the Assets panel. You can use the saved links in the Assets panel to quickly create new links to websites and email addresses to which you have already linked in your site.

Specify Favorite Assets

To help keep track of items that you use frequently, you can make your asset lists more manageable by organizing the assets into a Favorites list inside each asset category. Taking a few minutes to create a Favorites list of images, links, and other elements that you use regularly makes it easier to add those elements to your pages as you create them. And remember, as your site grows and evolves, you can add and remove elements from each of your Favorites lists.

Specify Favorite Assets

Add an Asset to the Favorites List

1. Click the **Assets** tab to open the Assets panel.

2. Click a category.

3. Right-click (**Control** + click) an asset.

4. Click **Add to Favorites** on the menu that appears.

   Dreamweaver adds the asset to the category's Favorites list.

5. Click **Favorites** (⊙ changes to ⊙).

Ⓐ The selected asset appears in the Favorites category.

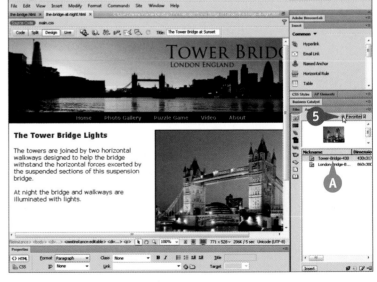

Nickname a Favorite Asset

1. Click a category.

2. Click **Favorites** (⦿ changes to ⦿).

Note: You cannot nickname regular assets; they must be designated as favorites.

3. Right-click (Control + click) an asset.

4. Click **Edit Nickname** on the menu that appears.

5. Type a nickname.

6. Press Enter (Return).

The nickname appears in the Favorites list.

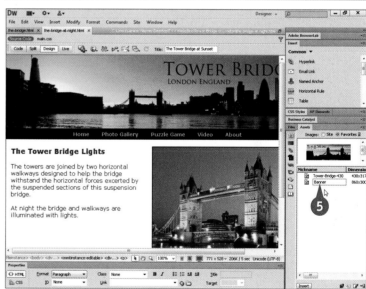

TIPS

How do I remove an item entirely from the Assets panel?

To delete an asset, you need to delete the corresponding file from the Files panel. Click **Window** and then click **Files** or click the **Files** tab to open the Files panel. Click the name of the file and then press Del or Backspace.

How do I add items to the Assets panel?

You do not need to add items. One of the handiest things about the Assets panel is that every time you add an image, external link, email link, color, or multimedia asset to your website, Dreamweaver automatically stores it in the Assets panel.

Validate Your Code

Creating clean code that meets modern web standards is an important part of good web design. Clean, efficient code loads faster in web browsers, and errors in code can lead to a variety of problems with the appearance and functionality of your pages. To help ensure that the code for your web pages is free of errors, Dreamweaver includes a feature that makes it easy to use the code-validation tools provided by the World Wide Web Consortium (W3C), which sets code standards on the Internet.

Validate Your Code

1 Click **File**.

2 Click **Validate**.

3 Click **Validate Current Document (W3C)**.

The W3C Validator Notification dialog box appears.

4 Click **OK**.

Ⓐ The Validation tab group appears with a list of any code errors.

⑤ Double-click any of the listed errors.

Dreamweaver opens Code view to display the error.

⑥ Correct the code error by editing, deleting, or replacing the code.

In this example, there is an extra paragraph tag in the code that should be deleted.

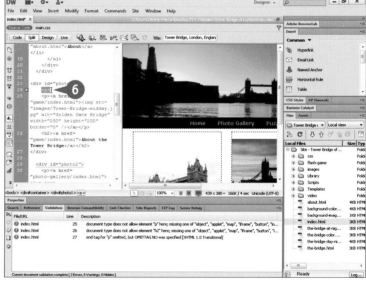

TIP

How do errors appear in my code?
There are many ways that errors can appear in your HTML code. If you manually enter code, any typos, extra spaces, or other errors can cause problems. Even if you only use Dreamweaver's Design view and let the program write all the code for you, you can end up with extra tags and other code errors when you copy and paste content or make changes that Dreamweaver does not interpret correctly. No matter how you create your HTML code, it is always a good practice to validate the code for your pages before publishing them to the World Wide Web.

Make Design Notes

esign notes enable you to add information about the development status of any or all of the pages in your site. This feature is especially useful when you are working on a website with other people because you can leave notes for the others and relate them to specific pages in your site. For example, if you find a problem with a page or want another team member to review a specific page in the site, you can attach a design note with a request to have the page edited before it is published.

Make Design Notes

1 Open the web page to which you want to attach a design note.

2 Click **File**.

3 Click **Design Notes**.

The Design Notes dialog box appears.

4 Click ▼ and select a status for the page.

5 Click the Date button (🗓) to enter the current date in the **Notes** field.

A You can click **Show when file is opened** (☐ changes to ☑) to automatically show design notes when a file opens.

6 Click the **All info** tab.

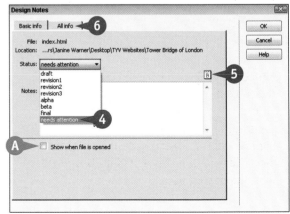

The All Info tab is displayed.

7 To enter new information in the Design Notes dialog box, click ⊞.

8 Type a name and an associated value.

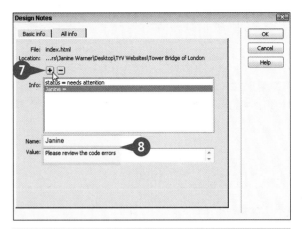

B The added value pair appears in the Info section.

C You can delete information by clicking it in the **Info** section and then clicking ⊟.

9 Click **OK**.

Dreamweaver attaches the design note to the page.

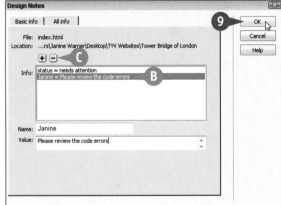

TIPS

How can I view design notes?
You can view design notes in two ways: First, files with a design note have a yellow bubble in the Site window. Double-click it to open the design note. Alternatively, you can open any file with an attached design note, then click **File**, and then click **Design Notes** to open the design note.

Are design notes private?
Although design notes are not linked to the page or displayed in a web browser, anyone with access to your server can view your design notes. If someone is especially clever and your server does not protect the notes folder, then he or she may find it, even without password access to your site. Ultimately, design notes are useful for communication among web designers, but they are not meant to protect important secrets.

Run a Site Report

Running a site report can help you pinpoint problems in your site, including redundant HTML code in your pages, before you upload the site to a web server. Site reports can also identify missing page titles. Page titles appear at the very top of a browser but not in the body of a web page, so they are easy to miss as you create new pages. But page titles are especially important because the text in your page title is what is used when someone bookmarks your page or saves it as a favorite in a web browser.

Run a Site Report

1. Click **Site**.

2. Click **Reports**.

   The Reports dialog box appears.

3. Click ▼ and select to run a report on either the entire site or selected files.

4. Click the reports that you want to run (☐ changes to ☑).

5. Click **Run**.

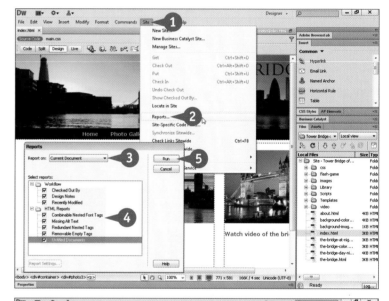

Ⓐ Dreamweaver creates a report and displays it in the Site Reports panel of the Results tab group below the Property inspector.

6. Click any tab across the top of the Results tab group to display a report in its own panel.

Change a Link Sitewide

The Change Link Sitewide feature in Dreamweaver can save you tons of time by automatically updating links throughout your site when they change. You can search for and replace all the hyperlinks on your site that use a specific address. This is helpful when a page is renamed or deleted and the links to it need to be updated. You can also use this feature to update links to other websites and to change an email address that you use throughout your website.

Change a Link Sitewide

1 Click **Site**.

2 Click **Change Link Sitewide**.

The Change Link Sitewide dialog box appears.

3 Type the old hyperlink destination that you want to change.

4 Type the new hyperlink destination.

Note: Email links must begin with `mailto:` and include the full email address. You must enter the full URL to change links to another website.

5 Click **OK**.

Dreamweaver finds and replaces all instances of the link. A dialog box asks you to confirm the changes.

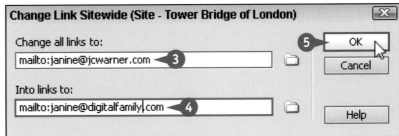

Find and Replace Text

The Find and Replace feature is a powerful tool for making changes to text elements that repeat across many pages. You can use Find and Replace to update text on a single page, but it is especially useful when you want to update something across all the pages in your website, such as the copyright date. You can also use Find and Replace to change or update HTML tags and other elements in the source code for any or all of your web pages.

Find and Replace Text

1 Click **Edit**.

2 Click **Find and Replace**.

The Find and Replace dialog box appears.

3 Click ⏷ and select whether you want to search the entire site or only selected files.

4 Click ⏷ and select the type of text that you want to search.

A For example, you can select **Text (Advanced)** to find text that is inside a specific tag.

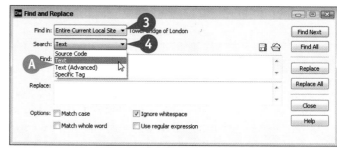

5 Type the text that you want to find.

B You can click **Find Next** to find instances of your query one at a time.

6 Type the replacement text.

7 Click **Replace** to replace the text instances one at a time.

C You can click **Replace All** to automatically replace all instances of your text search.

If you are using search and replace for the entire site, Dreamweaver asks whether you want to replace text in unopened documents. Click **Yes**.

D Dreamweaver replaces the text, and the details appear in the Search panel of the Results tab group at the bottom of the workspace.

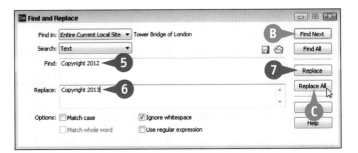

TIPS

How do I use the Find and Replace feature to alter HTML code?

Searching for a string of code is just like searching for other text and is a quick way to make changes to a website. For example, if you want to alter the body color for every page, you can search for the HTML <body> tag and replace it with a different color tag.

Can I use the Find and Replace feature to alter an HTML attribute?

Yes. You can replace attributes to achieve many things. For example, you can change the color of specific text in your page, such as changing color="green" to color="red" in <font> tags, or change the page background color across your site — for example, changing bgcolor="black" to bgcolor="white" in <body> tags.

Adding Interactivity with Spry and JavaScript

Using Dreamweaver's behaviors, you can create JavaScript features, such as rollover effects. Using the Spry widgets, you can create more advanced interactive features, such as drop-down menus.

Introducing Spry and Behaviors

Some of the most advanced website features are created by combining HTML and CSS with more advanced technologies, such as JavaScript. To help you create these features without having to write the code yourself, Dreamweaver includes a collection of widgets and behaviors that you can use on your web pages. You will find these features under the Spry menu and in the Behaviors panel. You can use Spry to create interactive features such as drop-down menus, tabbed panels, and tooltips. You can use behaviors to create rollover images, pop-up messages, and other effects.

Behavior Basics

Behaviors are cause-and-effect events that you can insert into your web pages. For example, you can use the Rollover Image behavior to add an image to a page and then replace that image with another image when a visitor rolls the cursor over the first image. Similarly, the Open Browser Window behavior causes a new web browser window to open when a user clicks or moves the cursor over an image.

Behaviors and Browsers

Because behaviors vary in complexity, they are written in various ways to ensure compatibility with older web browsers. The latest versions of both Internet Explorer and Firefox display most of Dreamweaver's behaviors well, and you can disable behaviors that may not work in older web browsers.

Behind the Scenes

Dreamweaver creates most behaviors with JavaScript and creates Spry features, such as drop-down menus, by combining JavaScript and XML. CSS is also a key component of many of these advanced features. Even if you are familiar with HTML code, you may be surprised by how complex JavaScript looks when you view the code behind your pages.

Create a Drop-Down Menu

You can create many interactive features using Dreamweaver's Spry widgets. One of the most popular is a drop-down menu, which makes it possible to include a drop-down list of links in a navigation bar. You can create horizontal Spry menus with links that drop down, and you can create vertical Spry menus with links that expand into the page from the left. Positioning the menu toward the top or left of your pages is a good practice because it makes the menu easy to find on each page and leaves room for the menus to expand when opened.

Create a Drop-Down Menu

Ⓐ If the Insert panel is not open, click **Window** and then click **Insert** to open it.

① Click ▼.

② Click **Spry**.

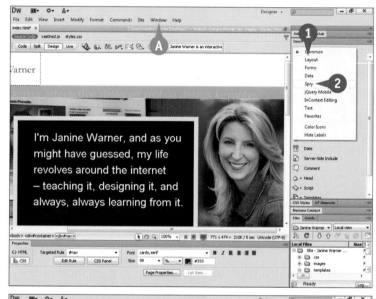

The Spry Insert panel appears.

③ Click to place your cursor where you want to add the menu.

④ Click **Spry Menu Bar**.

The Spry Menu Bar dialog box appears.

⑤ Click **Horizontal** (◎ changes to ◉).

⑥ Click **OK**.

A Spry menu bar appears in the workspace.

⑦ Click the blue Spry menu bar.

Ⓑ If the blue bar is not visible, click **View**, then click **Visual Aids**, and click **Invisible Elements**.

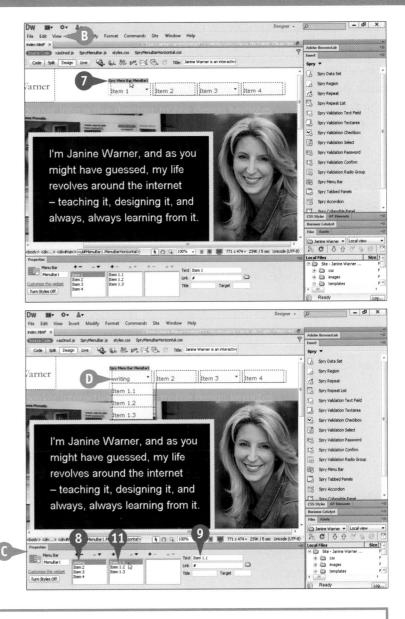

Ⓒ The menu bar properties appear in the Property inspector.

⑧ Click **Item 1**.

⑨ Type a name for the menu item in the **Text** field.

⑩ Press Enter (Return).

Ⓓ The name appears in the workspace and in the Property inspector.

⑪ Click **Item 1.1**.

TIP

What are Spry widgets?
Dreamweaver includes a set of features called *Spry widgets,* which are designed to make it easy to add a variety of complex features to your web pages. When you use Spry, you are adding AJAX (Asynchronous JavaScript and XML), which is a combination of XML and JavaScript that can be styled using CSS. Think of a widget as a special feature that is more advanced than most dialog boxes and other features in Dreamweaver. With widgets, you can create complex features, such as drop-down menus, collapsible panels, and tabbed panels.

The next step in creating a drop-down menu is adding your own text to each of the menu items and subitems in the Spry menu bar. Using the Property inspector, you can enter names for all the items and subitems. You can also add or remove items and subitems using the plus (⊞) and minus (⊟) signs. For the best results, keep the names of each menu item and subitem short. One word is ideal; if you use more than three or four words, menus can get hard to read.

Create a Drop-Down Menu (continued)

⑫ Type a name in the **Text** field.

⑬ Press **Enter** (**Return**).

Ⓐ The name appears in the workspace and in the Property inspector.

⑭ Repeat steps **11** to **13** for the other subitems of Item 1.

⑮ Repeat steps **8** to **14**, replacing all the item and subitem names with the text for your navigation menu.

⑯ Click ⊞ to add an item or subitem.

Ⓑ A new item appears in the Property inspector and the workspace.

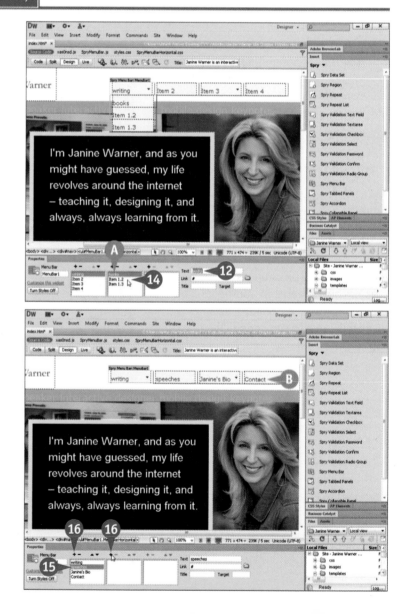

C You can click ☐ to remove any selected item or subitem.

17 Click to select any menu or submenu item that you want to turn into a link.

18 Type the URL in the **Link** field.

19 Press **Enter** (**Return**).

D You can click ☐ to browse to find any page in your site and set the link.

The item is linked, and the URL appears in the Link field in the Property inspector when the menu item is selected.

20 Click **File** and then **Save**.

E The page is saved, and Dreamweaver automatically creates a collection of special files that make the drop-down menu work.

Note: These files are saved in a folder named *SpryAssets* that Dreamweaver creates in your local root folder. This folder must be uploaded to your web server when you publish your site for the drop-down menu to work. Do not change the name or move the location of this folder.

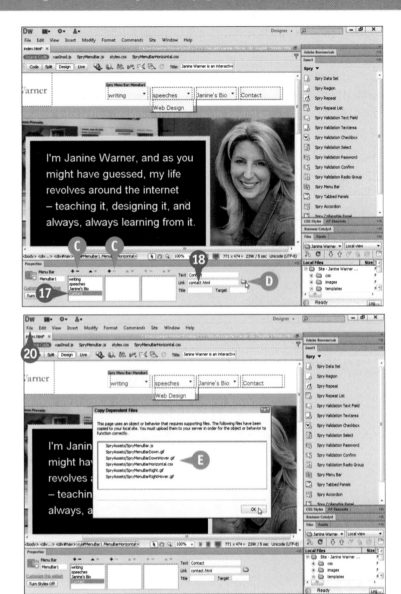

TIPS

What are Spry validation widgets?
The Spry validation widgets are designed to work with web forms to add validation features, such as confirmation that a check box has been selected or that a password has been entered properly.

Can I add more widgets and extensions to Dreamweaver?
Yes. Adobe hosts a Developer's section on its website where programmers can offer widgets and other add-ons for Dreamweaver. Some widgets are free; others cost money. You can learn more about widgets and extensions and download add-ons for Dreamweaver at www.adobe.com/devnet/dreamweaver.

Edit a Drop-Down Menu

After you have added a drop-down menu to your site, you will likely want to change the appearance to better match the design on your web pages. You can edit the colors, fonts, and other features of a drop-down menu by editing the corresponding CSS rules. The first challenge is to identify the Spry rule that corresponds to each element of the drop-down menu. After you have done that, you can alter the CSS rule settings to change the color, size, font, and other features.

Edit a Drop-Down Menu

Note: Add a drop-down menu, as shown in the previous section, "Create a Drop-Down Menu," and then follow these steps.

① Click **Window**.

② Click **CSS Styles**.

Ⓐ The CSS Styles panel opens.

③ Click + to open the style sheet that corresponds to the Spry menu.

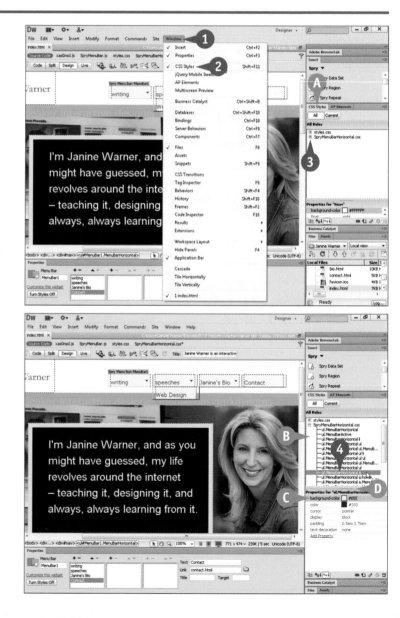

Ⓑ The Spry menu opens, and all the styles that control the appearance of the menu are listed in the CSS Styles panel.

Ⓒ You can click once on any style name to view and edit its definition in the CSS Properties pane.

Ⓓ You can click here and drag to expand the Properties pane.

④ Double-click the name of the style that you want to edit.

282

The selected style opens in the CSS Rule Definition dialog box.

5 Click to select a category.

6 Make your changes to the style.

In this example, the gray background color is changed.

Ⓔ You can click **Apply** to preview the changes.

Ⓕ You can make other changes in other categories as well, such as **Type**.

7 Click **OK**.

The style change is reflected in the workspace.

Ⓖ In this example, the background color of the drop-down menu was changed to white, and the text color was changed to dark blue.

Ⓗ You can click any other style to edit it in the Properties pane or double-click to open it in the CSS Rule Definition dialog box.

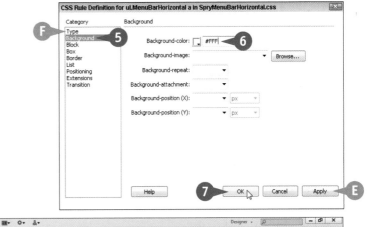

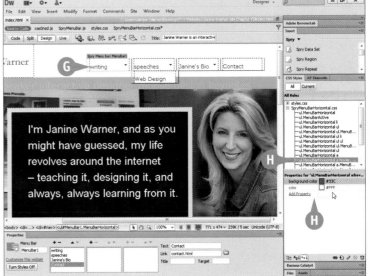

TIP

How do I know which style corresponds to the menu items?
When you click the name of a style in the CSS Styles panel, the rule is displayed in the Properties pane. By studying the style definition rules, you can deduce which style controls which formatting element. For example, if you click the style named `ul.MenuBarHorizontal a`, you can see that the style controls the background color, text color, cursor display, and padding for the active link style — which controls how any linked text appears when a web page is first loaded into a web browser.

Create Tabbed Panels

Dreamweaver's Tabbed Panels widget, available from the Spry menu, makes it easy to add a set of panels that can each contain text and images. The advantage of a tabbed panel is that you can use the space of a page more efficiently. Visitors to your site can cycle through the series of panels by clicking the tabs at the top of the panel set. Because the Spry widget uses AJAX, the web page does not have to be reloaded for the panels to change when a user clicks a tab.

Create Tabbed Panels

Ⓐ If the Insert panel is not open, click **Window** and then click **Insert** to open it.

① Click ▾.

② Click **Spry**.

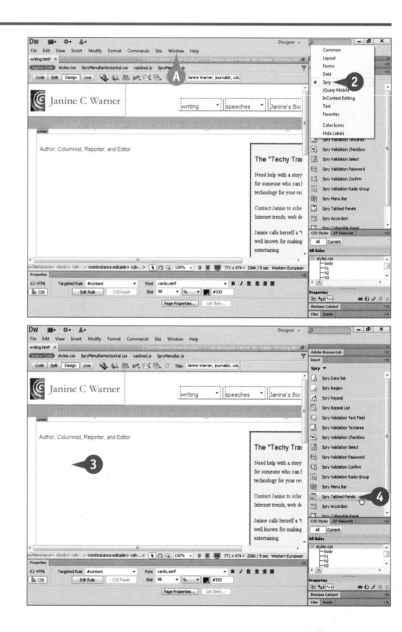

The Spry Insert panel appears.

③ Click to place your cursor where you want to add the panel set.

④ Click **Spry Tabbed Panels**.

A Spry tabbed panel appears in the workspace.

⑤ Click the blue Spry tabbed panel bar.

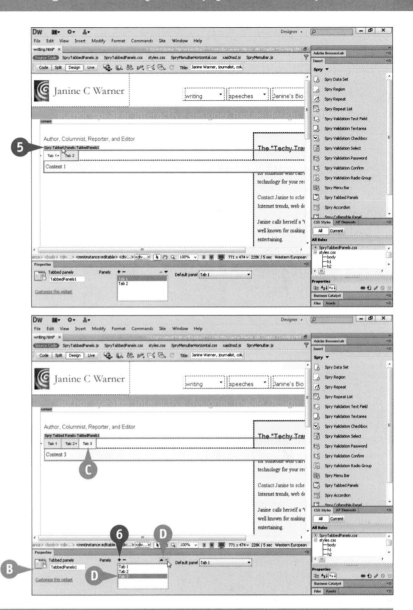

Ⓑ The tabbed panel bar properties appear in the Property inspector.

⑥ Click ➕.

Ⓒ A new tab is added to the panel group.

Ⓓ Click a tab in the Property inspector and click ▲ to move the tab up or ▼ to move it down.

TIPS

Can I add as many panels as I want?
Yes. But keep in mind that the more panels you include, the more space the panel group will take up in the browser, and the longer the page will take to download. Limiting a panel group to no more than eight items is a good practice.

When is it a bad idea to use tabbed panels?
If you are creating a mobile website design, tabbed panels and other similar features can be problematic because they are harder to open and close on a mobile screen and harder to navigate in such a small screen space. In addition, when you are designing mobile sites, you want to create pages that load as quickly as possible, so you are better off creating a series of small pages than a tabbed panel group.

Add Content to Tabbed Panels

You can insert images, video, and other elements into the panels just as you insert images and other elements into any web page. You can also edit the text on the tabs of each of the panels by selecting the text and replacing it with your own words in Dreamweaver's workspace. It is a good practice to keep the text in the tabs short so that visitors to your site can see multiple tabs at once and can easily switch between the contents of each tab.

Add Content to Tabbed Panels

Note: Insert a tabbed panel group, as shown in the previous section, "Create Tabbed Panels," and then follow these steps.

1 Click and drag to select the text on a tab.

2 Type to enter new text on the tab.

3 Repeat steps **1** and **2** for each tab.

4 Click the blue Spry tabbed panel bar.

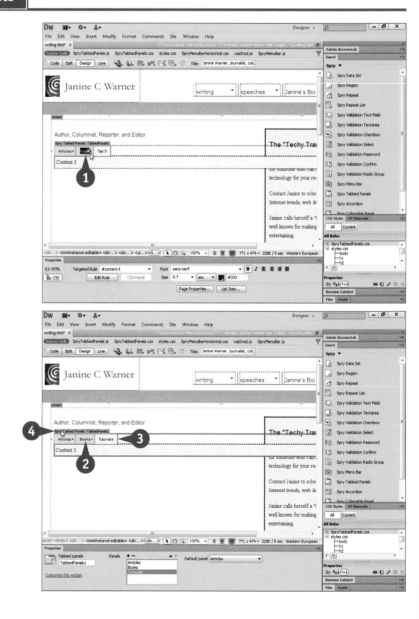

5 Click the name of a tab to select the panel.

A The selected panel is displayed in the workspace.

6 Enter any text, images, or other elements that you want in the tab area.

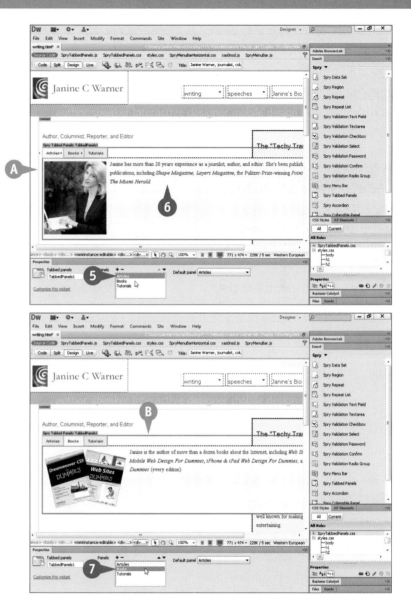

7 Repeat steps **4** to **6** for each panel.

B The new content is displayed in the panel in Dreamweaver's workspace.

TIP

Can I add multimedia to tabbed panels?

Yes. You can insert anything into a tabbed panel that you can insert into a web page, and you do so in much the same way. Just make sure that you have selected the panel in which you want to add content from the Property inspector while you have the blue Spry tabbed panel bar selected. A great way to make the most of a tabbed panel group is to include different kinds of content in each tab. For example, you could include text in the first panel, a slide show in the second panel, and then a video clip in the third.

Edit Tabbed Panels

You can edit the appearance of tabbed panels to better fit the design of your website by editing the corresponding style rules. By editing the style rules that correspond to each section of the tabbed panels, you can change the color, font, and other attributes of the panels and tabs. Remember, when editing the background, text, and link colors, it is best to use colors with good contrast to make text easy to read. For example, a dark text color with a light background or a light text color with a dark background works well.

Edit Tabbed Panels

Note: Insert a tabbed panel group and add content to it, as shown in the previous two sections, and then follow these steps.

1 If the CSS Styles panel is not open, click **Window**.

2 Click **CSS Styles**.

A The CSS Styles panel opens.

B You can click here and drag to expand the CSS Styles panel.

3 Click + to open the style sheet that corresponds to the tabbed panels.

C The styles that control the appearance of the tabbed panels are opened and listed in the CSS Styles panel.

D You can click once on any style name to view and edit its definition in the CSS Properties pane.

4 Double-click the name of the style that you want to edit.

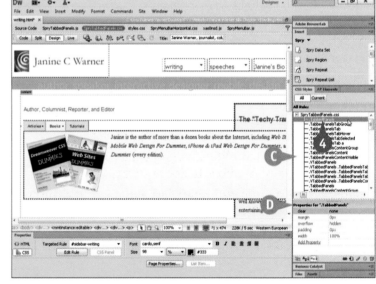

The selected style opens in the CSS Rule Definition dialog box.

5 Click a category.

6 Make your changes to the style.

In this example, the width is changed from 100 percent, which spanned the entire width of the page, to 550 px.

E You can click **Apply** to preview the changes.

7 Click **OK**.

The style change is reflected in the workspace.

8 Click to select the name of another style that you want to edit.

9 Edit the selected style in the Properties pane.

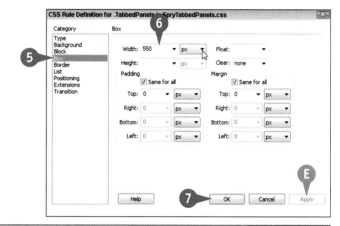

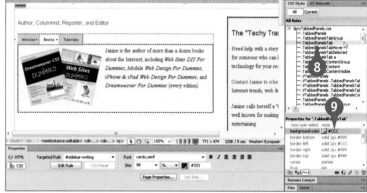

TIP

Can I use different colors for selected tabs?

Yes. The Spry panel tabs have separate styles for each of the three active link states: Tab, Tab Selected, and Tab Hover. You can specify different colors for each setting.

In this example, the Tab style is light blue, which will make links that are not actively selected light blue.

The Tab Selected style is an orange color. The tab for the selected section is displayed in the selector color.

Link styles can include different background colors, fonts, borders, and other variations to create attractive menu bars.

The Tab Hover style appears only when a user rolls the cursor over a tab.

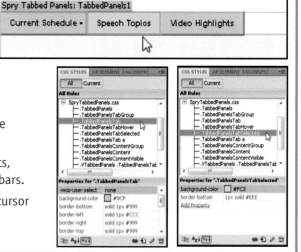

Using the Open Browser Window Behavior

You can use the Open Browser Window behavior to open a new window from within an existing window. When you use the Open Browser Window behavior, you can launch a new browser window with the click of a link, a rollover action, or any other trigger included in the Dreamweaver Behaviors panel, which is featured in this section. You can also specify the height and width of the new window to perfectly fit video and images in their own viewers or add other additional information, such as definitions.

Using the Open Browser Window Behavior

① Click **Window**.

② Click **Behaviors**.

Ⓐ The Behaviors pane opens in the Tag Inspector panel.

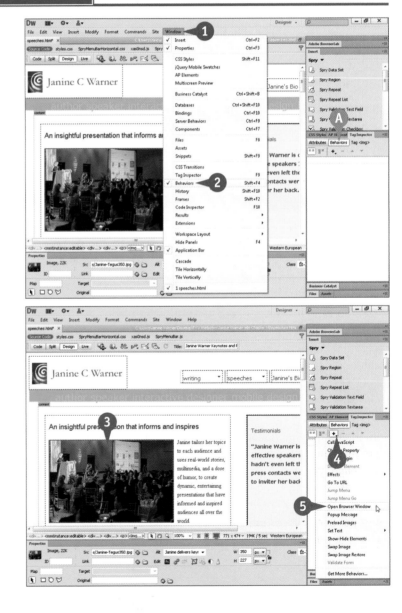

③ Click to select an image, selection of text, or other element that you want to serve as the trigger for the behavior.

④ ▾.

The list of behaviors is displayed.

⑤ Click **Open Browser Window**.

Note: You can select other behaviors from the list to apply those features.

The Open Browser Window
dialog box appears.

6 Click **Browse**.

The Select File dialog box
opens.

7 Click ▾ and select the folder
with the page to which you
want to link.

8 Click to select the file.

9 Click **OK**.

You are returned to the Open
Browser Window dialog box.

10 Type the window width in
pixels.

B If you leave the height
blank, the window will
expand to fill the content
automatically.

11 Select any attributes
that you want to include
(☐ changes to ☑).

12 Type a name.

Note: You cannot use spaces or
special characters.

13 Click **OK**.

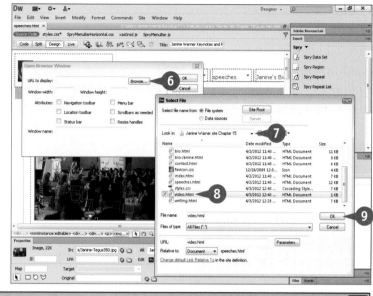

TIPS

What is the difference between behavior events and actions?
Think of an event in a behavior like a match and the action
like the flame on a candle. When you use a behavior on your
web page, you get to choose what kind of event you want to
serve as the spark. One common choice is `onClick`, which
triggers the action of a behavior when a user clicks a link.
Another common choice is `onMouseOver`, which triggers the
action of a behavior when a user rolls the cursor over a link.

**Can you combine actions and events
when you use a behavior?**
Yes, you can combine two triggers to
launch different events. For example,
you can swap one image for another
when the user rolls a cursor over an
image and then link to another page
with additional information when the
user clicks the image.

continued ▶ **291**

After you add a behavior, you can specify the event that will trigger the action of the behavior. With the Open Browser Window behavior, both the onClick and onMouseOver events are good choices. When you choose onClick, the event is triggered by the click of a mouse on the text, image, or other element that is associated with the behavior. With onMouseOver, the event is triggered by a mouse cursor rolling over the trigger element.

Using the Open Browser Window Behavior (continued)

14 Click here.

Note: Hint: Click just inside the line.

⊡ appears.

15 Click ⊡.

The drop-down list of functions appears.

16 Click to select an event to serve as the trigger for the behavior.

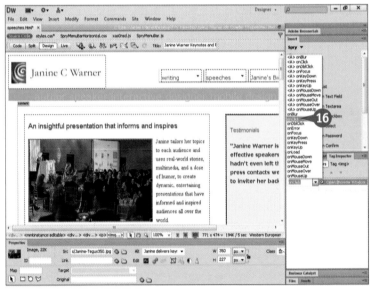

Ⓐ The event name is displayed in the Behaviors panel and is associated with the behavior.

17 Click 🖳 to preview the page in a web browser.

18 Click to choose a browser.

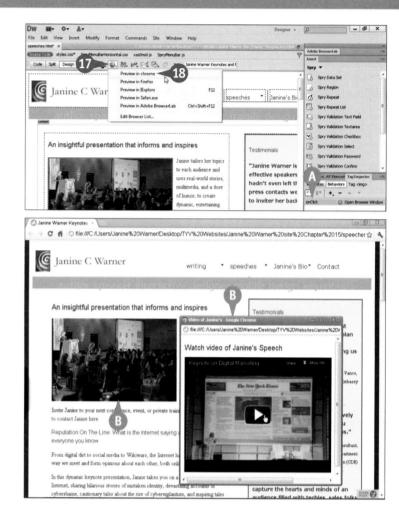

Ⓑ When you perform the trigger on the element, such as click the image in this example, the new browser window opens in the specified size.

TIP

Can I link images, text, and other types of files to behaviors?

Just about anything that you can use for a link in Dreamweaver you can associate with a behavior. Just select any image, section of text, or even a video or animation file and then click to select the Behavior action and events from the Behaviors panel. Note, however, that not all behaviors can be associated with all elements. If you notice that some of the behaviors are grayed out and unavailable, it is because those options cannot be used with whatever you have selected on the page. In some cases, you can infer from the name what you need — for example, you could guess that for Drag AP Element, you need to select an AP element to use that behavior. You can also learn a lot by trial and error. Select an element on the page, such as an image, and see which behaviors are active in the list.

Index

A

absolute positioning, 7, 211, 232
action compared to event, behavior, 291
Active links color option, 119
adding
    background images, 88–89
    button to a form, 150–151, 154–155
    check box to a form, 148–149
    content from Assets panel, 262–263
    drop shadow, 228–229
    header image, 216–217
    images, 216–219
    list/menu to a form, 152–153
    radio button to a form, 149, 150–151
    space around images, 80–81
    text field to a form, 146–147
    text shadow effect, 230–231
Adobe Dreamweaver
    code-completion feature, 55
    code-correction feature, 55
    CSS layout collection, 211
    defined, 4
    exiting, 15
    file transfer in, 239
    Help feature, 16–17
    installing, 10–11
    interface overview
        Document window, 32–33
        panels, 36–39
        Preferences, 40–41
        Property inspector, 34–35
        workspace layout options, 30–31
    interface tour, 12–13
    showing or hiding features, 14
    starting, 10–11
    visual interface to avoid coding, 45
Adobe Fireworks, 86
Adobe Flash, 6, 92–95, 261
Adobe Photoshop, 86
Adobe Shockwave, 261
AJAX (Asynchronous JavaScript and XML), 279
alignment
    captions with images, 221
    cell content in tables, 131, 139
    floating elements in CSS, 210, 220–221
    images, 78–79
    paragraphs, 63
    tables on web pages, 123
Alt (alternate text), using for images, 34–35, 77
anchor links, 108–109
animation files, 6
AP Divs, 7, 211, 232–235
App Developer layout, 30
Apple Safari, 26, 240
area of form, defining, 145
Assets panel
    adding content from, 262–263
    deleting an asset, 265
    Favorites list, 264–265
    introduction, 36–37
    library items, 158, 159, 161
    templates, 159
    working with site assets, 260–261
Asynchronous JavaScript and XML (AJAX), 279
audience, defining, 9
audio files, 6

B

background
    colors, changing, 90, 126–127, 219
    images, adding, 88–89
Background Activity dialog box, 252
behaviors, 276–277, 290–293
Behaviors panel, 97
block-formatting tags, 49
`<blockquote>` indenting tags, 65
blogs, as database-driven websites, 7
`<body>` tags, 48
borders, 81, 123, 227
box-shadow rule (CSS), 228
`<br />` break tag, 45, 49
broken hyperlinks, checking for, 117
browsers, web
    behaviors, relationship to, 277
    default link colors, 119
    defined, 5
    new browser window, opening linked page in, 115
    Open Browser Window behavior, 276, 290–293
    paragraph width, 63
    testing designs in, 4, 26–27, 46, 179, 240–243

Index

Q-R

S

Index

Read Less-Learn More®

Want instruction in other topics?

Check out these

All designed for visual learners—just like you!

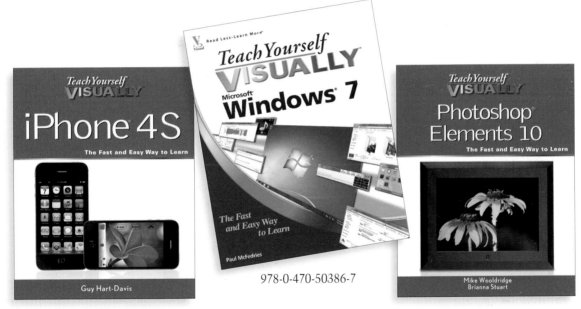

978-0-470-94219-2

978-0-470-50386-7

978-1-118-15173-0

Available in print and e-book formats.

For a complete listing of *Teach Yourself VISUALLY*™ titles and other Visual books, go to wiley.com/go/visual

Visual®
An Imprint of WILEY

Wiley, the Wiley logo, the VISUAL logo, Read Less-Learn More, and Teach Yourself VISUALLY are trademarks or registered trademarks of John Wiley & Sons, Inc. and/or its affiliates. All other trademarks are the property of their respective owners.